THE LAW AND THE EXPANDING NURSING ROLE

THE LAW AND THE EXPANDING NURSING ROLE

Editor:
Bonnie Bullough, R.N., Ph.D.

Associate Professor, Community Health Nursing,
School of Nursing; Associate Director, Pediatric Nurse
Practitioner Project, University Extension, University of
California at Los Angeles, Los Angeles, California

APPLETON-CENTURY-CROFTS/New York
A Publishing Division of Prentice-Hall, Inc.

Library of Congress Cataloging in Publication Data
Main entry under title:

The Law and the expanding nursing role.

Includes index.
1. Nurses and nursing—Legal status, laws, etc.—United States. I. Bullough, Bonnie. [DNLM: 1. Legislation, Nursing—United States. WY32 AA1 B9L]
KF2915.N8L3   344'.73'041   75-25601
ISBN 0-8385-5622-1

Copyright © 1975 by APPLETON-CENTURY-CROFTS
A Publishing Division of Prentice-Hall, Inc.

All rights reserved. This book, or any parts thereof, may not be used or reproduced in any manner without written permission. For information address Appleton-Century-Crofts, 292 Madison Avenue, New York, N.Y. 10017.

75 76 77 78 79 / 10 9 8 7 6 5 4 3 2 1

Prentice-Hall International, Inc., London
Prentice-Hall of Australia, Pty. Ltd., Sydney
Prentice-Hall of India Private Limited, New Delhi
Prentice-Hall of Japan, Inc., Tokyo
Prentice-Hall of Southeast Asia (Pte.) Ltd., Singapore

Printed in the United States of America

Contributors

Anita Berwind, R.N., M.N.
Coronary Care Specialist and Nurse Practitioner; Pediatric Nursing Instructor, School of Nursing, Los Angeles County Medical Center, Los Angeles, California; Formerly with the Department of Community Health Services, County of Los Angeles

Bonnie Bullough, R.N., Ph.D.
Associate Professor, Community Health Nursing, School of Nursing; Associate Director, Pediatric Nurse Practitioner Project, University Extension, University of California at Los Angeles, Los Angeles, California

Vern L. Bullough, Ph.D.
Professor of History, California State University, Northridge, California; Lecturer, School of Public Health, University of California at Los Angeles, Los Angeles, California

Sheldon Greenfield, M.D.
Assistant Professor, Department of Preventive Medicine and Public Health, School of Medicine, and School of Public Health, University of California at Los Angeles, Los Angeles, California; Staff Member, Training and Evaluation of Primex, University of California, School of Nursing, and University Extension, Los Angeles, California; Staff Member, Ambulatory Care Project, Beth Israel Hospital, Harvard Medical School; and Staff Member, Lincoln Laboratory, Massachusetts Institute of Technology, Boston, Massachusetts

Corine L. Hatton, R.N., M.N.
Clinical Specialist, Mental Health; Assistant Clinical Professor, School of Nursing, University of California at Los Angeles, Los Angeles, California

Lucie Young Kelly, R.N., Ph.D.
Nursing Consultant and Program Director, Office of Consumer Health Education, and Adjunct Associate Professor of Community Medicine, College of Medicine and Dentistry of New Jersey, Rutgers Medical School, Rutgers, New Jersey

Leonide L. Martin, R.N., M.S.
Assistant Professor, Department of Nursing, California State College-Sonoma, Rohnert Park, California: Formerly Assistant Professor, School of Nursing, University of California at Los Angeles; Family Nurse Practitioner, Family Practice Clinic, Santa Rosa, California

Patricia J. McClure, R.N., M.N.
Clinical Nurse Specialist, University of Wisconsin Hospitals, and Clinical Instructor, University of Wisconsin School of Nursing, Madison, Wisconsin

Wanda C. Nations, R.N., LL.B.
Chief, Patient Services (Ombudsman), Veterans' Administration Brentwood Hospital, Los Angeles, California

Ruth Roemer, J.D.
Researcher in Health Law, School of Public Health, University of California at Los Angeles, Los Angeles, California

Donna F. Ver Steeg, R.N., Ph.D.
Assistant Professor, School of Nursing and Co-Principal Investigator, Primex Project, University Extension, University of California at Los Angeles, Los Angeles, California

Joan P. Whinihan
Director of Communications, Washington State Nurses' Association, Seattle, Washington

Contents

Contributors   v
Introduction   1

SECTION I: THE LAWS GOVERNING NURSING PRACTICE: BACKGROUND INFORMATION   5

1. The First Two Phases in Nursing Licensure, *Bonnie Bullough* / 7
2. Licensure and the Medical Monopoly, *Vern L. Bullough* / 22
3. Statutory and Common Law as it Relates to Modern Nursing Practice, *Wanda C. Nations* / 33
4. Nursing Functions and the Law: Some Perspectives from Australia and Canada, *Ruth Roemer* / 38

SECTION II: THE VIEW FROM THE PRACTICE SETTING   51

5. Factors Contributing to Role Expansion for Registered Nurses, *Bonnie Bullough* / 53
6. Protocols as Analogs to Standing Orders, *Sheldon Greenfield* / 62
7. The Nurse in the Coronary Care Unit, *Anita Berwind* / 82
8. View from the Firing Line: Family Nurse Practitioner in California, *Leonide L. Martin* / 95
9. The Mental Health Clinical Nurse Specialist in Private Practice, *Corine L. Hatton* / 118
10. Nurses in Private Practice, *Patricia J. McClure* / 125

SECTION III: NEW NURSE PRACTICE ACTS AND OTHER APPROACHES TO THE LEGAL PROTECTION OF NURSES AND PATIENTS   133

11. Institutional Licensure, *Lucie Young Kelly* / 135
12. The Third Phase in Nursing Licensure: The Current Nurse Practice Acts, *Bonnie Bullough* / 153

13 The Political Process, or, The Power and the Glory,
    Donna F. Ver Steeg / 171
14 The Washington State Success Story, *Joan P. Whinihan* / 187

Implications and Conclusions 198
Index 205

THE LAW AND THE EXPANDING NURSING ROLE

Introduction

The role of the registered nurse is in a state of almost revolutionary change as nurses in both acute and ambulatory patient care settings take on a variety of new responsibilities. Partly a trend toward specialization, this change also involves significant expansion of the nursing role to include responsibility for functions that until recently were considered medical rather than nursing functions. Although the shortage of primary-care physicians is a major causal factor, other variables are also involved in these changes. Hopefully, the more efficient use of the talents of nurses will result in improved health care for the American people, and help to trim rapidly escalating health care costs.

For a time, the archaic medical and nursing practice acts made overt role expansion for nurses difficult. Although a variety of formal and informal coping mechanisms evolved to work around the laws, the laws remained a significant barrier to the open use of nurses in extended roles. This situation is now rapidly changing as state laws are revised. A variety of approaches are being used, and it is important that nurses and legislators understand the implications of the differing methods.

This book is aimed at a variety of audiences, including scholars who are interested in the interrelationship of the law and social change, nursing students, practitioners, educators, and those who plan and administer health care. The authors represent a variety of backgrounds, including law, sociology, history, public relations, medicine, and nursing.

The book is divided into three major sections. The first provides the background needed to put the current events into context. Two articles are historical. They were included to trace the genesis of some of the current problems of the profession as well as to provide a contrast with contemporary developments, because the changes taking place in nursing seem more exciting to those who understand the past position of nurses. The first of these two papers explores nursing licensure from the beginning of the twentieth century; the second, by Vern Bullough, summarizes the longer history of medical regulation, explaining how medicine achieved its current position of primacy in the health care field and what that position has and continues to mean for nurses. Basic information about nurse practice acts and other laws governing nursing is provided by Wanda Nations, as she discusses some of the methods nurses have used to cope with outdated laws. The final article in the section, by Ruth Roemer, offers a somewhat different approach. Role expansion for nurses is also occurring in other countries, and will probably in the future become a worldwide phenomenon. Thus, the discussion of the practice and legal situation of nurses as they expand their functions in Australia and Canada gives an added perspective to the developments in this country.

The second major section focuses on the practice setting, and the experiences with the law by nurses in the field. The authors and articles were selected to give some of the flavor of the broad scope of the role expansion taking place in nursing, as well as to explore the problems that nurses face as they break new ground. Four of the articles are by nurses who could be called "clinical specialists" because they have acquired clinical knowledge through experience and and advanced education; or they could be called "nurse practitioners" because of their expertise in diagnosis and treatment. The uncertainty about terms reflects the unsettled state of the field. Each of the four articles explores a different type of role expansion. Anita Berwind traces the background of the coronary care nurse; Leonide Martin tells about the difficulties and satisfactions of a family nurse practitioner in a new clinic; Corine Hatton discusses the role of the mental health nurse; Patricia McClure reports the development of a new private practice sector in nursing. The paper by Sheldon Greenfield approaches role expansion from a different perspective as the functions of protocols are explained. This paper was selected because of the growing importance of protocols, not only in guiding practice and furnishing legal protection for nurses but also in making medicine and nursing more scientific by committing some of the art to paper.

The section on practice is by no means comprehensive; there are a myriad of other practitioners, associates, and specialists who are carving out new roles and responsibilities for themselves. The selection is, however, sufficient to demonstrate the multifaceted character of the movement: the role expansion of these nurses differs both in direction and in degree. There are public health nurses, some of them with new titles, who are now doing well-baby care in clinics, with the support and consultation of physicians available, whereas they formerly did well-baby care alone in homes, without support. Their role change is minor, but what they were doing formerly is now made more explicit. On the other hand, there are practitioners like Ms. Martin who have taken on a whole range of new responsibilities for the primary care of varied patient populations.

The third and final section of the book examines the current and changing nurse practice acts, contrasting different approaches to the facilitation of role expansion. Lucie Young Kelly discusses the proposal for institutional licensure, pointing out why some authorities in the field support this idea but also indicating some of the negative implications for nursing of such a move. The two final papers, by Donna Ver Steeg and Joan Whinihan, offer some practical suggestions for nurses who may be willing to participate in the political process. Ver Steeg approaches from the point of view of the researcher; Whinihan describes in detail the actual campaign that led to the passage of the Washington State nurse practice act.

The role of the editor in this enterprise has been to write articles or comments where they are needed to fill in the gaps. Hopefully, the articles that were selected, plus the editorial comments, will give the reader a well-rounded picture and some of the flavor of excitement that surrounds what well may be the major development in nursing in the twentieth century: namely, the parallel development of an expanded nursing role and a broader legal definition of nursing.

Section I

THE LAWS GOVERNING NURSING PRACTICE: BACKGROUND INFORMATION

BONNIE BULLOUGH

1
The First Two Phases in Nursing Licensure

The history of nursing licensure in the United States can be divided into three major phases. The goals of the nurses who sought legislation, and the types of laws that were passed in response to their efforts, differed in each of these periods. The first phase coincided with the beginning of the twentieth century, when nurses began actively to campaign for state laws to register trained nurses. By 1923, nurses had succeeded in obtaining some type of licensing act in each of the states, although later amendments were sought to raise educational standards and facilitate the work of the state boards.

The second phase began in 1938, when New York, which tends to be a bellwether state in the field of nursing licensure, passed a mandatory act defining the scope of functions of registered and practical nurses. Following this precedent, the goal for the next three decades of nurses in other states was to seek definitions of nursing practice, to differentiate the roles of registered and practical nurses, and to make it illegal for unlicensed persons to work as nurses. The definitions of nursing developed in this period carefully differentiated between medical and nursing practice, particularly after 1955 when the American Nurses' Association approved a model definition that specifically disclaimed any independent role for nurses in diagnosis or treatment.

Phase three is the current phase. Its roots can be found in the decade of the sixties, with the development of intensive and primary care nursing, but the phase became overt in 1971, with the passage of amendments to the Idaho nurse practice act authorizing acts of diagnosis and treatment under rules and regulations to be drafted jointly by the boards of medicine and nursing.[1] The New York act, signed in 1972, allowed nurses to diagnose and treat in terms of a nursing regime.[2] Other states, including Arizona, Colorado, Washington, and California have moved to amend their nurse practice acts to allow diagnosis and treatment; but the changes are not taking place without social upheaval and great effort on the part of nurses.

This chapter traces the first two phases in some detail in order to set the background for an understanding of the current revolutionary phase in licensure.

Phase I: The Nurse Registration Acts

The year 1873 is usually thought of as the beginning of the modern era in American nursing, because three "Nightingale" schools were opened that year: Bellevue, Connecticut, and Massachusetts General hospitals. Although several earlier attempts had been made to establish training for nurses, these were the first schools to remain open for any significant length of time. These three schools, and the many that followed (using the same model), were successful partly because of the publicity that had been given the English nursing school started by Florence Nightingale and partly because of a growing awareness that the establishment of apprenticeship education led not only to better patient care but also to significant savings in the cost of running a hospital.[3(pp120-49)] The movement to establish nurses' training schools rapidly gained momentum. In 1880 there were 15 schools; in 1890 there were 35; in 1900 there were 432; and in 1910 the number reached 1023.[4(p141)] To put these figures in perspective, it is necessary to realize that in 1972 there were only 1,363 schools of nursing in the United States.[5]

The rapid growth of hospital training programs, particularly in the period between 1890 and 1900, created a problem for the new graduates. Because the hospitals were staffed primarily by students, most of the graduating nurses were forced to seek employment as private duty nurses, and as such they often worked in the homes of their patients. Here it was necessary to compete with untrained nurses, correspondence school graduates, or ex-classmates who had failed or dropped out of the arduous two-year courses. Moreover, the traditional linkage of the nursing role with that of the wife and mother or the domestic servant had prevented the growth of the image of the nurse as an educated practitioner. The popular literature of the period still referred to the "born" nurse, or intimated that the requisite skills of the nursing role could be acquired intuitively.

Within the ranks of trained nurses, and particularly among nursing educators, there was, however, a growing sense of self-identity. These people were ready to take the beginning steps towards the professionalization of nursing. The precursor to the National League for Nursing (at first called the Society for Superintendents of Training Schools in United States and Canada) was founded in 1894, and in 1896 the organization that was to become the American Nurses' Association (originally the Nurses' Associated Alumnae of United States and Canada) was established. Primary objectives in the formation of both these organizations was to gain control over the profession and to stem the untrammeled growth of substandard nursing schools.[6,3]

As soon as the initial work of organizing was completed, members of both groups turned their attention to seeking state licensure as a mechanism for accomplishing their goals. Sophia Palmer, one of the founders of both organizations and first editor of the *American Journal of Nursing,* made the first public statement supporting licensure in a paper read before the New York State Federation of Women's Clubs in 1899. She argued that nursing's greatest need was for a law that would control the schools. She asked that the schools be placed under the supervision of the Regents of the University of the State of New York, the pattern for other types of professional licensure in the state. The Regents would then be responsible for appointing a board to examine and register nurses.[4(p 44)] Lavinia Dock, the superintendent who was the driving force behind the establishment of the Nurses' Associated Alumnae,[7] wrote an article for the first issue of the *American Journal of Nursing* favoring licensure, although she pointed out that it could not solve all of the problems of the profession.[8] In her presidential address before the third annual meeting of the Nurses' Associated Alumnae, Isabel Hampton Robb outlined the two priorities of nursing as the support of the growth of the professional organizations and the campaign for registration for nurses in each of the states.[9]

Although the process of professionalization was also beginning among nurses in other countries, there were no extant governmental registration programs for those nurses at the time American nurses started to consider the idea. Most European countries did not institute any type of nursing licensure until about 1920.[10(pp 248-52)] Although the medicine and pharmacy act of the Cape Colony had mentioned nurses in an act passed in 1891, the first nurse registration act was enacted in New Zealand in 1901. This act encouraged American nurses to push forward, but it also came at a time when they were already committed to the goal of registration.

It is interesting to note that although the English experience was used as a model for nursing education in this country, England did not furnish a model for nurse registration. This was because the British scene was dominated by the strong figure of Florence Nightingale, who did not approve of individual licensure for nurses. In 1886 a proposal was made by a committee of the Hospitals' Association to create a body of examiners, not connected with the training schools, to test nurses and to keep a list of those who qualified. The objective was to create a standard of excellence in nursing and to protect the hospitals and public against employing incompetent nurses. Nightingale fought against this proposal because she felt that technical competence should be secondary to good character. Although she agreed that training programs should include instructions in how to carry out nursing procedures, in her estimation the primary goal of training and related experiences (such as the requirement that students live in closely supervised nurses' homes) was to build character.[11(pp 351-54)] She felt that she had "raised nursing from the sink" by emphasizing culture and moral standards, and that the new focus on competence rather than character would destroy her life's work.[11(p 352)] Nightingale felt that the then current model, in which the former student was kept closely tied to the training school, or affiliated with some other institution, so that the matron could give on-going surveillance and thus be able to vouch not only for the technical competence of the nurse but also for the character, was a better one for protecting the public. This Nightingale system was in many ways the precursor to what is now being called a "new" proposal for institutional licensure.

In 1888 the British nurses organized an association, and tried several times to obtain a royal charter that would allow them to test and register nurses; but they were defeated because of Nightingale's influence, and nurse registration did not become a reality until 1919.[10(p 251)]

American nurses were not unaware of the controversy that raged over licensure in England. Florence Nightingale was revered, and most of her tenets were followed. But, Ethel Gordon Bedford Fenwick, one of the leaders of the proregistration forces in England, was the more influential figure on the issues of organization and registration. She visited this country in 1892 to prepare an exhibit for the Chicago World's Fair, and apparently spent much of her time visiting with Isabel Hampton Robb and other American nurses to urge them to organize and to later seek registration.[4 (pp 125, 142)] Her arguments seemed most reasonable to American nurses; there is little evidence in any of their writings that they were particularly concerned about any negative consequences that might follow from a possible shift in emphasis from character to technical competence, and so the objections of Florence Nightingale and her followers were of little influence.

In looking for a model for the type of registration they wanted, nurses necessarily turned to other professions. Dock, in her article for the *American Journal of Nursing,* cited the example of medicine, although she also noted that dentistry had been able to control educational standards through the efforts of the schools rather than the state.[8] Palmer mentioned physicians, pharmacists, dentists, and teachers.[4(p 144)] Because of the close association of medicine to nursing, medicine undoubtedly furnished the major model as well as the major barrier to nurses in their search for professional status. As outlined in Chapter 2, state medical practice acts had been enacted in all the states by 1895. A Supreme Court decision in 1889 had held that occupational licensing laws were a valid exercise of the police powers of the states, so the way was open for the nurses to proceed.

The 1889 decision also pointed up the fact that licensure could not be conceived on a national basis, as it was and is in most countries. The federal government has only those powers listed in the constitution which were granted to it by the original colonies or added by amendments, and these powers do not include the right to regulate occupational groups. As a result, the drive for registration had to be carried out separately in each of the states. To facilitate this this effort the Nurses' Associated Alumnae moved to set up constituent state organizations so that the local membership could do the necessary work for lobbying for the registration acts.[12(pp41-59)]

The North Carolina nurses were the first to succeed.[13] A nurse registration act was passed there in March of 1903. Three other registration acts were passed that same year in New Jersey, New York, and Virginia. The North Carolina act allowed for licensure by waiver for the rest of that year. Anyone from a "reputable training school," or anyone who could produce a certificate signed by three registered physicians stating that she or he had been working for at least two years as a nurse, was entitled to be listed by the county clerk as a registered nurse. Starting in 1904, only those persons who were certified by the Board of Examiners could be listed as registered nurses. The Board was instructed by the law to examine the applicants to make sure they were of good character, knowledgeable in anatomy, physiology, invalid cookery, household hygiene, and medical, surgical, obstetric, and practical nursing. Certification by the Board allowed the applicant to use the initials "R.N." and to have his or her name entered on the registry kept by the county clerk.[14]

The campaign in New Jersey met with so much opposition that the that the statute which passed was weaker than the one in North Carolina. The term *trained* nurse was used, rather than *registered* nurse. Applicants were required to have completed two years of practical and theoretical training before applying, but no examination was required and no board of examiners was set up. New Jersey also included provisions for nurses from "foreign states," if their training was comparable to that offered by New Jersey schools. The New York law created a Board of Examiners, appointed by the Regents of the State University of New York from a list of names supplied by the State Nurses' Association.[14(pp312-14)] The provisions of the law matched those proposed by the members of the nursing organization. Nurses were particularly pleased with the all-nurse board, which was felt to be preferable to the mixed nurse and physician board mandated in North Carolina.

One by one the other states followed suit: By 1910 twenty-seven states had passed nurse registration acts, and by 1923 all the states then in the Union, plus the District of Columbia and Hawaii, had licensure for nurses on their books. The Alaskan and Puerto Rican acts came later.[14(pp 306-7)] Although state governments had the constitutional right to pass these acts, this does not mean that legislation was ordinarily planned by or initiated by members of the legislatures. Rather, the first steps usually were taken by nurses who contacted friendly representatives for their assistance. Programs of local, state, and national nurses' associations often featured "how to" seminars to help nurses with the lobbying process.[15,12(pp 97-108)] This pattern is not unusual. In fact, even though the professions often speak of public control by means of state licensure, the professions themselves have participated and continue to participate significantly in the licensing process.[16]

What little opposition there was to early nursing licensure tended to come from hospital administrators, people who ran correspondence courses to prepare nurses, mental hospitals, and occasionally from charitable organizations that sponsored home nursing programs. Physician opposition came usually from doctors who administered hospitals or nursing homes, rather than from active practitioners.[12(p 98),17] Such opposition was sufficient to cause nurses to lower their sights, from their original goal of protection of the term "nurse" to the term "registered nurse," although it was not sufficient to stop the movement in any state. Often, nurses could marshall enough lobbying power to pass a nurse registration act in a single session of the legislature; but if that was not possible they would try again and again until the bill passed. Sometimes they settled for a weak bill and planned their strategy for revision. One of the most common compromises that had to be made was to settle for a board of examiners that included one or more physicians. As the original registration acts went through successive revisions, other goals emerged. Nurses worked actively to obtain legislative sanction to close schools connected with small or highly specialized hospitals, including mental hospitals, and to make high school graduation a preentry requirement for nursing education.

None of the original registration acts included a definition of nursing in terms of the scope of practice of the profession. They might more accurately be called nurse *registration* acts rather than nurse *practice* acts. The term "registered nurse" was defined as a person who had attended an acceptable nursing program and passed a board examination, rather than a person who engaged in a specific type of practice. This definition placed the emphasis on the educational process, and early reform efforts tended to be focused on improving training. Some of the laws became quite elaborate in their requirements for specific theoretical or clinical content. A comparative study of six professions done in 1938 indicated that the educational process in nursing was more regulated than that of the other five professions analyzed.[18]

Phase II: The Development of Definitions of Practice and Mandatory Licensure

The second phase in the development of nursing licensure started in 1938, when the first mandatory practice act was passed in New York. This law established two levels of nurses, registered and practical, and restricted nursing functions to members of these two groups.[19,20] This event marked the beginning of a new drive among nurse activists. Although there was unfinished business, with 19 states still not requiring high school graduation for registration and 17 states still including one or more physicians on their boards,[18] the primary goal for reform became mandatory licensure. By 1939 there were three national nursing organizations: the American Nurses' Association, the National League for Nursing Education, and the National Organization of Public Health Nurses. The boards of directors of these three groups met in January of that year to celebrate the success of the New York nurses and to approve a recommendation favoring "licensure for all those who nurse for hire."[19,21] This became the rallying slogan for the second phase of nursing licensure.

Although mandatory licensure can be thought of as a long-time aspiration from the beginning of the century when abortive attempts were made to restrict the title "nurse," the goal did not seem realistic until the New York nurses broke the barrier. Their efforts, and those of nurses in several states that followed the precedent, were facilitated by the development of licensure for practical nurses. The employment patterns for nurses were changing in this period from private duty to hospital nursing, and hospital administrators argued with some justification that all nursing functions did not require the standard three-year training period that was by then the norm. The development of the practical nurse as the basic bedside practitioner allowed registered nurses to more successfully argue for licensure for all practitioners.

In 1918, Virginia had passed an act regulating attendants.[22] A few other states had followed suit, but most of the early legislation was aimed at attendants in mental hospitals rather than practical nurses in general hospitals. In 1944 15 states had provisions for some type of auxiliary personnel.[20] However, the major impact of the New York precedent of full recognition for practical nurses was not felt until the period immediately after World War II, when the shortage of nurses created pressure for the stratification of the nursing role and the concept of team nursing developed.[3(pp 182-215)] By 1960 all the states and territories had licensure for practical nurses, although in two states the title is "vocational" nurse.[23,24(pp 9-10)]

Besides its connection with the stratification of the nursing role, mandatory licensure also had another interesting ramification. In order to pass a mandatory act of any kind, it was necessary to spell out the scope of practice of the occupation that was being protected against encroachment. The older nursing laws made it illegal for an unauthorized person to use the title "registered nurse," but not illegal for such a person to practice nursing. Once the new mandatory laws made it illegal for an unauthorized person to practice nursing, a definition of the scope of practice had to be written into these laws. The 1938 New York act indicated that:

A person practices nursing within the meaning of this article who for compensation or personal profit (a) performs any professional service requiring the applications of principles of nursing based on biological, physical and social sciences, such as responsible supervision of a patient requiring skill in observation of symptoms and reactions and the accurate recording of the facts and carrying out of treatments and medications as prescribed by a licensed physician, and the application of such nursing procedures as involve understanding of cause and effect in order to safeguard life and health of a patient and others; or (b) performs such duties as are required in the physical care of a patient and in carrying out of medical orders as prescribed by a licensed physician, requiring an understanding of nursing but not requiring the professional service as outlined in (a).[14(p 316)]

This definition of nursing became the model for other legislation, with Louisiana, Arkansas, and West Virginia adopting the same language and other states using modifications. By 1946, ten states Hawaii had adopted some sort of a definition of nursing.[14(p 315-8),25] Thus, a statement about the scope of practice became inexorably tied to the movement to gain mandatory licensure, and even came to be thought of as a goal in and of itself. Nurses and the legal advisors of the day advocated that the scope of practice be defined in nurse practice acts.[26,14(p 47)]

The process of defining nursing and passing mandatory nurse practice acts was facilitated in 1955 when the Board of Directors of the American Nurses' Association adopted a model definition of nursing. Professional and practical nursing practice were defined as follows:

The term "practice of professional" nursing means the performance, for compensation, of any acts in the observation, care and counsel of the ill, injured or infirm or in the maintenance of health or prevention of illness of others, or in the supervision and teaching of other personnel or the administration of medications and treatments as prescribed by a licensed physician or a licensed dentist; requiring substantial specialized judgment and skill and based on knowledge and application of principles of biological, physical and social science. The foregoing shall not be deemed to include any acts of diagnosis or prescription of therapeutic or corrective measures.

The practice of practical nursing means the performance for compensation of selected acts in the care of the ill, injured, or infirm under the direction of a registered professional nurse or a licensed physician or a licensed dentist; and not requiring the substantial specialized skill, judgment, and knowledge required in professional nursing.[27]

This definition became the new model for changing nurse practice acts. By 1967 15 states had incorporated the language of this model into their state laws and 6 states had used the model with only slight modifications.[28] A notable aspect of this model act, as well as the other similar definitions of practice that were used is the disclaimer, which clearly spells out the fact that nursing did not include any acts of diagnosis or the prescription of therapeutic measures. Before the era of mandatory licensure, nurse registration acts did not define nursing. As a result, they did not include any such disclaimer. The fascinating thing about the disclaimer is that it was made not by the American Medical Association, but by the American Nurses' Association. Although a reasonable assumption might be that the nurses felt the disclaimer necessary to avoid medical opposition to the new practice acts, there is little evidence of overt pressure by medical people. In effect, organized nursing surrendered before any battle over boundaries could occur.

The reasons for this collective behavior by nurses are complex and involve some speculation. Some nurses, particularly those in university settings, were beginning to evolve an ideological position calling for a separation of the function of nurses from that of physicians. They naturally supported such disclaimers because they felt that the nursing role should emphasize psychological support rather than medical diagnosis or treatment.[29-32] Others welcomed the protection of the pretense that they did not make decisions.[33] However, probably the major reason for support of the disclaimer in the model practice act and the various state acts was a type of alienation, or anticipatory self-discrimination. Rather than risk a rebuff or a possible boundary dispute with medicine, nurses almost unconsciously decided to avoid admitting their role in the patient care decision-making process. Similar patterns of anticipatory self-discrimination are a fairly common phenomenon among minority groups; the ghetto walls are often as well-policed from the inside as the outside. Feelings of powerlessness and fear prevent people from challenging discriminatory practices.[34,35]

Actually, by 1955, when the model act was formulated by the ANA, nurses were a fairly well-educated group of workers. Although there were still a few states that did not require high school graduation for licensure, this requirement had become a dead issue because the schools themselves, aided by standards developed by the National League for Nursing, had moved to uphold the standard. A trend to move educational programs into colleges and universities was developing, and although only about 15 percent of the schools were collegiate the movement was already a significant factor in motivating the diploma schools to improve their programs and move away from the old apprenticeship model.[36] National pool examinations had been developed to upgrade state board examinations and to facilitate the movement of nurses between jurisdictions.[37] The standard training period was three years, and with the improved academic content a substantial body of knowledge could be imparted to the student nurses in that length of time.

With this background, nurses in 1955 were observing patients, collecting data about their conditions, arriving at decisions, and acting on those decisions to care for their patients. They were, in short, making diagnostic and therapeutic decisions. Although recent developments in intensive and primary care have greatly expanded the role of nurses in medical decision making, the scope of practice statements enacted in this period were outdated at the time they were written.

Various coping mechanisms evolved to attempt to deal with this situation of immediate obsolescence. One of these mechanisms was the joint statement. The first joint statement was promulgated in California in 1957. Representatives of the California Nurses' Association met with representatives of the medical and hospital associations to draw up a statement regarding nurses doing vena punctures. The statement they adopted authorized agencies to allow nurses with proper preparation to start intravenous fluids.[38] Following this precedent, similar statements were made by joint committees in Ohio and Pennsylvania; in California, subsequent conferences of the three original organizations supported nurses performing other procedures. As the nursing role was extended in the intensive care units, new kinds of statements emerged. In 1966, the Michigan Heart Association passed a resolution approving the use of defibrillators by coronary care nurses. Reporting this resolution, Harvey Sarner pointed out that the Michigan Heart Association was in fact improperly taking on the role of the Michigan legislature.[39(pp 89-90)] Although his argument would probably hold true also for the joint statements, position papers by the professional organizations and other groups continued. In 1968, the Hawaii Nursing, Medical and Hospital Association approved nurses doing cardiopulmonary resuscitation.[40(pp 110-27)] The joint statements were given further support when permanent joint practice commissions were set up in various states in response to recommendations by the National Commission for the Study of Nursing and Nursing Education.[41] These joint practice commissions are now drafting statements supporting expanded functions for nurses.

The joint statements were apparently effective to some degree in preventing legal problems for nurses. In 1967, ten years after the first joint statement was made, the California Nurses' Association reported that not a single nurse who had followed criteria set up under one of the statements had been indicted.[42] Of course, the truth of the matter is that nurses have not ordinarily been sued for exceeding their scope of practice unless negligence was in some way involved. For example, in the often cited case of *Barber* v. *Reiking* (Washington: 411 P.2d 861 [1966]), a practical nurse who was employed in a physician's office was found negligent for exceeding her scope of practice. She was giving an injection to a child who moved, and the needle broke off in his buttock. Surgical removal of the needle proved difficult and was not accomplished for nine months. The family sued both the physician and nurse, and after a lengthy court battle both were found negligent because the mandatory nurse practice act of the State of Washington at that time reserved injections to registered nurses.[40(p 114),43]

In a more clearly negligent case, a practical nurse was charged with a violation of the medical practice act for going into a New York bar and grill during the 1947 smallpox scare and injecting some 500 people with water, claiming it was smallpox vaccine.[44] Neither of these cases would have emerged without negligence, and in the second case the fraudulent actions of the nurse are more noteworthy than her violations of the scope of practice rules. Medical boards have been unwilling to indict nurses for practicing medicine as long as they were working under physicians' directions. The traditional attitude of medical people has been that nurses are permitted to perform any function that physicians care to delegate to them.[39(pp 16-17)] These functions have of course included acts of diagnosis, in spite of the legal prohibitions that existed in the medical and nurse practice acts. On the other hand, in at least one case an occupational health nurse was found negligent because she failed to diagnose a basal cell carcinoma (*Cooper* v. *National Motor Bearing Company* 136 Cal App 2d 229, 288 P 2d 581[1955]).[45] Thus the fiction that nurses did not diagnose rested on shaky legal grounds.

The legal crisis was escalated by the rapid development of the new roles of nurses in acute and primary care. In 1971 a special committee appointed by the Secretary of the Department of Health, Education, and Welfare announced that it saw no legal barriers to role expansion for nurses.[46] This statement merely caused confusion, because of the incongruence that had developed between the state statutes and the decisions of courts and boards. The Attorneys General of Arizona and California added to the uncertainty when they issued statements, based on the statutes of their respective states, that nurses could neither diagnose nor treat patients.[47,48] The feeling, particularly among nurses working in expanded roles, was one of confusion and concern, although few of them actually suffered any negative legal sanctions.

Phase II in the development of nursing licensure might be described as ending on this growing note of concern over the legality of much of nursing practice. Still, most of the other goals of the past had been accomplished. Nurses in all states were registered, and educational standards were reasonably high. Mandatory licensing acts had been passed in 42 states for registered nurses and in 28 states for practical nurses.[24(pp 65,73)] There were still a few physicians sitting on boards of nursing, but a new element of consumer representation was adding a different flavor to the boards and helping to dilute the power of the remaining physicians.[49]

Phase III began when the first new nurse practice acts were passed—acts that honestly admitted that selected nurses or all nurses could diagnose and treat patients. Probably the starting date for Phase III is 1971, when Idaho amended its nurse practice act to authorize acts of diagnosis and treatment.[1] Nurse practice act revisions followed in New York, South Dakota, and Tennessee in 1972. Since then the pace has been increasing as society—and nurses themselves—reassesses the role of the nurse in the health care team. These changes in the role and in the legal status of nurses are probably the most significant developments in nursing in this century. The remaining portion of the book will examine these changes from a variety of vantage points.

REFERENCES

1. IDAHO CODE, § 54-1413.
2. New York Education Law § § 6901, 6902 (Supp. 1972).
3. V.L. BULLOUGH & B. BULLOUGH, THE EMERGENCE OF MODERN NURSING 120-49 (2d ed. 1969).
4. L.L. DOCK, A HISTORY OF NURSING, VOL. III (1912).
5. AMERICAN NURSES' ASSOCIATION, FACTS ABOUT NURSING 96 (1974).
6. M.M. ROBERTS, AMERICAN NURSING: HISTORY AND INTERPRETATION 20-30 (1961).
7. H.E. MARSHALL, MARY ADELAIDE NUTTING: PIONEER OF MODERN NURSING 79 (1972).
8. L. Dock, *What We May Expect from the Law*, AM. J. NURS. 8-12 (October 1900).
9. *Address of the President, Isabel Hampton Robb, before the Third Annual Convention of the Associated Alumnae of Trained Nurses of United States*, 1 AM. J. NURS. 97-104 (November 1900).
10. L.R. SEYMER, A GENERAL HISTORY OF NURSING (1933).
11. C. WOODHAM-SMITH, FLORENCE NIGHTINGALE (1951).
12. R.M. WEST, HISTORY OF NURSING IN PENNSYLVANIA (1933).
13. V. ROBINSON, WHITE CAPS: THE STORY OF NURSING 282-3 (1946).
14. M.J. LESNICK & B.E. ANDERSON, LEGAL ASPECTS OF NURSING (1947).
15. *The Biennial*, 34 AM. J. NURS. 603-27 (June 1934).
16. R.C. DERBYSHIRE, MEDICAL LICENSURE IN THE UNITED STATES (1969).
17. *Nursing Legislation, 1939: What the State Nurses' Associations Accomplished*, 39 AM. J. NURS. 974-981 (September 1939).
18. *Statutory Status of Six Professions*, 16 RES. BULL. NAT'L EDUC. ASS'N 184-223 (September 1938).
19. *Editorial*, 39 AM. J. NURS. 275-7 (March 1939).
20. *Trained Attendants and Practical Nurses*, 44 AM. J. NURS. 7-8 (January 1944).
21. E.M. JAMIESON & M. SEWELL, TRENDS IN NURSING HISTORY 533-4 (1944).
22. 18 AM. J. NURS. 929 (July 1918).
23. N. Stevenson, *Curriculum Development in Practical Nurse Education*, 64 AM. J. NURS. 81-6 (December 1964).
24. NATIONAL CENTER FOR HEALTH STATISTICS, U.S. DEP'T OF HEALTH,

EDUCATION AND WELFARE, PUBLIC HEALTH SERVICE PUB. 1758, STATE LICENSING OF HEALTH OCCUPATIONS (1968).
25. G. HARRISON & J.H. HARRISON, THE NURSE AND THE LAW 4-5 (1945).
26. M. Jacobsen, *Nursing Laws and What Every Nurse Should Know about Them*, 40 AM. J. NURS. 1221-6 (November 1940).
27. *ANA Board Approves a Definition of Nursing Practice*, 55 AM. J. NURS. 1474 (December 1955).
28. E.H. Forgotson, R. Roemer, R.W. Newman & J.L. Cook, *Licensure of Other Medical Personnel*, in REPORT OF THE NATIONAL ADVISORY COMMISSION ON HEALTH MANPOWER, VOL II 407-92 (1967).
29. F.R. Kreuter, *What Is Good Nursing Care?* 5 NURS. OUTLOOK 302-4 (May 1957).
30. D.E. Johnson, *A Philosophy of Nursing*, 7 NURS. OUTLOOK 198-200 (April 1959).
31. M. ROGERS, REVEILLE IN NURSING (1964).
32. *American Nurses' Association's First Position on Education for Nursing*, 65 AM. J. NURS. 106-11 (December 1965).
33. L. Stein, *The Doctor-Nurse Game*, 16 ARCH. GEN. PSYCHIATRY 699-703 (June 1967).
34. B. Bullough, *Alienation in the Ghetto*, 72 AM. J. SOCIOL. 469-78 (March 1967).
35. B. BULLOUGH, SOCIAL-PSYCHOLOGICAL BARRIERS TO HOUSING DESEGREGATION, UNIV. OF CALIF. HOUSING, REAL ESTATE & URBAN LAND STUDIES PROGRAM (1969).
36. AMERICAN NURSES' ASSOCIATION, FACTS ABOUT NURSING: A STATISTICAL SUMMARY, 1955-1956 at 76 (1956).
37. B.E. ANDERSON, THE FACILITATION OF INTERSTATE MOVEMENT OF REGISTERED NURSES (1950).
38. G.C. Barbee, *Special Procedures: I.V.s, Blood Transfusions and Skin Testing*, in PROCEEDINGS: INSTITUTE ON THE MEDICO-LEGAL ASPECTS OF NURSING PRACTICE 41-4 (1961).
39. H. SARNER, THE NURSE AND THE LAW (1968).
40. N. Hershey, *Legal Issues in Nursing Practice*, in PROFESSIONAL NURSING: FOUNDATIONS, PERSPECTIVES AND RELATIONSHIPS (E.K. Spalding & L.E. Notter eds. 1970).
41. NATIONAL COMMISSION FOR THE STUDY OF NURSING AND NURSING EDUCATION, AN ABSTRACT FOR ACTION (1970).
42. S.H. WILLIG, THE NURSES' GUIDE TO THE LAW 75 (1970).
43. H. CREIGHTON, LAW EVERY NURSE SHOULD KNOW 19 (1970).
44. N. Hershey, *Nurses' Medical Practice Problems, Part I*, 62 AM. J. NURS 82-3 (July 1962).
45. I.A. MURCHISON & T.S. NICHOLS, LEGAL FOUNDATION OF NURSING PRACTICE, 91, 109-11 (1970).
46. EXTENDING THE SCOPE OF NURSING PRACTICE: A REPORT OF THE SECRETARY'S COMMITTEE TO STUDY EXTENDED ROLES FOR NURSES 6 (November 1971).
47. 71 OP. Ariz. Att'y Gen. 30 (August 6 1971), cited in A.M. Sadler, Jr. & B.L. Sadler, *Recent Developments in the Law Relating to Physicians' Assistants* 24 VAND. L. REV. 1205 (November 1971).
48. CV 72 OP. CALIF. ATT'Y GEN. 187 (1973); Indexed letter from Calif. Att'y Gen. (October 4, 1972).
49. L.Y. Kelly, *Nursing Practice Acts*, 74 AM. J. NURS. 1310-9 (July 1974).

VERN L. BULLOUGH

2

Licensure and the Medical Monopoly

Discussion of change in nursing roles cannot be undertaken without considering modification in the roles of physicians. Since both roles are regulated by the state, the problem becomes a legal as well as an inter-occupational one. The difficulty is compounded because medicine, by law as well as by custom, has been given control over the whole health field; other health occupational groups, such as nurses, dentists, pharmacists, therapists, technicians, and even psychologists, have only been able to assume certain delegated or specified responsibilities and duties. In effect, by exercise of the state licensure powers a medical monopoly has been created, and this monopoly has both good and bad effects.

On the one hand it has been argued that medical licensure raised the level of medical practice by setting a high standard. Licensure eliminated the quacks and incompetents, and provided some guarantee to the patient that the physician consulted was qualified. Thus, medical licensure was a successful effort by the state to protect the public against unqualified practitioners.[1-5] Conversely, it can be claimed that medical licensure handicapped the effective delivery of health care by giving a monopoly to a small self-regulated group, whose interests were not necessarily in better medical care but rather in bettering the standing of their profession. By restricting the number of practitioners, licensure allowed the physician to raise his or her economic standards and achieve a much higher social status than might otherwise have been warranted. The state, rather than acting to protect its citizens by licensure, gave a monopoly to a few to exploit the public; it further increased such exploitation by giving one segment, the physician, control over all other health fields and specialists. In sum, the state thwarted the public interest by creating a pyramid of medical practitioners, which guaranteed wealth and power to those at the top and then gave them the means of perpetuating their power.

Probably the truth, if there is such a thing, lies somewhere between these two extreme points of view; but since the purpose of a book such as this is to encourage the rethinking of traditional assumptions, I would like to present the case for the second more strongly than the first. I realize that nurses and other health professionals and paraprofessionals are also licensed by the state, but since the physicians dominate the field these other groups have never been able to assert themselves quite so much either in control of their own area of specialty or in subsuming other areas of health care under their control.

Perhaps the best way to deal with the problem of licensing is to understand why we have licensing at all. The answer is not as simple as it might seem. Opposition has often existed to giving any professional group a monopoly over a field. One of the most ardent opponents was Adam Smith, often looked upon as the intellectual founder of capitalism. Smith was consulted in 1774 for advice about giving university-trained physicians an exclusive monopoly on the practice of medicine—a monopoly that they enjoyed in many of the continental countries but did not then have in England. Smith opposed the granting of any such monopoly by the government because, he claimed, the universities would abuse their right, and no examination or degree that they awarded could "give any tolerable security that the person upon whom it had been conferred was fit to practice physic" (an eighteenth century term for medicine). Indeed, he argued that if the Royal College was given a medical monopoly the price of medical care would rise to double or triple the sum it then cost, and there would be ever-continuing attempts to limit the number of practitioners in order to keep medical fees high.[6]

Although Smith still exercises great influence on economic thinking, this aspect of his writing is generally ignored even by some of his most fervid supporters. A good example of what Smith predicted appeared in an editorial by Arthur D. Lisbin, M.D., past president of the Los Angeles Pediatric Society.

Everybody is trying to practice medicine! Senate Bill 968 was just passed and is now in the Assembly. This bill would allow school nurses, or certified personnel (whatever that term means) to do routine exams on all school children during school time and on school premises. There is no financial screening, nor is there any indication of whether or how these examiners will be supervised by physicians. . . . I don't know about the rest of you, but I am neither licensed, nor do I teach history or math in my office, and I don't think our educators should be practicing medicine in their schools! Their purpose is teaching and I am sure there are lots of improvements to be made in that direction before they look for involvement in new fields. . . . A similar bill was defeated several years ago because of the Academy's opposition to it. Again, the Academy is opposed to the bill. . . .[7]

Lisbin's real objection to the bill seemed to be that there was no financial screening; his pocketbook became the judgment for what constituted the best interests of his profession.

Smith was not the only one concerned with the dangers of a state monopoly through licensure, and over the years writers and critics both within and without medicine have been concerned. Some opposed licensure for conservative reasons; others, for more liberal reasons. William Osler, for example, one of the greats of modern medicine, felt that licensure as practiced in the United States and Canada was "provincialism run riot";[8] Henry Sigerist, the founding father of medical history in this country, opposed the administration of state tests or examinations to determine qualifications for medical practice.[3] In spite of such opposition various government units, encouraged by the organized medical profession, decided that the guarantee of some minimum standards was essential to the public interest. In the process of establishing these standards they severely curtailed the number of physicians, raised the cost of medical care, gave the physician a medical monopoly, and helped create some of the difficulties that other health professional face today.

The controversy among various allied health groups is an old one. In fact, the basis for the medical monopoly can be traced back to the Middle Ages, when medicine was just beginning to emerge as a profession. At that time, physicians in the newly-emerging universities argued that in the best interests of the public welfare they ought to be allowed to control the practice of medicine, because they were better educated than other would-be practitioners—namely the barbers, surgeons, pharmacists, midwives, and so forth.[9] Though the physicians never quite achieved an absolute monopoly, they did force other groups of medical practitioners to define their roles vis-à-vis the university trained physician; by achieving the dominant position in the pyramid of health care, they managed to eliminate many groups of practitioners altogether—primarily and most notably, Jews and women.

One of the reasons for the physicians' failure to achieve absolute control in the medieval period was their own status demands, which made them unwilling to do certain medical procedures (particularly surgical ones) that they considered beneath their dignity. The traditional alliance of the apothecary with the greengrocer made controlling this group more difficult. Another reason was the lack of sufficient numbers of university graduates to serve all segments of the population. The university-trained physicians tended to be concentrated in the larger cities and to serve the richer clients, while the lesser-trained practitioners served in the villages or market towns; providing that the latter group did not threaten the former, its members were allowed to practice. In England the issue was complicated by the fact that London, the largest city and the nation's capital, lacked a university until the nineteenth century. To remedy this the London physicians organized into a college, that was given a charter as the Royal College of Physicians in 1518. By 1522, the Royal College controlled examination and licensing throughout England. Similar authority was given to the London Company of Barber-Surgeons in 1540, to the London Society of Apothecaries in 1617, and to the Surgeons' Company in 1745; but usually effective control of such groups was limited to the London area. Further adding to the difficulties was the failure of the medical schools at Oxford and Cambridge to keep up with developments in curriculum or medical expertise in the seventeenth and eighteenth centuries. When the kingdoms of England and Scotland were merged under the rule of James I, at the beginning of the seventeenth century, large numbers of Scottish university physicians began to move to London. In many cases university degrees in medicine were worth little more than the parchment on which they were printed, and the real training in London took place in the various hospitals. Outside of London most people were treated by village surgeons or apothecaries, who were trained through an apprenticeship system.[10]

Neither the British Crown nor the British Parliament extended professional regulations to any of the overseas provinces. Here the practice differed from that of Spain, which established the medical code of Castile in the Spanish-American colonies in the sixteenth century. Because physicians, like the upper classes in general, did not migrate overseas, and because for a long period no American city was large enough to maintain a medical college, American medical practitioners at first were rather free-enterprise types. Clergymen often practiced medicine on the side. In other cases individuals simply set themselves up as practitioners. A few went to Europe, particularly to Edinburgh, for some training, before attempting to practice. Generally, would-be medical practitioners served a brief period of apprenticeship under other practitioners before setting out on their own. Regardless of training, most quickly claimed to be doctors of medicine—a term that the Americans applied with egalitarian abandon to all types of practitioners. In Great Britain and on continental Europe, the term *doctor* had been reserved to those who graduated from the higher faculties of the university, primarily those who intended to teach. Admission to these faculties came only after earning a baccalaureate degree. In America, however, all medical practitioners, whether surgeons, barbers, physicians, or apothecaries, called themselves or were called *doctor*; a term that originally meant "to teach" (from the Latin *docere*, to teach) became a euphemism for all medical practitioners.

The first American medical school was founded in Philadelphia in 1765. Its founders hoped to control the issuance of licenses in the colonies, but this plan was thwarted by the opposition of the Royal College of Physicians in London. In order to bring about some regulation New York City enacted its own licensing procedures, followed by New Jersey, but the initial governmental efforts in this direction collapsed during the American Revolution. Following the Revolution medical societies were organized in the newly independent states, and these societies began to advocate state tests and licensing, usually in order to protect themselves against their would-be rivals. Legislatures usually granted the requests for licensing acts, although the specifics varied widely from state to state. In some states a state examining board was created; in others medical societies were granted the power to test and license; in still others, various regions had permission to do their own testing. Regardless of procedures, however, the medical societies had control of licensing. The result was a kind of self-policing, the purpose of which was not so much to protect the public as to protect the profession.

This system failed, largely because graduates of medical schools (as distinguished from those trained by apprenticeship) did not have to undergo the same licensing procedures as others, and in effect were licensed by the colleges from which they graduated. In the nineteenth century there was a rapid proliferation of medical schools, many of them adherents of particular medical philosophies. Since most of the schools were proprietary ones, run for profit, the number of licensed medical practitioners increased rapidly and standards dropped just as rapidly. So did the cost of medical care. Just how well educated a physician might be was indicated by an 1850 survey of practitioners in eastern Tennessee, which found that of the 201 physicians in the area (for a population of 164,000 people), 35 (17 percent) were graduates of some sort of regular medical school; 42 (20 percent) had taken a course of lectures but never graduated; and 27 (13 percent) were botanic or natural healing practitioners. The others (almost 50 percent) generally had received no instruction other than their own reading, and even this had been limited.[4(pp 31-32)]

Even a diploma from a medical school was no guarantee of competence. Most schools depended upon student fees for their operation, and it was to the advantage of the proprietors to take in as many students as possible and graduate them as quickly as they could. It was not until the last part of the nineteenth century, when a few of the leading universities began paying medical professors salaries, that some of the incentive for awarding medical degrees was lost. Concern with the university's right to proclaim anyone a physician led to the founding of the American Medical Association in 1847. The call for the organizing meeting was made in 1846 by the New York State Medical Society in an effort to raise the level of professional competence and status, and the Society tried to restrict its appeal to those who were members of "regular" societies and "approved schools." Gradually, certain standards were adopted that eventually led to better premedical training, minimum periods for medical schooling, strengthened state boards of licensing, and stronger professional societies. In 1873 Texas became the first state to pass a modern registration act requiring state examination and registration. In 1881 a West Virginia statute was challenged by opponents, and not until 1889 did the Supreme Court decide that this type of licensure was a valid exercise of the police power of the state. The result was further encouragement of state licensing, and by 1895 all the states had passed registration laws for physicians.[5(pp 1-8)] In almost every state the boards of licensing worked in collaboration with the state medical societies, which were also usually cooperating with the AMA.

This collaboration proved a handicap because efforts by the physicians to raise standards further met with fear that the cost of medical care would also increase and a suspicion of the motives of the medical profession. The AMA felt that to go further it strongly needed outside support. This support came from the Carnegie Foundation for the Advancement of Teaching, which commissioned a survey of medical education under the direction of Abraham Flexner, a nonphysician. His report, published in 1910, had great effect on public opinion and on state licensing.[11] The almost immediate result was the establishment of ever-stricter licensing standards, elimination of the worst of the so-called diploma mills, and a gradual decline in the number of medical graduates. Typically in most states the governor appointed a Board of Medical Examiners, selected from a list of practicing physicians recommended by the state medical association. These boards operated, and continue to operate, with considerable autonomy in determining the qualifications of applications for licensure, although certain statutory requirements must be kept in mind.

Medical licensing, however, did not solve all the problems affecting the medical profession, and has created problems for other members of the health care field. One of the difficulties with licensing as it has existed in the past, is that there has been little effective check on the continued competence of the physician who continued to practice for decades after he was licensed. A physician at the beginning of his career might well have been aware of most of the developments in medicine, but licensing guaranteed his competence for life without any effort to ascertain if he still retained competence. An incompetent could continue to practice with little fear that he would be denounced by the organized medical profession. In the United States, medical licensure gave the physician the right to practice in all fields of medicine, even though he knew little or nothing about most of them. Gradually, volunteer boards have developed to certify specialists, although in order to gain support these boards have had to "grandfather" in a number whose background was dubious. Although many hospitals insist on board certification for their staff members, even present American medical practice goes on the assumption that a physician is competent in all areas of medicine.

Still another difficulty is the control the physician has over all other medical groups, caused by the general claims of the medical practitioner and the political backing these claims have through the state licensing board. Though there are large numbers of disinterested physicians, it is probably asking far too much of any profession to give away any of its powers or even claims of powers without a struggle, or to deal with other health professionals without keeping its own interests in mind. Some states have attempted to insist that at least one member of the Board of Medical Examiners represent the general public, but this tokenism is particularly ineffective. Medical examiners generally look upon the health field as their own preserve and resent any encroachment, however slight. This control is like leaving direction of colleges and universities entirely in the hands of the professors, doing away with state lay boards of education or boards of regents and consultation with students. From personal experience in academic life, I find that I often disagree with the lay boards; but I think it is absolutely essential we have this kind of interaction with the public. Otherwise the professional, and I include myself, would be more likely to think in terms of his or her own professional needs rather than the needs of the public. The problem in education is to harmonize professional needs with public wants, and this kind of give-and-take is lacking in medicine except through direct appeal to the legislature. Inevitably, when any segment of the health care pyramid attempts to extend or modify its role the legislature must be appealed to for support. This is the only direct way of modifying or checking the medical dominance.

Further complicating the problem is that the Board of Medical Examiners in most states does not necessarily represent the latest trends in medicine or even the majority of medical opinion. This is not the result of any kind of conscious conservatism, but rather of the nature and demands of medicine and the political process. Most beginning physicians are not particularly interested in the political arena either of their profession or of state government; the most interested physicians tend to represent the older, often even semiretired, members of the profession, and much too often their interests reflect the concerns of a few decades ago rather than the needs of today or the future.[5(pp 40-41)] Thus, medical boards today are dominated by general practitioners, because they are the most common medical practitioners of the past. This means that far too many physicians in a position of power are basically unaware of current demands—or, if aware, tend to dismiss them. Obviously this is a generalization with many exceptions, but it helps to explain why both the AMA and the various Boards of Medical Examiners often seem to be fighting the battles of the last generation rather than those of the present.

This history helps to explain why there is so much difficulty in modifying the traditional nursing role. It also explains why there are so many mixed feelings in the nursing profession itself about a change in the nursing role. The same theories that apply to the medical establishment tend to apply to the nursing establishment although nurses, lacking the power of physicians, have always been more subject to public and legislative pressure. Licensure in nursing was about a generation behind that of medicine.[12] This delay meant that the primary power position in the health field had been preempted by the physician, forcing nurses to define their role in terms of the physician even more than did dentists and pharmacists, who were earlier on the scene. From the first, the nursing role has been defined as more limiting than it really was because nursing was a woman's profession while medicine generally was restricted to men. Therefore nurses, even before they became nurses, learned to play the male–female game; because the role of women was very narrowly and strictly defined, the role of nurse's (one of the largest women's occupations) also was very narrowly and strictly defined. The rigid definition of theory, however, was not carried out in practice, because nurses pretended to leave most of the decisions to the male physicians while in effect quietly making decisions of their own or manipulating the physicians to make the desired decisions.[13] Thus, though the nurse lacked formal power, she had a great deal of informal power if she was able to mask her power and decision-making. This ability to masquerade as innocent also protected her from any responsibility for her decision. Many male physicians never did catch on to the game, and still hark back to this model. Unfortunately the world keeps changing; developments in medicine and nursing, as well as rising consciousness among women, led to a demand for change. Increasingly, the strains of the game have begun to show, although both sides have been slow to rethink the old rules. Such rethinking as has been done has more likely come from the nurses than from the physicians, because in any pyramid of power it is those at the bottom who are most likely to demand change. Nurses have been encouraged in their new demands by the demands of other women who have been at the bottom of the pyramid of power and prestige in a variety of occupations.[14]

The growing importance of the hospital in medicine has added to the difficulties. As the physician has become more and more specialized he has become more and more a part of an institution, whether it be a Health Maintenance Organization, a hospital, or simply a group practice. Nursing went through the shift into the hospital much earlier than medicine itself; but this shift has entailed a real vacuum in primary patient care because specialization tends to increase fragmentation. Though there have been, and continue to be, attempts in medical schools to encourage the general practitioner (often renamed family practitioner), the rewards in medicine today go to the specialist — not only monetary rewards, but also prestige and, perhaps more important, the ability to deal with many of the real problems afflicting patients. The general practitioner, even though an emotionally appealing ideal to most physicians, will be difficult to produce in the quantities needed unless he or she is given the same kinds of rewards received by the specialist, or unless we develop a multi-level medical education and certification program in which the standards for the general practitioner are different (and somewhat lower) than for the specialist. The first alternative would raise the price of medical care to astronomical heights, primarily to salve the egos of the practitioners. The second alternative is somewhat more attractive. In fact, we implement this program today on an informal basis by importing foreign medical graduates to meet our needs.[15-17] But in the long run, this practice is even more threatening to the medical profession and goes contrary to the tradition built up over the past few decades. Moreover, the supply of foreign graduates is always in danger of declining if standards are raised. The third alternative is to move up another member of the health team, namely the nurse; to give official recognition to what she has been doing in the past; and allow the nurse to further extend her role. Of the options available, this last seems the most logical, but the problem lies in dealing with the boards of medical examiners, who feel their position threatened by any but the first alternative. Thus, the solution in most states will be a political one, with the legislature acting to modify traditional roles to meet changing needs. If this proves to be the case, nurses and other members of the health professions should keep in mind that too often in the past the boards of medical examiners have worked to benefit the members of their own profession and only indirectly to improve health care. When change does come, as it undoubtedly will, medicine will remain at the top of the pyramid: but there will be some chance for movement among other members of the health profession. Reform has long been overdue.

REFERENCES

1. This traditional view is effectively summarized by E. Forgotson, R. Roemer, & R. Newman, *Legal Regulation of Health Personnel in the United States,* in REPORT OF THE NATIONAL ADVISORY COMMISSION ON HEALTH MANPOWER II, Appendix VII, 279–541 (1967).
2. *See also* R. Roemer, *Legal Systems Regulating Health Personnel: A Comparative Analysis,* 46 MILBANK MEM. FUND Q. 431–71 (October 1968).
3. *See also* H.E. Sigerist, *The History of Medical Licensure* in HENRY E. SIGERIST ON THE SOCIOLOGY OF MEDICINE M. Roemer ed. (1960) The article originally appeared in 104 J. AM. MED. ASSOC., 1060 (1935).
4. R.H. SHRYOCK, MEDICAL LICENSING IN AMERICA, 1650–1965 (1967).
5. R. DERBYSHIRE, MEDICAL LICENSURE AND DISCIPLINE IN THE UNITED STATES (1969) for historical background to the American situation.
6. The letter which Smith wrote on this subject is perhaps most readily available in JOHN RAE, LIFE OF ADAM SMITH 372–80 (1895, reprinted 1965).
7. *Newsletter of the Los Angeles Pediatric Society* (January 1974).
8. W. OSLER, AEQUANIMITAS 276 (1944) Osler, however, was not opposed to licensure *per se.*
9. For a lengthy discussion of this see V. L. BULLOUGH, THE DEVELOPMENT OF MEDICINE AS A PROFESSION (1966).
10. *See* F.N.L. POYNTER, THE EVOLUTION OF MEDICAL PRACTICE IN BRITAIN (1961).
11. A. FLEXNER, MEDICAL EDUCATION IN THE UNITED STATES AND CANADA, CARNEGIE FOUNDATION FOR THE ADVANCEMENT OF TEACHING, BULLETIN NO. 4 (1910).
12. V.L. BULLOUGH & B. BULLOUGH, THE EMERGENCE OF MODERN NURSING 112–3, 152–3 (2d ed. 1969).
13. *See, for example,* L. Stein, *The Doctor-Nurse Game,* 16 ARCH. GEN. PSYCHIATRY 699–703 (1967).
14. *See* V.L. BULLOUGH, THE SUBORDINATE SEX (1973), with a final chapter by B. Bullough.
15. *See, for example,* INSTITUTE OF INTERNATIONAL EDUCATION, OPEN DOORS REPORT ON INTERNATIONAL EXCHANGE (1966).
16. D,M, Greely, AMERICAN FOREIGN MEDICAL GRADUATES, 41. J. MED. EDUC. 641–50 (1966).
17. T.D. Dublin, *Foreign Physicians: Their Impact on U.S. Health Care,* 185 SCIENCE 407–14 (August 2 1974).

WANDA C. NATIONS

3
Statutory and Common Law as it Relates to Modern Nursing Practice

In California, the practice of medicine was recognized as a profession that required regulation by the state for the good of the public approximately 100 years ago. Because it was considered to be a profession, minimum standards of education and training were prescribed by the state. The administration and enforcement of medical training and standards were then delegated to the Board of Medical Examiners of the state of California.

Nursing was also recognized as a profession that should be regulated by the state for the public good. Like medicine, minimum standards of education and training were prescribed by the state. The California Board of Nursing Education and Nurse Registration was delegated to administer and enforce the minimum nursing standards set forth in the California Nurse Practice Act.[1]

A license to practice nursing is granted by the state in which the nurse performs her work, after the Board of Nursing Education and Nurse Registration approves the qualifications of the licensee. The licensing of nurses and other health workers, including physicians, is carried out under the police power of the state: the power vested in any state to make all manner of laws it considers necessary and essential to protect and promote the public health, safety, and welfare of its citizens. This power is inherent in the lawmaking body of the state. The California Nurse Practice Act came into being through legislative action in 1939.[1] It has been amended by legislative action approximately 20 times. It is contained in its entirety in the Business and Professions Code of the State of California.[1] The word *code* is an ancient one, going back to the Emperor Justinian. In the context in which it is used here,

A "code" implies compilation of existing laws, systematic arrangement into chapters, subheads, table of contents, and index, and revision to harmonize conflicts, supply omissions and generally clarify and make complete body of laws designated to regulate completely subjects to which they relate.[2]

Therefore, the California Nurse Practice Act is a complete collection of laws relating to professional nursing in California. The primary purpose of this act is to protect the citizens of the state from unskilled and incompetent persons who might present themselves to the public as Registered Nurses, and might practice or offer to practice nursing within the state.

Many nurses believe the Nurse Practice Act is that law which requires them to successfully complete a prescribed course of study, pass the state board examination, and obtain a license to practice nursing. Of course, it is this law and much more. It not only specifies how to obtain a license, it also regulates and controls nursing practice. It describes what nurses can do to practice professional nursing, as defined in Section 2725 of Article 2 of the Laws Relating to Nursing Education, Licensure—Practice with rules and regulations.

The Act prohibits nonregistered persons from using the letters RN after their names and from practicing professional nursing. In Washington, in 1966, a practical nurse working in a doctor's office negligently gave a polio immunization injection to a two-year-old boy. The needle broke off and was left in the body of the infant because the physician could not immediately remove it. Surgery was later necessary to remove the broken needle. The court in this case said:

In accordance with the public policy of this state, one who undertakes to perform the services of a trained or graduate nurse must have the knowledge and skill possessed by a registered nurse. The failure of nurse Reiking to be so licensed raises an inference that she did not possess the required knowledge and skill.[3]

In Washington, at that time, a practical nurse could not administer a hypodermic injection. In California, as well as other states, a Licensed Vocational Nurse with prior instructions and demonstrated competence can, at the direction of a licensed or legally authorized medical doctor, administer hypodermic medications and withdraw blood for testing. The Nurse Practice Act has penal provisions that make it unlawful for one who is not duly licensed to practice nursing, to use the title Registered Nurse, the letters RN, or the words Graduate Nurse or Trained Nurse. Any violation of this provision should be reported to the executive secretary of the State Board of Nursing.

The law specifically defines what nurses cannot do. Nurses are forbidden to practice medicine. This appears to be a reasonable provision of the law, and is obviously designed to protect the public from persons who are unqualified, unskilled, and incompetent to practice medicine. Nurses are aware of this section of the law. Physicians, employers in hospitals, public health departments, schools, and other employers are also aware of it. However, nurses are constantly frustrated and in conflict over what their license permits them to do and what physicians and employers expect them to do. It is no longer uncommon for school nurses and office nurses to independently suture simple lacerations, remove sutures, and give antitetanus vaccine to injured patients and students. They are taught these procedures and then instructed to perform them by a supervising physician whose licensing act also prohibits anyone other than a licensed medical doctor to practice medicine. Every day nurses perform procedures that go far beyond nursing practice as it is defined by law. It is not uncommon for nurses to deliver babies in hospitals, and it is very common for nurses to dispense drugs from hospital pharmacies during evening and night hours and on weekends and holidays. The only conclusion that can be drawn is that nurses are practicing medicine and pharmacy, which only medical doctors and pharmacists are legally entitled to do. Nurses are also often professionally responsible for intensive care units, emergency departments, surgery recovery rooms, and many other patient care departments. They perform these tasks because their employers and supervising physicians require them to do so as an integral part of their jobs.

Some states, including California, have incorporated into the practice of nursing a series of papers called *joint statements.* In California, joint statements are issued cooperatively by the California Nurses Association, the California Medical Association, and the California Hospital Association. These statements are legal position papers regarding emerging questioned areas of nursing. Their purpose is to relieve nurses' fears about the possibility of liability for violation of the Medical Practice Act — a criminal offense. Joint statements define conditions and provide guidelines under which a nurse may perform procedures that traditionally and legally belong in the province of medicine. Attorneys believe joint statements would permit them to defend a nurse against a criminal charge of practicing medicine if such a defense were ever necessary. The first joint statement was issued in California in 1957. It was instigated by Mrs. Grace Barbee, who was then legal counsel for the California Nurses' Association. She saw a need to develop some protection for nurses who were performing procedures that extended outside the scope of the Nurse Practice Act. To Mrs. Barbee, there was a clear and obvious need to establish some way of identifying those areas of nursing that previously had been loosely designated "community" standards of practice or "common" standards of practice. Joint statements permit a nurse, with proper training, to expand her role and perform procedures traditionally and legally performed by doctors. Joint statements are examples of cooperative efforts between hospitals, physicians, and nurses to clarify some grey areas of practice and to legitimize some specific procedures that nurses have long been doing.

Joint statements are not law in the same way that the nurse practice acts are law. They do not come about through legislative action. However, with widespread use and acceptance they may very well be called common laws—customs that prevail among the public and are recognized as such by the courts. Joint statements, like nurse practice acts, are designed to protect the public. They also serve to protect nurses and to establish accepted standards of practice.

Many nursing practices are protected neither by legislation nor by joint statements. If these practices are common practices, performed by properly trained nurses, they too can be defended—but with more difficulty and less certainty of outcome, especially if they are in direct conflict with legislated public policy. Fortunately, joint statements can be added to, changed, or amended by agreement of the issuing parties. In comparison, nurse practice acts can be said to be set in concrete. To change an act requires a complicated set of procedures and persuasive activities to get a change through the state legislative body. A majority of the states nursing associations and medical societies have established liaison for the purpose of developing and and issuing joint statements. Judging from the numerous statements developed, tacit agreement exists that each time a medical task is transferred from one category of worker to another new learning will be required. New knowledge and demonstrated skills are necessary for establishing an acceptable standard of practice.

In recent years, nursing has been in a state of constant evolution. It has expanded to admit a new category of nurse—the nurse practitioner. Nurse practitioners now number several thousand, and the number is growing rapidly. Nurse practitioners have special training and can work independently or interdependently. Their expanded role requires them to learn and perform some skilled procedures that usually are considered to be within the realm of medicine. Among these procedures are the performance of physical inspections and examinations, the taking of medical histories, pelvic examinations, insertion of intrauterine devices, and prescribing some medication. Obviously, this category of nurse is providing an important and valuable service. However, this expanded role presents some interesting and serious legal concerns: Is this nurse protected by a nurse practice act? Is she protected by a joint statement? If she is working with a physician in a hospital or in a clinic, to what extent is she liable for her own acts? Is she jointly liable with the physician, hospital, or clinic? What are the legal relationships between other nurses and the nurse practitioner who verbally or in writing "orders" a treatment plan? If the nurse has malpractice insurance, does it cover her in the part of her work that has expanded into areas considered to be the practice of medicine?

Conclusion

The role of nursing has expanded rapidly to meet the increased health care needs of the public. Legislative acts and joint statements, however well intended, have not kept pace with the extended practice of nursing. There is an urgent need for legislation that, while protecting the public, will permit nurses to meet the health care needs of the public within the scope of their qualifications, knowledge, and demonstrated skills. Physicians, hospitals, and other employers who require nurses to perform some medical tasks in the course of their employment should join with nurses to bring about needed changes in legislation.

REFERENCES

1. Business and Professions Code of the State of California, ch. 6, arts. 1, 7, §§ 2700, 2830.
2. Gibson v. State, 214 Ala. 38, 106 So. 231, 235.
3. Barber v. Reiking, 411 P. 2d 861 (Washington 1966).

RUTH ROEMER

4

Nursing Functions and the Law: Some Perspectives from Australia and Canada

The problem of what a nurse does, should do, or is allowed to do is neither new nor unique to the United States. Scope of practice questions are not novel because nursing functions have been expanding ever since nursing began. This process of change is reflected in enlarged nursing functions in health care institutions, in the enrichment of curricula of nursing schools, in rulings of licensing boards, in joint statements of the nursing and medical professions as to functions appropriately performed by nurses, and even in advisory opinions of attorneys general of some states.[1]

Several general forces explain this dynamism in nursing functions. First, scientific and technologic advances, commonly referred to as the biomedical revolution, have impelled new tasks and functions. Would anyone have thought a generation ago that nurses would be performing complex tasks, making critical decisions, and monitoring highly sophisticated equipment in intensive and coronary care units? Second, advances in nursing education have contributed to enlarged functions, especially since many nurse practice acts define professional nursing as acts based on knowledge and application of scientific principles acquired in an approved school of professional nursing. The introduction of new subjects into the curriculum, more profound

The research on which this paper is based was supported by Public Health Service grant NO1-MI-34090(P) (Milton I. Roemer, M.D., Principal Investigator).

examination of certain fields, the teaching of new techniques, and more interdisciplinary studies have all given the nurse a richer background for performance of nursing tasks, for supervision of auxiliary personnel, and for decision-making and nursing assessments. Third, increasing recognition of health care as a human right drives toward expanded nursing functions. Acceptance of the idea that health care is a human right is expressed in measures to improve the organization of health services and thereby increase access to care, such as the recently-enacted federal legislation to promote health maintenance organizations. This acceptance is also reflected in such measures to improve the quality of care as the requirement in the 1972 Social Security Act for professional standards review organizations to monitor institutional care under Medicare, Medicaid, and the maternal and child health program. Perhaps the clearest acknowledgment that health care is a right is contained in such measures to spread the financial burden of health services through social insurance as Medicare, which has now been extended to include the totally disabled as well as the aged; and the proposals for some form of national health insurance, which seems more likely to be enacted than ever before. The concept of health care as a human right raises questions about how the limited resources of a country, including its manpower, are to be allocated to provide the needed services. Who will provide the care? Who will and can do which tasks?

The same forces that have impelled the evolution in nursing functions in the United States are also operative in other countries. Scientific advances, improved education, and increasing recognition of health care as a human right are compelling reexamination of the roles of health personnel and the ways that health services are organized and financed in many countries. It is natural that this scrutiny should turn to the key health profession of nursing—the health profession that has the largest numbers and the longest tradition of service. Nevertheless, the issue may arise in different ways, and change may occur at different rates, depending on the particular conditions in each country. The example of Belgium may be relevant.

In Belgium in 1971, a significant upheaval occurred in the health field when the Belgian nurses organized themselves to conduct an inquiry among doctors on the subject of nursing functions. In interviews with doctors nurses asked whether nurses could properly perform certain specific procedures. The doctors replied, in essence, that nurses could do all these procedures perfectly, that they did them every day, and, in fact, that without nurses' doing these procedures the hospitals would not be able to function.[2] But the tasks listed were all functions that nurses were not legally authorized to do. For example, the Belgian law authorizes nurses to do intramuscular injections but not intravenous injections; but nurses actually do intravenous injections commonly. Although the Belgian nurses by their own initiative had demonstrated the need to update the law, this updating has not yet been done. Despite general concurrence by doctors about the expanded scope of nursing functions, Belgian nurses are still awaiting action by prestigious (but conservative) academic groups in medicine and changes in the legislation governing nursing functions to match the realities of what nurses are trained to do and what they actually do.

In resolving questions concerning nursing functions and the law in our own country, it may be helpful to examine the experience of two countries that resemble the United States in several ways—Australia and Canada. All three countries are large, English-speaking, common law countries. All consist of federated states or provinces, with major authority for health matters vested in the states but considerable influence still exerted by the federal government. All are characterized by pluralistic health systems, with multiple public and private agencies and varied patterns of organizing medical care.

Of course, just as there are similarities, there are also differences. Some of these differences are historical, social, and cultural, with greater influence of the United Kingdom on both Australia and Canada than on the United States. Some of the differences relate to the health care system, and the most important of these is probably the system of financing health care. In both Australia and Canada, social financing of health care is more developed than in the United States.

In Australia, the National Health Act encourages enrollment in voluntary health insurance programs with the aid of government subsidies. People obtain medical care through private physicians and voluntary or public hospitals, with reimbursement of fees or charges for insured persons made partly by the insurance plan and partly by the state and Australian governments. The membership in insurance plans of low-income families and certain other groups (eg, people receiving unemployment insurance and migrants during their first two months in Australia) is subsidized by the Australian government. The Pensioner Medical Service, funded nationally, provides general practitioner care to recipients of social service pensions and their dependents. Prescribed drugs are a public benefit for all people, except for a one dollar charge per prescription to each patient.[3] (In August 1974, Australia amended its health insurance law to cover the entire population with comprehensive benefits.)

The Canadian system of financing health care also differs from ours. In 1957, the Canadian Parliament enacted a national program of hospital insurance, with each province entering the program in different years thereafter. A similar Federal–Provincial program for physician care was enacted in 1966. Now all ten provinces of Canada have entered the system, so that a national health insurance system for both physician care and hospitalization operates across Canada.[4]

Within these health service systems, as in our own, nursing functions are in transition. Before turning to current developments in nursing practice, however, it may be helpful to sketch briefly the kinds of nursing personnel in each country and the educational and regulatory systems in operation. From this review, two contrasting approaches emerge—with perspectives, perhaps, for the United States.

Nursing Functions in Australia

Australia has two levels of nurse: the registered nurse, with three years' training and a basic certification in general or psychiatric nursing; and the nursing aide or enrolled nurse, with one year's training and practical experience. Nursing assistants are untrained personnel. Basic nursing education for registered nurses in Australia is generally provided in hospital schools of nursing. The Nurses' Registration Board in each state is responsible for setting the required curriculum and for the final examinations leading to registration, except that very recently the most populous state, New South Wales, has separated the regulation of education and of registration into two agencies. Postbasic education in hospitals or colleges provides specialist qualifications for registered nurses in midwifery, geriatrics, intensive care, obstetrics, infant care, and other specialties. Australia has the interesting system of regulating specialist qualifications through its Nurses' Registration Boards. A nurse who has completed basic training and midwifery is "double-certificated"; a nurse who has completed basic training and also obstetrics and infant care is "triple-certificated."

Although nursing education in Australia still is conducted predominantly as an apprenticeship system, it is beginning to change. Basic nursing programs are now being offered or planned in academic institutions, called Colleges of Advanced Education. For some time, Colleges of Nursing have offered postgraduate training—both full-time courses in nursing administration and other specialties, and also shorter courses as a form of continuing education—and these colleges are beginning to offer basic training in an academic setting for the first time. The trend is in the direction of separating nursing education from nursing service. One of the major problems facing the nursing profession and the health services of Australia is the serious loss of of nurses from the profession. An estimated 60 percent of nursing graduates from 1957 to 1966 were no longer in practice in 1967.[5] Explanations for this wastage include family reasons, job dissatisfaction, inadequate salaries, difficult hours, lack of child care facilities, and others. It is hoped that improved education and improved working conditions will retain larger numbers of professional nurses in active practice.

Because the vast majority of Australian nurses are employed in hospital settings, the most dramatic change in nursing functions has been in the development of intensive care units, where nurses have been called on for new functions because of new technology. Authorization for new functions has come about in two ways. One way is that the State Hospital Commission, which regulates hospital services and reimbursement, issues general instructions on the appropriate scope of practice for nurses. Under these instructions, hospitals can make specific determinations. Another way is that, in some cases, the Nurses' Registration Board specifies what a nurse may properly do. Thus, the Nurses' Board of Western Australia issued a policy on the role of the nurse that set forth the conditions under which a nurse may apply a defibrillator, may institute intravenous therapy, may assist in epidural injections, or may administer simple analgesics.[6]

The legal scope of nursing practice has not been a prominent issue in the hospital setting in Australia. Some moderate expansion of general nursing functions has occurred, and nurses now take blood samples, cross-match blood, and start intravenous therapy. But when asked about authorization for new functions, representatives of Nurses' Registration Boards and governmental officials in health services reply that once a nurse is properly educated and registered, her functions tend to be the responsibility of the institution that employs her. This attitude toward the problem of scope of practice— more matter-of-fact than that in the United States—may be related to the relatively low incidence of malpractice actions in Australia.

In the context of community health services, however, nursing functions in Australia are a more lively issue. Australia has not in the past had a generalized public health nurse in the American sense. Rather, specialized nurses have provided well-baby care in baby health centers, care in child health centers for children with physical or emotional problems, school health services, and home nursing services.[7] As mentioned, nurses receive postbasic training in various specialties, including psychiatric and geriatric nursing.[3(p 255-6)] Recently, a new type of nurse has emerged in conjunction with the national initiative of the Labor Government to develop community health centers. The community health nurse is a registered nurse, with additional training for ambulatory care in the community, who will replace the various specialized nurses now functioning in different settings. The community health nurse will provide clinic services and domiciliary care; she will work with infants, children, adults, and the aged in connection with physical and psychosocial problems.

The community health nurse is just now evolving. Neither her functions nor her training are fully defined as yet. In some places, community health nurses are functioning in a capacity analagous to that of generalized public health nurses in the United States. In others, they are assuming responsibility for home nursing services, with a strong mental health component. In South Australia, where primary doctors are in short supply, they may serve as community practice nurses to extend the reach of the limited supply of doctors.

In 1973 the Karmel Committee, reporting to the Australian Universities Commission on Medical Education, recommended development of registered nurses to work in an expanded role in conjunction with doctors in community health centers and as practice nurses in large group practices.[8] In this capacity, nurses would assist in screening the degree of urgency of calls, carry out certain procedures, interview patients, and take histories. The Karmel Committee favored offering a graduate program to prepare nurses for these functions, rather than creating a separate program for "assistant doctors." With continuing funding provided by the Australian government for development of community health centers, the community health nurse is already becoming a pivotal member of the health team in those centers.

Current training programs for community health nursing vary in length and depth. In Melbourne, the College of Nursing Australia is offering a one-year postgraduate program leading to a diploma in community nursing. In other places, shorter courses with considerable on-the-job instruction are offered." The curricula also vary, some being developed along traditional public health lines and others incorporating a new component on diagnostic techniques, history taking, and patient assessment.

Ample precedent exists in Australia for expanded functions of nurses. So-called bush nurses have long been the main source of medical care for aborigines and others in vast stretches of central Australia. In fact, the outstanding record of the bush nurses is cited as clear demonstration of the capacity of registered nurses to undertake an expanded role.

Nursing Functions in Canada

Canada has two main classes of nurse: the registered nurse and the registered nursing assistant. There are also untrained personnel: orderlies, nurse's aides, practical nurses, and psychiatric aides. A variety of educational programs exists for the registered nurse in Canada, as in the United States: diploma programs (in both hospitals and community colleges), baccalaureate programs, and postbasic programs. Canada, again like the United States, has developed clinical nurse specialists in various fields. The registered nursing assistant is generally trained in ten-month programs. The regulatory system consists of registration by the College of Nurses or similar body in each province, and the prerequisites for registration include graduation from an approved nursing school, passing a national examination designated by the College, and payment of the registration fee. In Quebec, as of July 1976, proficiency in the French language will also be required, unless special exemption is granted.

Unlike Australia, in Canada considerable explicit attention has been directed to the issue of nursing functions. In 1964, the Royal Commission on Health Services in its exhaustive study of existing health services and future needs addressed issues related to the supply of nurses. In 1969, the Task Force Reports on the Costs of Health Services in Canada opened discussion of manpower utilization by underlining the importance of more efficient use of registered nurses, suggesting specific ways of assigning certain tasks to less-qualified personnel. In October 1970, the Canadian Nurses' Association issued an official statement that manpower needs can be met effectively and economically by expanding the role of the nurse.[10]

Provincial commissions and committees, established in several provinces to consider problems of health services and health manpower, have urged expanded roles for nurses. In Ontario, the Committee on the Healing Arts gave extensive consideration to the practice of nursing, the relations of nurses with other health workers, and the functions of different kinds of nurses.[11] A study prepared for the Committee on the Healing Arts urged that nursing recognize its role as interdependent with that of medicine and strengthen cooperation with the medical and hospital associations, rather than concerning itself solely with those functions not shared with physicians.[12] Perhaps in response to this suggestion, one of the recommendations of the Committee on the Healing Arts was that a definition of the practice of medicine be developed incorporating the idea of interdisciplinary team practice. In the Castonguay–Nepveu Report the Commission of Inquiry on Health and Social Welfare in Quebec recommended a regionalized system of health care in which local community health centers would play a large part in providing ambulatory service.[13] Similarly in Nova Scotia, in the Report of the Nova Scotia Council of Health, emphasis was placed on the role of the community health nurse, who would function in association with the physician in provision of primary care.[14] The movement for community health centers in Canada received strong impetus from the Hastings report on that subject; community health centers assume a central role for nurse practitioners in provision of ambulatory care.[15]

In April 1971, a national conference was convened to discuss the question of assistance to the physician. Consensus was reached at this conference that the registered nurse is the most logical worker to fill the role of physician's assistant.[16] In effect, the decision was reached not to go the route that had been followed in the United States—perhaps because Canada had no returning military veterans, but more likely because of Canada's exceptionally high supply of nurses (active and inactive)—a ratio of 1 nurse per 182 people.[17] Instead, the decision was made to look for assistance in primary care to professional nurses who have thorough scientific grounding, who have experience in working in close relationships with physicians, and who have a portable qualification.

In April 1972, the Report of the Committee on Nurse Practitioners to the Department of National Health and Welfare of Canada recommended guidelines for developing educational programs for nurse practitioners to serve as initial contact for entrance into the system of care, to assess the individual's health status, and to determine the need for medical, nursing, and other intervention.[18] The Committee recommended that the development of nurse practitioners be regarded as the highest priority in meeting primary health care needs; that the nurse practitioner function as part of a multidisciplinary health team; and that educational programs to train nurse practitioners be developed—as indeed they had already begun to develop at McMaster University and other places. The position was taken (wisely) that since widespread acceptance of nurse practitioners depends on attitudinal change, the rate of development should be gradual.

Finally, a joint statement of the Canadian Nurses' Association and the Canadian Medical Association endorsed expanding roles for nurses, particularly for primary health care in appropriate forms of team practice.[19] The role and responsibilities proposed include well-child care and prenatal and postnatal care. In the absence of a physician, the nurse would perform triage and initial evaluation, and also deal with emergencies. (The Northern Outpost nurse would have particularly broad functions, as in the past.) In association with a physician she would carry out certain procedures, provide health supervision for stable patients with chronic illness, and provide supportive and social services. Training programs for nurses with extensive experience or university preparation could be short-term training, whereas nurses from two- or three-year programs might require more extensive additional training for these roles. Educational programs should be developed jointly by nursing and medical faculties. Supervised clinical practice is a key aspect of the education.

A number of Canadian studies have documented the effectiveness of nurse practitioners in providing health care. One study deserves special mention. From July 1971 to July 1972, in a large suburban Ontario practice of two family physicians who had been unable to accept new patients for two years, a randomized, controlled trial was conducted to assess the effects of substituting nurse practitioners for physicians in provision of primary care.[20(p 251),21] In this carefully designed study involving nearly 5,000 patients, the care provided by nurse practitioners was found to be safe and effective. Not only could increased numbers of patients be seen but the participation of nurse practitioners contributed to improving the work of the physicians. The study suggested further that if appropriate financial arrangements were made these might serve as an inducement to physicians to employ nurse practitioners and, at the same time, result in lower overall costs of care. The authors of this article acknowledge that neither the concept of the nurse practitioner nor its evaluation is new. Outpost nurses "have established an enviable record of clinical accomplishment in isolated areas in the Canadian North and Maritime provinces." [20(p 255),22]

Insights for the United States

From this brief review of Australian and Canadian developments in nursing functions, it is clear that both countries are moving, each in its own way, toward varied uses of professional nurses in expanded roles. Australia is taking steps to prepare community health nurses in conjunction with its development of community health centers. These steps are being taken with a minimum of brouhaha, with few reverberations from registration boards, and in a low key. Canada has made an explicit decision to develop nurse practitioners as the middle-level medical personnel, thus rejecting the concept of the physician's assistant. This policy is being implemented cautiously in conjunction with federal and provincial decisions on organization of health services, particularly in development of community health centers; but not excluding the possibility of using nurse practitioners in family practices. Legal authorization for the functioning of nurse practitioners has not received great emphasis. The Canadian view seems to be that the necessary will be done and legal measures must flow from sound health practices.

In some ways, the United States has moved farther in the direction of developing new kinds of personnel to provide primary medical care than either Australia or Canada; it has undertaken development of both the physician's assistant and the nurse practitioner. Hundreds of training programs have been established for both types of personnel, and legal authorization has been provided in many states. Legislatures in 33 states have authorized the functioning of physician's assistants either by regulatory or delegatory legislation.[23] In 21 states nurse practice acts have been amended to authorize expanded functions for professional nurses.[24] In 17 jurisdictions, the nurse-midwife is authorized to provide a wide scope of maternity care including normal deliveries.[25]

This momentum in the United States seems related to the very low proportion of general practitioners among American doctors. By contrast, the slower and more variable development of nurse practitioners in Australia and Canada would seem related to the high proportion and total supply of GPs in those countries available for primary care. In the United States, where GPs are in such short supply, perhaps if nurses had been more aggressive in recognizing their joint role with physicians, instead of insisting on their separate role and functions, nurse practitioners would be fully accepted now. A genuine opportunity to work as a nurse practitioner might serve to draw back into nursing some of the approximately 300,000 inactive nurses—30 percent of all registered nurses in the United States.[26]

In view of the legal controversy that has developed concerning authorization in law for nurse practitioners, some form of legislative action now seems necessary. Such action not only allays any doubts as to the authorized scope of practice but serves affirmatively to express a policy in favor of the development of nurse practitioners.

At least three methods are available for providing legal authorization. One method is to follow the pattern first established by the State of Idaho, which amended its nurse practice act to authorize nursing functions by rules promulgated jointly by the nursing and medical licensing boards. This approach is a statutory version of the joint statement, under which the medical and nursing professions enter into an agreement as to what constitutes accepted custom and practice. A second method is to bring nurse practitioners under the physician's assistant legislation. The third is to modernize and broaden the definition of professional nursing as defined in the nurse practice acts. The method of choice ought to be the one that provides clear authority with a minimum of delays and administrative inconvenience. By this criterion, the Idaho pattern seems inadvisable because it necessitates initial legislation followed by agreements, often painstakingly arrived at, between the two professions on each specific nursing function. The inflexibility of this mechanism militates against this approach.

The second suggestion—to bring nurse practitioners under the physician's assistant legislation—suffers from some of the same defects. Defining the functions of nurse practitioners under this legislation and to distinguishing these functions from those of physician's assistants would cause delays and would fragment regulation of the nursing profession by placing different kinds of nurses under different legal authority. Moreover, use of the physician's assistant framework might tend to restrict the functions of nurse practitioners to a specific list, thus inhibiting desirable flexibility.

The third option—amendment of the definition of professional nursing in the nurse practice acts—seems to be the simplest and clearest solution. Successful precedent exists in several states for this approach.

In conclusion, the enactment of federal legislation to encourage development of health maintenance organizations (P.L. 93-222) makes clarification of the role of nurse practitioner a high priority. This legislation authorizes federal subsidy for development of HMOs, providing health services on a prepaid basis to enrolled persons through health professionals who are members of the staff of the HMO, through medical groups, or through individual practice associations (partnerships, corporations, or other arrangements). Organized frameworks, of which the HMO is one important example, can use most effectively a wide range of personnel in team provision of health care. As health maintenance organizations grow—and in other frameworks as well—the nurse practitioner will be a key member of the health team.

REFERENCES

1. *See* N. Hershey, *Expanded Roles for Professional Nurses*, 3 J. NURS. ADMIN. 30 (November–December 1973).
2. Personal communication from Dr. Jozef Van Langendonck, Institute of Social Security, Catholic University of Leuven, Belgium.
3. For an excellent account of the National Health Scheme of Australia, *see* J.C.H. DEWDNEY, AUSTRALIAN HEALTH SERVICES (1972).
4. For a comprehensive historic and analytic description of social insurance programs for health services in Canada, *see* J.E.F. Hastings, *Federal-Provincial Insurance for Hospital and Physician's Care in Canada*, INT. J. HEALTH SERV. 4 at 398 (November 1971).
5. ROYAL AUSTRALIAN NURSING FEDERATION AND THE NATIONAL FLORENCE NIGHTINGALE COMMITTEE OF AUSTRALIA, SURVEY REPORT ON THE WASTAGE OF GENERAL TRAINED NURSES FROM NURSING IN AUSTRALIA (1967).
6. Nurses' Board of Western Australia, *Policy on the Role of the Nurse*, 3 AUS. NURS. J. 4 at 43–44 (October 1973).
7. S. SAX, MEDICAL CARE IN THE MELTING POT, AN AUSTRALIAN REVIEW 50 (1972).
8. EXPANSION OF MEDICAL EDUCATION, REPORT OF THE COMMITTEE ON MEDICAL EDUCATION TO THE AUSTRALIAN UNIVERSITIES COMMISSION (Peter Karmel, Chmn., 1973).
9. Sister Mary Paulina, *Nurses Have a Role in Community Health Services*, HOSP. & HEALTH ADMIN. 7, (November–December 1971).
10. *See* D. Morgan, *The Future Expanded Role of the Nurse*, CAN. HOSP. 75 (May 1972).

11. REPORT OF THE COMMITTEE ON THE HEALING ARTS (ONTARIO), VOL. 2, (1970).
12. V.V. MURRAY, NURSING IN ONTARIO, A STUDY FOR THE COMMITTEE ON THE HEALING ARTS (1970).
13. REPORT OF THE COMMISSION OF INQUIRY ON HEALTH AND SOCIAL WELFARE, VOL. IV (Gov't of Quebec, 1970).
14. HEALTH CARE IN NOVA SCOTIA, A NEW DIRECTION FOR THE SEVENTIES, THE REPORT OF THE NOVA SCOTIA COUNCIL OF HEALTH 73-6 (1972).
15. THE COMMUNITY HEALTH CENTRE IN CANADA, REPORT OF THE STUDY ON COMMUNITY HEALTH CENTRES PRESENTED TO THE MINISTERS OF HEALTH (John E.F. Hastings, Study Director, July 1972).
16. MINISTRY OF NATIONAL HEALTH AND WELFARE NATIONAL CONFERENCE ON ASSISTANCE TO THE PHYSICIAN, THE COMPLEMENTARY ROLES OF THE PHYSICIAN AND THE NURSE (1972).
17. *Nursing in Canada: From Pioneering History to a Modern Federation*, 15 INT. NURS. REV. 1 at 29 (1968). This ratio compares with the ratio of one nurse per 300 population in the United States. *See* U.S. DEP'T OF HEALTH, EDUCATION AND WELFARE, HEALTH RESOURCES STATISTICS, HEALTH MANPOWER AND HEALTH FACILITIES, 1971 (1972).
18. REPORT OF THE COMMITTEE ON NURSE PRACTITIONERS TO THE DEPARTMENT OF NATIONAL HEALTH AND WELFARE, CANADA (April 1972).
19. *The Expanded Role of the Nurse: A Joint Statement of CNA/CMA*, Can. Nurse 23-5 (May 1973).
20. W. Spitzer, D. Sackett, J. Sibley, R. Roberts, D. Kergin, B. Hackett & A. Olynich, *The Burlington Randomized Trial of the Nurse Practitioner*, 290 NEW ENGL. J. MED. 5 (January 31, 1974).
21. *See* W. Spitzer, D. Kergin, M. Yoshida, W. Russell, B. Hackett, & C. Goldsmith, *Nurse Practitioners in Primary Care III. The Southern Ontario Randomized Trial*, 108 CAN. MED. ASSOC. J. 1005 (April 21, 1973).
22. *See* C. Keith, *What Is Outpost Nursing?* CAN. NURSE 41 (September 1971).
23. H.S. COHEN & L.H. MIIKE, DEVELOPMENTS IN HEALTH MANPOWER LICENSURE: A FOLLOW-UP TO THE 1971 REPORT ON LICENSURE AND RELATED HEALTH PERSONNEL CREDENTIALING, U.S. DEP'T OF HEALTH, EDUCATION AND WELFARE PUB. NO. (HRA) 74-3101, Table 1 at 11 (June 1973).
24. For example, *see* N.Y. EDUCATION LAW, § § 6901, 6902 (Supp. 1972); IDAHO CODE ANN., § § 54-1413 (Supp. 1972); N.H. REV. STAT. ANN., § 326-A:2 (Supp. 1972); ARIZ. REV. STAT. ANN., § 32-1601 (Supp. 1972); WASHINGTON LAWS OF 1973, ch. 133 (effective June 7, 1973); NEV. REV. STAT., ch. 632 (Supp. 1973); CALIF. BUS. AND PROF. CODE, § § 2725-2726 (Supp. 1974).
25. Information provided by the American College of Nurse Midwifery.
26. *See Primary Care by the Nurse*, 290 NEW ENGL. J. MED. 5 at 282, (January 31, 1974) for the statement that according to the 1972 Inventory of Registered Nurses, prepared by the American Nurses' Association Statistics Department, out of 1,127,657 registered nurses in 1972, only 778,470, or 70%, are employed full or part-time.

Section II

THE VIEW FROM THE PRACTICE SETTING

BONNIE BULLOUGH

5
Factors Contributing to Role Expansion for Registered Nurses

In the articles included in this section several of the new work roles for nurses are examined. One is written by a physician who participated in projects to develop protocols to be used as mechanisms for for guiding the practice of nurses and paramedical personnel. The others are by nurses who have done research about, or participated in, one of the new work roles. In order to place these views from the practice setting in context, this paper will trace some of the causes of the movement for role expansion for registered nurses.

Probably the first factor is simply the coming of age of nursing education. The determined struggles of the dedicated nurses of the past to raise educational standards and move the training of nurses out of the hospitals and into the mainstream of the educational system have at last succeeded. These efforts can be dated from 1899 when Teachers College, Columbia University, reluctantly allowed two registered nurses to enter; or from 1909 when the University of Minnesota started the first baccalaureate program[1]; or from 1923 when the Goldmark report advised that nursing education be strengthened, shortened, and taken out of the control of the hospitals[2]; or even from 1952 when the community college nursing project was established.[3]

It does not matter which beginning date is used. Suffice it to say that the struggle was a long and difficult one. Finally, in 1972 a watershed was reached. For the first time in the history of American nursing education there were more nurses graduated from collegiate than diploma schools: 21 percent of the new graduates were from baccalaureate programs, 37 percent from associate of arts programs, and 42 percent from diploma programs. Only a decade earlier, 14 percent of the graduates were baccalaureate, 3.7 percent associate of arts, and 82 percent hospital diploma school graduates.[4(p 72-3)] The associate of arts graduates increased tenfold in this period. Moreover, even these figures do not tell the whole story of educational improvement. The competition from the collegiate schools and the rising expectations of nurses and the community forced the existing hospital schools to alter their programs by hiring more and better prepared instructors, affiliating with colleges, and avoiding exploitation of their students. Although these costly improvements are a major factor in the continued closing of hospital programs, they have also substantially improved the quality of education in the diploma schools.

The better initial education of the current graduates is supplemented by postbasic training. There are approximately 16,000 registered nurses enrolled in colleges and universities working towards doctorates or master's or bachelor's degrees.[4(p 109)] The number seeking master's degrees has been increasing each year; currently, approximately 3 percent of the employed nurses hold this degree. Although the number working toward the baccalaureate degree has remained stable over the last decade,[4(p 10)] several predictors point toward a radical change in the near future. Twenty years ago the colleges gave blanket credits to diploma nurses for their hospital education. This practice is now uncommon, and fewer diploma nurses have been willing to come back to school with no credit for the three years they spent in nursing school. Increasingly, however, these diploma nurses are being replaced by associate of arts graduates, who are in a different position because they have at least two years of bona fide college credit. For a period, the university nursing schools resisted accepting these students, partly because the founders of the community college nursing programs had indicated that the associate of arts nursing program was a terminal one,[3(p 4-5)] and partly because their nursing courses were all lower division, while the baccalaureate programs featured upper-division nursing courses.

The current graduates of the associate of arts schools do not, however, agree with the founders. Many of these nurses selected the community college on the basis of geography or finance rather than any lack of ability, and they feel as entitled to finish their college education as the next American. Because of pressure from this group of nurses there is a beginning but growing trend for the baccalaureate schools to accept the associate of arts registered nurses for advanced study.[5] The new move is not without attendant problems. The career ladder students have already mastered many of the basic training theories and procedures, so their educational needs are different from those of the generic students. Although they must necessarily spend a portion of their time strengthening their backgrounds in the behavioral and biological sciences, they also need some upper-division nursing to justify their majors. Most of the schools pioneering in the development of curricula for these students are offering hospital or community nursing specialties as the advanced focus. These nurses therefore are becoming beginning clinical specialists or nurse practitioners, and acquiring skills that were, until recently, available only in master's degree programs, hospital in-service, or extension courses. As the number of associate of arts graduates continue to grow and the need for nurses with specialty training increases, this trend for upper-division specialty training can be expected to escalate.

A parallel trend is also taking place at the practical nurse level, as more practical nurses seek advanced education; approximately 11 percent of the admissions and 14 percent of the graduations from the associate level programs are practical nurses.[4(p 90)] The basic role of the practical nurse is also being extended. In one study in which the total nursing role was broken down for analysis into 306 tasks, practical nurses were able to perform 270 (or 88 percent) of the tasks.[6] The large number of functions now carried out by these workers creates pressure from below for registered nurses to seek role expansion.

The improvements in nursing education, the growth of the career ladder concept, and the pressure from practical nurses are factors within nursing supporting a change in the nursing role. There are outside factors as well. Probably the factors outside the profession are even more important, particularly some of the trends in medicine. In the years preceding and following the famous Flexner report, which came out in 1910, medical schools were upgraded and many of the substandard schools closed. Although this reform actually decreased the number of physicians relative to the population only slightly, it did cause the number to stay almost stable for the next half century,[7] and it is only in the last few years that the number has started to slowly climb to reach a current ratio of approximately 170 physicians and osteopaths per 100,000 population.[8(p 183)] During that same 65-year-period there was a rapid escalation in medical knowledge, a growing consumer demand for better health care, and an increasing recognition of the need for better distribution of care to more segments of the society. In effect, the long-term results of an almost stable output of physicians relative to the population was to create a shortage of physicians and a significant increase in their incomes.[9]

Adding to this basic shortage was the trend toward specialization in medicine. Specialists now outnumber general practitioners more than three to one.[8(p 183)] These two trends converge to create a serious gap in the health care delivery system. The most serious shortage is not the overall one, but the shortage of primary physicians available to care for people with ordinary illnesses, for a modest fee, and to perform basic diagnoses so that patients can be referred for appropriate specialty care. Of course, general practitioners are not the only physicians who give primary care: many pediatricians, internists, and most osteopaths are also involved in this type of practice, although the first two groups are probably overtrained for this role and their fees tend to reflect their lengthier training. However, even if all the potential primary practitioners are added up, they still amount to less than half the practicing physicians,[8(p 194)] whereas at the time of the Flexner report most doctors gave primary care. This situation furnishes the strongest impetus for role expansion of registered nurses into ambulatory primary care.

Inside the hospital advancing medical technology is probably the most potent factor extending the responsibility of nurses. New lifesaving procedures have developed which involve complex equipment and often call for on-the-spot diagnostic judgments. These situations are most common in the various intensive care units of the hospital, including the coronary and respiratory care units as well as the trauma and postoperative recovery rooms. In these units nurses are responsible for monitoring patients, making decisions about their conditions, and acting on those decisions—often without time to seek consultation. As is discussed in Chapter 3 of this section, there was some early brief consideration given to manning these units with full-time physicians, but the costs to hospitals was prohibitive; so they have evolved as nursing units, and there is little thought now of any other manpower alternative.

On the ambulatory scene, physician's assistants compete with nurses for the direct patient-care role. For a time, physician's assistants seemed to many people the most likely answer to the shortage of primary-care physicians. The first and most well-known physician's assistant training program was started at Duke University in 1965 by Eugene Stead with four students, all of whom were ex-corpsmen. The two-year program included basic sciences and the less complex medical skills that would be needed in the practice of the student's prospective employer.[10,11] The second major program was the Medex course for ex-independent duty corpsmen set up in Washington state. This program was established with federal financing for the purpose of providing high level technical assistance to primary physicians, particularly in the rural areas of the state where the shortage of doctors was acute.[12] There are now 50 accredited educational programs for physician's assistants and 37 states have passed some type of law allowing them to practice.[13] These licensing statutes tend to follow two basic patterns: one is to increase the power of the physician to delegate tasks to other workers, including nurses; the second is to give the responsibility for regulation some specific body, in most cases the Board of Medical Examiners.[14]

The development of physician's assistants did not actually predate the development of nurse practitioners. There were public health nurses working in an expanded role in northern California as early as 1962, and probably in informal types of primary-care situations much earlier.[15] In the out-patient setting, nurses were responsible for the long-term management of patients with chronic illnesses at Massachusetts General Hospital in 1962.[16] The Colorado program to train nurse practitioners, established by Henry Silver and others, was started in 1965—the same year the Duke physician's assistant program was started.[17,18] Yet it seemed to the public that physician's assistants were the first on the scene. The media no doubt played a significant role here. Physician's assistants were new and newsworthy. Various types of paramedics were seen on the television screen heroically saving lives, while the nurses apparently stayed behind a desk or spent their time quietly suffering from unrequited love for the doctor–hero.

It cannot be denied, however, that the highly visible physician's assistant movement was an important factor in the development of nurse practitioners. It demonstrated publicly that the delegation of a significant number of medical tasks was possible. Once this became apparent, some physicians remembered that nurses existed, and thought about them as perhaps better-prepared assistants, probably more tractable, and certainly more plentiful than ex-independent duty corpsmen.[19] The American Academy of Pediatrics furnished leadership in this area, sponsoring conferences, research, and pronouncements supporting practitioners whom they termed nurse associates.[20] In 1971, after a series of negotiations, the Academy issued a joint statement with the American Nurses' Association suggesting guidelines for short-term courses for the preparation of the associates.[21] Although these negotiations were broken off for a year, in 1974 the academy remained supportive of the idea of nurse associates.[22] The American Medical Association followed the lead of the Academy, and in 1970 issued an official statement supporting the expansion of the role of the nurse.[23]

The physician's assistant movement also gave courage to nurses to rethink their own traditional avoidance of overt expansion of their functions onto the medical turf of diagnosis and treatment. For example, when the Los Angeles urban Medex program was started there was some advance publicity, which may well have been spurious, indicating that the starting salaries for physician's assistants would be $18,000. While this is a modest income relative to that of physicians, it was about $7,000 more than public health nurses with bachelor's degrees were making at the time. The county of Los Angeles was said to have budgeted two positions for the assistants when they graduated. When public health nurses called the salary discrepancy discriminatory, they were told by agency officials that the physician's assistants were expected to be more valuable than nurses because of their medical skills. Nurses talked among themselves for several months about this situation, and some of the nurses who subsequently entered the UCLA pediatric nurse practitioner course mentioned the possible future salary discrepancy as a minor, but nevertheless significant, motivating factor in their decisions to become nurse practitioners.

Major trends also exist in society related to role expansion for nurses. The first such factor is the women's liberation movement. Although nurses have not been conspicuous in the leadership of this movement, they have not been entirely absent. For example, Wilma Scott Hiede, a nurse, was president of the National Organization of Women. However, nurses have reaped benefits from the movement. As the norms of society have changed to allow more autonomy for all women, nurses suffer fewer self-doubts about taking on more responsible roles. Faculty members who have been teaching in nurse practitioner programs over the last few years report that they are now seeing less evidence of inner conflict associated with the change in roles from the traditional to an expanded role. The liberation movement, with its emphasis on less sex stereotyping, may also be helping to bring more men into the field. Approximately 6 percent of the new students entering nursing schools are men—roughly double the percentage of five years ago.[4(p 89)] Because these young men were not socialized to expect female subordination they are somewhat reluctant to play doctor–nurse games, and they serve as healthy catalysts for their classmates in these changing times.

A second trend in society that may well contribute to the development of the nurse practitioner is the changing age distribution among the population. The number of people in the postretirement age group is growing, and it is this age group that suffers most from chronic illness. While these illnesses sometimes need the highly technical skills of physician specialists, the patients also need long-range monitoring, emotional support, and health teaching related to the management of their symptoms. This is a cluster of tasks for which nurse practitioners, with their dual background in the behavioral and biological sciences, are well suited. Undoubtedly, the role of nurses in the management of chronic illnesses will increase.

In summary, factors that have helped stimulate the current changes in the nursing role include the improvements and changes in nursing education, the upward push of the licensed practical nurses as they expand their functions, the acute shortage of primary-care physicians created by the overall shortage and the trend toward specialization, the development of the physician's assistant programs, the women's liberation movement, and the changing age distribution of the population. Although the trend towards specialization in medicine is probably the major factor, the other variables also contribute significantly to the movement now in progress.

There is also another factor which should not be overlooked. Sociologists and political scientists have long been interested in the complex interrelationship between the law and social change.[24,25] In some cases it is possible to trace changes in the law to changes that have already occured in the society;[26] in other cases, the opposite causal sequence can be traced, with new laws creating significant changes in the society.[27] Here, both processes can be observed. Before 1971 the nurse practice acts, which forbade nurses the right to overtly participate in diagnosis and treatment, were a deterrent to role expansion. Employers worried about malpractice suits and the legitimacy of billing patients for nurses' services; nurses worried about the morality and safety of violating existing laws. The laws were a significant barrier to role change. As the laws were revised, this barrier was removed or lessened, but something else is happening now. As the momentum for changes in state nurse practice acts grows, an excitement is being generated and a bandwagon psychology in developing; more nurses are now willing to think about obtaining specialty training so they can move into one of the expanded roles. Thus the changing laws themselves become a factor supporting the revolution taking place in nursing.

REFERENCES

1. V.L. BULLOUGH & B. BULLOUGH, THE EMERGENCE OF MODERN NURSING 153-4, 173 (2nd ed. 1969).
2. J. GOLDMARK & THE COMMITTEE FOR THE STUDY OF NURSING EDUCATION, NURSING AND NURSING EDUCATION IN THE UNITED STATES (1923).
3. M. MONTAG & L.G. GOTKIN, COMMUNITY COLLEGE EDUCATION FOR NURSING (1959).
4. AMERICAN NURSES ASSOCIATION, FACTS ABOUT NURSING (1974).
5. J. LYSAUGHT, INDIVIDUALIZATION, ARTICULATION, CONCENTRATION: EMERGENT FORCES IN NURSING EDUCATION, IN ACTION IN NURSING: PROGRESS IN PROFESSIONAL PURPOSE (J. Lysaught ed. 1974).
6. L.A. WOOD & T.E. FREELAND, THE UCLA ALLIED HEALTH PROFESSIONS PROJECT; NURSING OCCUPATIONS: PROGRESS REPORT 31 (1971).
7. R. FEIN, THE DOCTOR SHORTAGE: AN ECONOMIC DIAGNOSIS 66 (1967).
8. U.S. DEP'T OF HEALTH, EDUCATION AND WELFARE, P.H.S. PUB. NO. 73-1509, HEALTH RESOURCES STATISTICS: HEALTH MANPOWER AND HEALTH FACILITIES (1973).
9. U.S. DEP'T. OF HEALTH, EDUCATION AND WELFARE, VITAL AND HEALTH STATISTICS, P.H.S. PUB. NO. 1000, SERIES 14, NO. 1, HEALTH MANPOWER UNITED STATES 1965-67 at 12 (1968).
10. BULLETIN OF DUKE UNIVERSITY, PHYSICIAN'S ASSISTANT PROGRAM: 1969-1970 at 1-4.
11. E.A. Stead Jr., *Training and Use of Paramedical Personnel,* 277 NEW ENGL. J. MED. 800-1 (October 12, 1967).
12. *National Center for Health Services Research and Development,* 5 FOCUS 8-9 (Summer 1970).
13. AMERICAN MEDICAL ASSOCIATION, ACCREDITED EDUCATIONAL PROGRAMS FOR THE ASSISTANT TO THE PRIMARY CARE PHYSICIAN (March 1974).

14. W. Dean, *State Legislation for Physician's Assistants*, 88 HEALTH SERV. REP. 3-12 (January 1973).
15. E. Siegel & S. Bryson, *Redefinition of the Role of the Public Health Nurse in Child Health Supervision*, 53 AM. J. PUBLIC HEALTH 1015-24 (June 1972).
16. B. Noonan, *Eight Years in a Medical Nurse Clinic*, 72 AM. J. NURS. 1128-30 (June 1972).
17. H. Silver & L. Ford, *The Pediatric Nurse Practitioner at Colorado*, 67 AM. J. NURS. 1143-44 (July 1967).
18. H. Silver, L. Ford & S. Stearly, *A Program to Increase Health Care for Children: The Pediatric Nurse Practitioner Program* 39 PEDIATRICS 756-60 (May 1967).
19. A. Bergman, *Physician's Assistants Belong in the Nursing Profession*, 7 AM. J. NURS. 975-7 (May 1971).
20. *Executive Board Initiates Child Health Manpower Training Program in a Major Effort to Improve Pediatric Care*, 20 NEWSLETTER: AMER. ACAD. PEDIATRICS 1, 4 (July 1, 1969).
21. *Guidelines on Short-Term Continuing Education Programs for Pediatric Nurse Associates*, 71 AM. J. NURS. 509-12 (March 1971).
22. Letter to Pediatric Nurse Associates from the American Academy of Pediatrics, January 16, 1974, signed by Robert G. Frazier, M.D., Executive Director (unpublished).
23. Committee on Nursing, *Medicine and Nursing in the 1970's: A Position Statement*, 213 J. AM. MED. ASSOC. 1881-3 (September 14, 1970).
24. W.G. FRIEDMANN, LAW IN A CHANGING SOCIETY (1964).
25. S. NAGEL, THE LEGAL PROCESS FROM A BEHAVIORAL PERSPECTIVE (1969).
26. C.T. Dienes, *Judges, Legislators and Social Change*, 13 AM. BEHAV. SCIENTIST 511-21 (March/April 1970).
27. T. LEWIS, THE IMPACT OF SUPREME COURT DECISIONS: EMPIRICAL STUDIES (1969).
28. H.L. Ross, D. Campbell & G. Glass, *Determination of the Social Effects of a Legal Reform*, 13 AM. BEHAV. SCIENTIST 494-509 (March/April 1970).

SHELDON GREENFIELD

6
Protocols as Analogs to Standing Orders

A *protocol,* as the term will be used here, is an instrument that guides a practitioner in the collection of data and recommends specific action based on that data.[1-4] Because adequately validated protocols represent a proven strategy in the workup and management of specific problems, they are mechanisms to insure both high standards of quality of medical care and careful audit. As an explicit set of directions, constructed and approved by licensed physicians, their relation to the law as analogs to standing orders is a tantalizing subject.

In this chapter I will explore the relation of protocols to the law by discussing first the conceptualization of the protocol as an instrument in medical care, then the development and validation of protocols, and finally their potential for widespread use in the practice of medicine. The focus in this presentation will be on the protocol systems for primary care developed by the Ambulatory Care Project, Beth Israel Hospital, Boston.

The Protocol Concept

The protocol concept originated in response to the national call

This is a revised version of "Protocol Management of Dysuria, Urinary Frequency, and Vaginal Discharge," by Sheldon Greenfield, Gerald Friedland, Sally Scifers, Arthur Rhodes, W.L. Black, and Anthony L. Komaroff, that originally appeared in *Annals of Internal Medicine* 81:451-452, 1974.

for nonphysicians to compensate for the physician shortage. By helping to guide and audit performance, protocols not only could assure certain high standards of quality of care, but also could conserve physician time by facilitating the delegation of clinical care responsibilities to providers and practitioners other than physicians. The conceptual framework for the protocol is that an instrument representing the sequential decision-making processes of the physician allows a person with minimal knowledge of the medical content to collect the data appropriate for a particular patient. Further, because protocols are far more explicit and individualized for the particular patient than "guidelines," they allow the nurse to take independent action where indicated. The combination of specificity for the individual patient and the standardization of patient care justify delegation to the nurse of responsibility from the initiation of data collection through the disposition, including the decision to send the patient home without seeing the physician.

In order to be satisfied that the protocols possess these capabilities, at least several conditions have to be met. These conditions are: (1) A significant fraction of complaints in a primary-care clinic or facility would have to fall into a relatively small number of categories. A practitioner using protocols must be able to handle a great majority of visits with a relatively small number of protocols. Prior studies of primary care practice have supported this contention.[5-13] Further, our own data, collected at the Kaiser facility at Inglewood, California, confirm these analyses of the distribution of chief complaints (Table 1).[14] In summary, it is generally held that between eight and twelve chief complaints or problems will represent somewhere between 50 and 80 percent of primary care practice. (2) Once the critical number of protocols are constructed, the practitioners must be able to collect the data—that is, perform adequate history and physical exam—and be able to follow the logic with minimal error. We do not assume that past medical training is helpful; rather, we define and delimit the job to be done, select the group of skills necessary to accomplish the job, and test whether the selection of skills is appropriate and whether these skills can be performed by nurses with no experience apart from basic nurse training. (3) If the data are collected properly the deductive logic must lead to the proper decision or series of decisions, and hence to a proper outcome of the encounter. Both the second and third conditions must be determined experimentally by validation trials.

Table 1. Distribution of Presenting Complaints
Kaiser–Inglewood Clinic, March 1973

Complaint	Number
URI	797
Abdominal pain	289
Headache	237
Back pain	182
Chest pain	175
Legs/feet	165
Return to work slip	158
Rash, skin	127
Dizziness, etc.	118
Return visit	113
Arms/hand	98
Gynecologic	94
Side pain	88
Urinary	87
Blood pressure	85
Ears (no other URI)	85
Nausea, vomiting, diarrhea	73
Total patients	2909
Total complaints	3842
Protocol coverage by complaint	2422 (63%)

Development and Validation of Protocols

The last twenty years of medical research has gone, by and large, into the study of the mechanisms of disease. Very little work has gone into the scientific basis for the solving of clinical medical problems as patients present these problems to physicians. Thus, the data on which to base most of the decisions made in medical practice are not available. How high must a fever be in combination with sore throat and tender enlarged lymph nodes to make a diagnosis of streptococcal pharyngitis? Does pain in the groin accompany a backache often enough so that groin pain need not point to a gastrointestinal or genitourinary condition in a patient complaining of back pain? Will patients with certain serious back diseases be detected by a single question attempting to ascertain whether the pain is relieved by bed rest? How often are the symptoms dysuria and frequency caused by vaginitis rather than urinary tract infection? Such clinical questions go on and on. The strategies for solving clinical problems are not, by and large, taught in medical school, either because not enough is known about them or because it is assumed that after a physician has spent many years on the wards as a medical student and house officer, he or she can easily integrate organ system pathophysiology and patient problems.

Protocols attempt to accomplish the standardization of diagnostic and management strategy in an explicit and concise manner. Beginning with a complaint, the intellectual processes of the practitioner unfold, each step dependent on preceding responses or physical findings. Decisions about what historical and physical information to collect and what action to take are generally based on two considerations: one is the frequency of a condition or a diagnosis sought; the other is the importance or value placed on making the diagnosis or, more precisely, defining the condition.[15] For example, diphtheria is so rare in adults in the northern United States that it is not unreasonable to leave it out of the differential diagnosis of a person with sore throat. On the other hand, although bacterial meningitis is very rare in patients with the chief complaint of headache alone; it is easy to diagnose and is treatable; thus great importance is placed on its detection.

One of three outcomes is chosen as the protocol comes to a final decision about the individual patient. One outcome is to refer the patient to the physician because of potential complexity of diagnosis or management. For example, if the patient with backache is found to have a high fever the patient should be worked up by a physician for osteomyelitis, epidural abscess, or other serious infectious processes. Another outcome is that the physician reviews the protocol data, having the option of examining one of the physical findings or checking over part of the history. A third outcome is the protocol recommendation that a patient can be sent home safely without seeing the doctor. This latter possibility, which obviously has great value in conserving physician time, makes it mandatory for protocols to be adequately validated.

Our protocol for dysuria, urine frequency, vaginal discharge, and vaginal irritation will serve as an illustration for protocol development. The major logic pathways are shown diagramatically in Figure 1. A patient presenting with dysuria and/or frequency has the relevant history taken by the nurse administering the protocol. Pertinent parts of the physical examination are performed, including palpation for costovertebral tenderness, temperature, and blood pressure. Next, a urinalysis is performed and a urine sample is cultured. If the urinalysis shows at least 20 or more white cells or 2+ bacteria per high power field in a centrifuged sediment, the patient is treated for presumptive urinary tract infection. If the urinalysis is negative, a pelvic exam is done to determine whether the urinary tract symptoms are due to vaginitis. If vaginitis is not present the patient is considered to have urethral syndrome or urethritis, is informed about the nature of the condition, and is not treated with antibiotics pending culture results. A patient complaining of either vaginal discharge or irritation of the vulva receives a pelvic exam, which includes examination for gross abnormalities, inspection and palpation of the cervix for purulent discharge and tenderness, and examination of a wet mount of

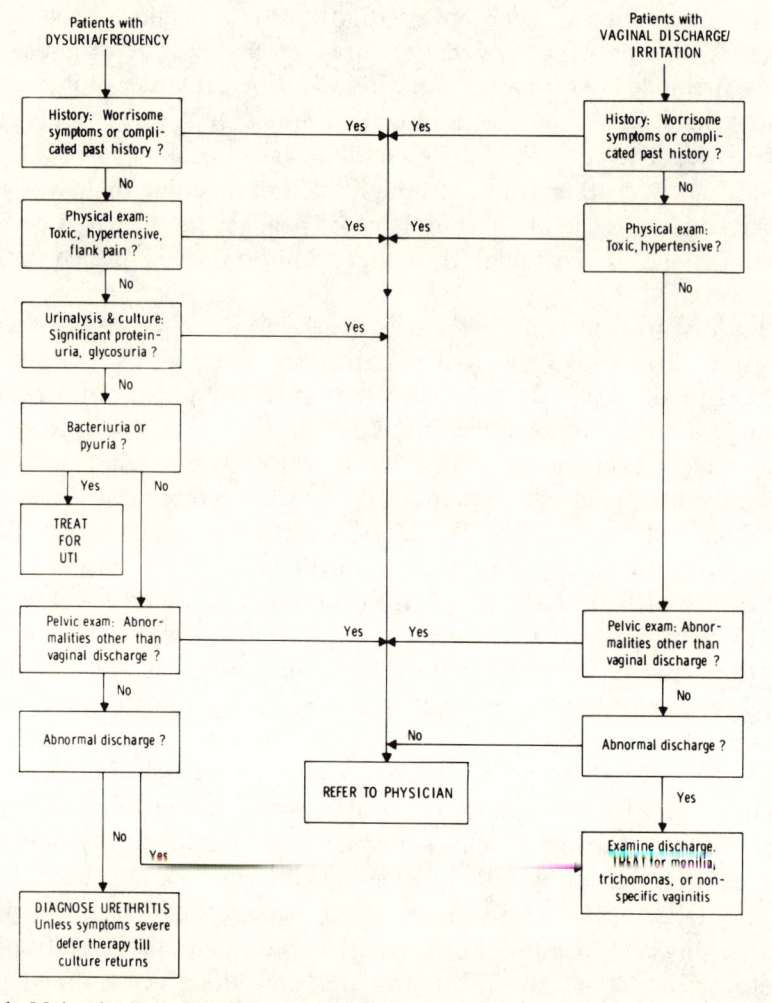

Fig. 1. Major logic pathways through the UTI/Vaginitis Protocol. The protocol itself specified what is meant by phrases such as "worrisome symptoms" and "toxic." In addition to the logic shown above, the protocol contains many other minor pathways and logic branch points.

the vaginal discharge. The patient is treated for monilia or trichomonas if present. If neither are detected on wet mount, the patient is treated for nonspecific vaginitis.

Patients are automatically referred to the physician if they are on a return visit for any of the above symptoms, are older than age 45, have had a recent gynecologic procedure, are pregnant, or have diabetes, severe abdominal pain, back pain, incontinence, hypertension, significant fever, or any vaginal abnormalities on observation. A history of recurrent urinary tract infection or chronic kidney disease and a history of medications recently inserted vaginally are reasons for verbal consultation with the physician after the workup is completed, but in these instances the physician need not see the patient.

Urinary tract infections are treated with sulfisoxazole. In the presence of sulfonamide allergy, tetracycline or ampicillin is used. Mycostatin suppositories are prescribed for monilia infection and metronidazole for trichomonas infection. Sulfonamide vaginal suppositories are used in the treatment of nonspecific vaginitis.

The accuracy of the initial diagnosis is checked when the culture returns, and treatment is modified if necessary. Patients are advised to return if rash, fever, chills, or vomiting develop, or if the symptoms continue for more than three days in the case of urinary tract infection or seven days in the case of vaginitis.

As might be expected, the actual decisions made during a history and physical exam are extremely complicated. The actual logic pattern of the urinary tract infection–vaginitis protocol is shown in Figure 2. Every attribute or data bit is included for a specific reason; it follows that the answer to every question must be linked to a decision, such as pursuing a symptom or sign further, initiating treatment, referral to the physician, and so forth. W. L. Black has taken this branching logic tree and combined it with a data collection sheet, as is shown in Figure 3. This form allows the nurse to check off the presence or absence of an attribute, guided by a set of internal instructions based on color-coding and special symbols. For example, a dot means to skip the following questions and go on to the next set of questions.

It can be seen that making the intellectual process of the practitioner explicit is a difficult task. We not only ask that the decisions be clearly made for each data bit or attribute, but further that the presence of each must be justified in some way by whatever literature is available or by personal practice experience in the absence of supporting data. For example, if there is no known level of fever at

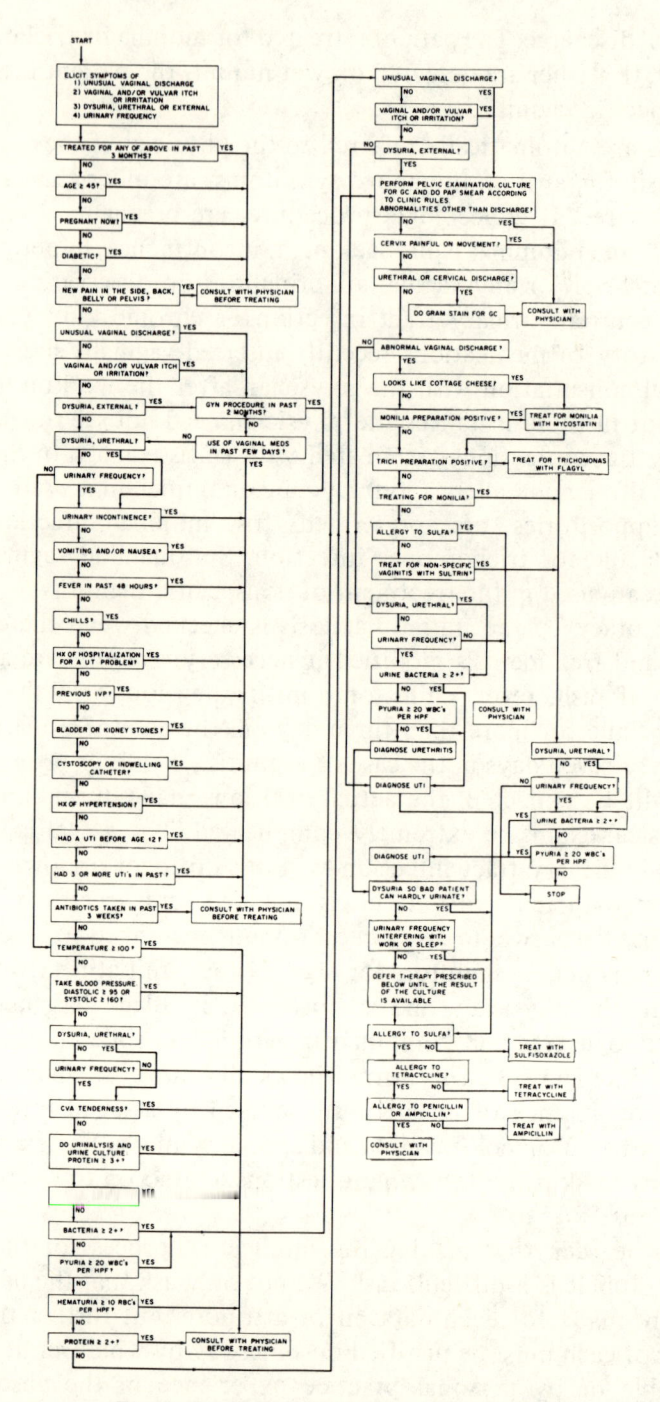

Fig. 2. Logic tree of UTI/Vaginitis Protocol.

which a decision to treat or not to treat with an antibiotic is made, we require that the protocol developer say that a temperature level of 102 F is chosen arbitrarily. In that way, other practitioners can address themselves concretely and specifically to that piece of information.

Therefore, the initial construction of the protocol can take as long as several weeks or even months. In the Beth Israel Hospital Ambulatory Care Program, protocols have been initially constructed by general physicians rather than by specialists. An expert on backache who might be an orthopedic or neurologic surgeon or a rehabilitation physical medicine specialist has expert knowledge in the disease causing backache. However, the specialist is more inclined to be disease-oriented than a generalist, and is less likely to do an examination appropriate for primary care. An illustration of this principle is that the specialist almost always orders an X-ray of the lumbar spine in the person with backache. The general practitioner might well not order the X-ray if he knows that of 400 or 500 patients presenting to him with backache, only 1 or 2 will have a serious disease that would be detected by X-ray and not by history or physical exam.[16] Moreover, many back X-rays will show minimal to moderate osteoarthritis, which may not actually be the cause of the patient's backache but may be a coincidental finding. Some surveys have shown that as many as 40 or 50 percent of patients of middle age or older may have some minimal degenerative joint disease changes on spinal X-ray. Therefore, from the point of view of the general practitioner an X-ray may not be a cost-efficient test to order, even though the specialist might consider it to be mandatory.

Once the protocols have gone through the initial development by the generalists, they are then reviewed by experts in the field and finally by a larger panel of general physicians. It is not enough, however, to construct an "armchair" strategy for the workup of a complaint. Too few of the decisions necessary in clinical practice are supported by data to make those decisions. Therefore, to be valid a protocol has to be field tested. Adequate field testing to validate the protocol has been one of the major thrusts of the Beth Israel Hospital Ambulatory Care Program, and we have undertaken to devise methodology for the validation of protocols as we validate a critical number of protocols for use in practice. At the time of this writing, protocols adequately validated now include those for urinary tract infection,[4] vaginitis,[4] upper respiratory tract infection,[2] low back pain,[16] and headache. Chronic disease protocols for diabetes and hypertension have also been validated.[3]

U.T.I./VAGINITIS PROTOCOL© (12/73)

Unit #: Date:
Name:
Chief complaint(s) _____
Birthdate: Phone:
Provider:

yes no SUBJECTIVE

- Vaginal discharge, unusual
  - Days duration _____
- Vaginal/vulvar itch/irritation
  - Days duration _____
- Pain/burning on urination
- Inside urethra
- Outside on a raw area
  - Days duration _____
- Unusually frequent urination
  - Days duration _____
- Rx for any of above in past 3 mo
- Age ≥ 45
- Pregnant now
- Diabetic
- New pain side/back/belly/pelvis
- Severe
- Any blue boxes checked
- Gyn procedure in past 2 mo
- Meds inserted into vagina in past few days
- Any grey boxes checked
- Incontinence (prior to UTI Sx)
- Vomiting/too nauseated to eat
- Fever by Hx in past 48 hrs
- Chills, teeth chatter
- Hx of hospitalization for UT prob.
  - Kidney X-ray (IVP)
  - Bladder/kidney stones
  - Cystoscopy/in-dwelling catheter
  - High blood pressure
  - Had a UTI before age 12
  - Past UTI's ≥ 3
- Antibiotic taken in past 3 weeks

OBJECTIVE

- Temperature ≥ 100 _____
- Systolic BP ≥ 160 or Diastolic ≥ 95
  - BP: _____
- A Any grey boxes checked
- CVA tenderness

Do urinalysis and culture

- Bact ___ WBC ___ RBC ___
- ≥ 3+ protein
- Any sugar _____
- Bact ≥ 2+ or WBC ≥ 20? Dx UTI
- ≥ 10 RBC
- A ≥ 2+ protein

A Stop — Any blue boxes checked
- Any red boxes checked? *Consult MD*
  Do Pelvic (Pap & GC culture)
- Abnormalities - not discharge
- Cervix painful on movement
- Urethral/cervical discharge?
  Do GC gram stain _____
- Abnormal vaginal discharge
- Looks like cottage cheese? *Dx monilia*
- Monilia prep positive? *Dx monilia*
- Trich prep positive? *Dx trichomonas*
- Any vag dx? *Dx non-specific vaginitis*

- Any dx yet?
- Any greys? *Dx urethritis*

Stop — Any reds? *Consult MD*
Stop — Will consult MD for other reasons

PLAN (also see back of protocol)

- Dx of trichomonas? *Rx Flagyl*
- Dx of monilia? *Rx Mycostatin*
- Dx of non-specific vaginitis?
- Stop — Sulfa allergy? *Consult MD   Rx Sultrin*

- Stop — Dx of UTI/urethritis
- Dx of urethritis/vaginitis
- Dysuria so bad pt can hardly urinate
- Frequency interfering with work or sleep? *Rx as below but tell pt to wait for culture result before beginning med*

- Sulfa allergy? *Rx Sulfisoxazole*
- Tetracycline allergy? *Rx Tetracycline*
- Penicillin/Ampicillin allergy?
  Consult MD   Rx Ampicillin

© The Beth Israel Hospital Association and Massachusetts Institute of Technology 1974

Fig. 3. UTI/Vaginitis Protocol.

INSTRUCTIONS TO PATIENTS

If Dx vaginitis: Tell patient to return in 1 week if no relief. Give patient information sheet.

If Dx UTI/urethritis: Tell patient to return if rash, fever vomiting or chills occur. Give patient information sheet.

If urine culture done: Tell patient to call back for culture results in 3 days.

The chart below indicates what the patient should be told at that time.

Ampicillin 250 mg #40
1 QID X 10

Flagyl 250 mg #30 TID X 10 (Consult MD about also treating consort.)

Mycostatin vag. tabs 100,000 U #30
1 BID X 15 - - even during period

Sulfix Sulfisoxazole 0.5 gm #80
2 QID X 10 with full glass of water

Sultrin triple sulfa vag. supps. #20
1 BID X 10 - - even during period

Tetracycline HC1 250 mg #40
1 QID X 10 on an empty stomach

CULTURE POSITIVE	CULTURE NEGATIVE
If no UT Rx given: Arrange for therapy.	*If no UT Rx given:* Continue vaginitis meds as directed.
If UT Rx given; pt told to wait: Begin med; return in 3 days if Sx persist and in 3 weeks for reculture.	*If UT Rx given; pt told to wait:* Don't take med. Return in 1 week if Sx persist.
If UT Rx given; pt told to start: Return if Sx still present; otherwise continue meds and return in 3 weeks for reculture.	*If UT Rx given; pt told to start:* Stop UTI/urethritis med. Return if dysuria/frequency still present or if they recur.

For the most recent edition of this protocol and/or further information, write:
Ambulatory Care Project, Beth Israel Hospital, 330 Brookline Ave., Boston, Ma. 02215

NOTE:
On actual hospital form...
- will be red
- will be blue
- will be yellow
- will be grey

What is adequate validation? How are we to be satisfied that a protocol can be used safely and with highest quality available medical care? At first glance it would seem to be enough if the patients seen by the nurses administering the protocols could be found to have done the proper workup as certified by physicians seeing the same patients. That would be what we would call a validation of process. However, we know that many of the steps physicians take are not necessarily related to a proper outcome; thus, it is also necessary to test for the outcome of the encounter. Further, even if outcomes are determined, how are we to know whether the achieved outcome represents good medical care? If, upon testing a protocol for low back pain, the nurses found that 80 percent of their patients experienced symptomatic relief, how are we to know that physician-provided care could not have achieved 90 percent? The literature does not tell us what to expect about the relief of symptoms for chief complaints, because most of the studies in the literature deal with diseases rather than complaints. Therefore, we have decided to compare ourselves to physicians in practice. If the nurses using a protocol are as effective as physicians in a well-controlled trial, we could say that the protocol administered by a nurse is an adequate mode of delivery of care.

As a concrete example of adequate validation of a protocol I will briefly describe the protocol validation study for the complaints of dysuria, frequency, vaginitis in women. The study, conducted at the UCLA Student Health Service, was designed to compare the performance of a protocol-guided nurse to the performance of a group of physicians with respect to history taking, physical examination, simple laboratory observations, and management. The study design is depicted in Figure 4. Women presenting with either dysuria, urine

STUDY DESIGN

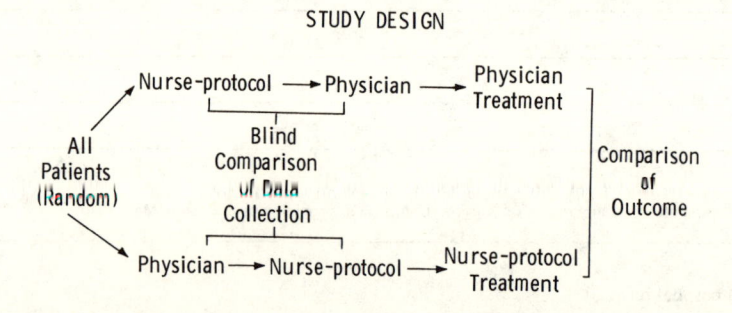

Fig. 4. A randomized crossover study design to compare both process and outcome. The patients followed the treatment recommendations of the practitioner they saw last.

frequency, vaginal discharge, or vaginal irritation were randomly allocated to one of two groups. One group was seen first by the nurse, an RN without prior practitioner experience, and then by one of a group of 13 participating physicians. The physicians were advised to the study goals and design, and all inquires were answered; however, the protocol decision logic was not reviewed with any physician. Patients assigned to the other group were seen first by a physician and then by the nurse. Neither the physician nor the nurse knew the other's findings. The nurse performed her own examination of urine sediment and vaginal smear without knowledge of the Student Health Laboratory examination of the same specimens.

The nurse on the protocol form, and the physician on a similar form that did not include any decision logic, recorded their respective histories and physical findings; after ascertaining the laboratory results, they committed themselves on paper to a presumptive diagnosis and plan. The group of patients seen last by physicians followed the physician's recommendations (physician group). The other group, those seen by the nurse, followed the protocol disposition and therapy (nurse–protocol group). In this group, the nurse presented to the physician the protocol recommendations regarding treatment or the need for referral to a physician, and requested that the physician indicate on a special sheet his judgment about these protocol decisions. The physician was asked, in effect, whether the protocol action was reasonable, not whether it corresponded exactly to what he or she had recommended or would recommend. If the physician was opposed to the nurse–protocol disposition or therapy in this group of patients seen last by the nurse, the physician's decisions prevailed and these patients were removed from the analysis of outcome results.

The patients were asked to telephone two days later for the results of the urine culture. If the urine culture was positive the patient was asked to return for a repeat culture one week after termination of therapy. Within a week following the clinic visit all patients were contacted by telephone to ask about presence, absence, or alleviation of symptoms, and to inquire about complications.

The results showed favorable comparison between physicians and the nurse–protocol. Concordance between physicians and the nurse with respect to history is recorded in Table 2. Of the 146 histories, 139 were essentially identical. Of the 7 discrepancies, there were 6 cases in which an error was made by the physician. In 4 cases, the

Table 2. Data Collection Concordance Between Physicians and Nurse-Protocol (N-P)

	Identical	Physician Error	N-P Error
History	139	6 (4)	1 (0)*
Physical exam	137	0	9 (0)

*( ) Resulting in altered diagnosis or management.

physicians concurred that they had erred in not pursuing symptoms suggestive either of vaginitis or of urinary tract infection, and management was altered upon discovery of the other condition. In 2 cases, physicians agreed that they had not acquired a presumptive history of past urinary tract problems. There was 1 patient in whom the nurse did not detect a past history of significant urinary tract infection.

Concordance was similar with respect to physical examination. Of the 146 cases, 137 had virtually identical physical examination. In 9 cases the nurse was considered to have made an error, based on concurrent physician assessment. These were not independently verified. In no case did any of these physical exam errors result in a different management decision. In 5 cases the nurse did not recognize the cheesy character of vaginal discharge, but monilia was seen on wet mount; in 4 cases physicians noted costo-vertebral angle tenderness, which the nurse had not noted, but did not specifically diagnose pyelonephritis, and did not alter management of routine urinary tract infection.

Evaluation of nurse laboratory work indicated that the laboratory findings agreed with the nurse's findings in 54 of 58 urinalyses performed. In the 4 cases where there was disagreement, the physician who had seen the patient examined the sediment himself and confirmed the nurse's observation. With respect to wet mounts of vaginal secretions, in 9 cases of 39 in which the nurse detected monilia the laboratory failed to note the presence of monilia. In all these cases, the nurse findings were confirmed by the physician upon review. The nurse failed to note monilia on one specimen that was found to be positive by the laboratory. There was no independent judgment made on the specimens reported negative by both nurse and laboratory.

The protocol's diagnostic accuracy was evaluated in those cases in which the patient would have gone home without seeing a physician. The nurse using the protocol made the decision to refer the patient to the doctor in 16 cases, or 11 percent. Concordance of diagnosis in the remaining 130 patients is seen in Table 3. The diagnoses were made after review of the laboratory work in the case of both physicians and nurse. It can be seen that agreement was virtually complete. In 2 cases the diagnosis of vaginitis was pursued and confirmed by the nurse when the physician had noted only urinary

Table 3. Diagnosis Concordance Between Nurse-Protocol and Physician for 130 Patients

N-P Diagnosis	Urinary tract infection	Urethral syndrome or urethritis	Monilia	Nonspecific vaginitis	Trichomonas	Urinary tract infection and vaginitis	Other*
Urinary tract infection	28						
Urethral syndrome or urethritis		6					
Monilia			37				
Nonspecific vaginitis			1	41			
Trichomonas					1		
Urinary tract infection and vaginitis	2					8	
Other*							6

*Includes no pathology found, trichomonas and monilia together, suspect allergic reactions to vaginal insertions.

tract infection to be present; in both instances, upon review, the physician agreed with the nurse-protocol diagnosis and therapy. In one case the laboratory found monilia on a gram stain of vaginal discharge; this woman had been diagnosed as having nonspecific vaginitis by the nurse.

There was virtually complete agreement with regard to therapy as well. In 1 case the physician agreed with the nurse-protocol diagnosis but preferred another treatment. In the other 129 cases, physicians judged the protocol treatment plan to be "reasonable." In all, physicians concurred with the nurse-protocol diagnosis and management (specific therapy or referral) in 144 of 146 cases.

In addition to prescribing specific treatment, the protocol recommended review of the record in consultation with the physician in 11 cases. Nine of these were reviewed for a suspect past history of urinary tract disease. Two were reviewed for recently having taken medication that might potentially interfere with diagnosis and therapy. There was agreement on the need for review of all these 11 records.

All 16 patients referred to the physician by the protocol were referred appropriately, according to the physician. Of the 16 referrals, 7 were due either to a return visit for the same complaint or for medication recently taken that would interfere with the diagnosis and therapy. Three were for symptoms and signs of generalized toxicity and the remainder were for miscellaneous reasons. The protocol did not fail to refer any patient whom the physicians felt had to be examined by a physician.

Symptomatic outcome was evaluated in the nurse–protocol group and the physician group. A total of 76 patients were allocated to the nurse treatment group; of these, 8 did not receive nurse–protocol management because of referral (6 cases), physician disagreement (1 case), or no identifiable pathology (1 case). Similarly, 5 patients of the 70 assigned to the physician group were excluded from analysis of specific therapy because of referrals to sub-specialists or other complications. Symptomatic outcome for the remaining 68 patients treated by nurse–protocol and 65 patients treated by physicians are recorded in Table 4. Of the 65 patients who received physician treatment, all but 2 reported alleviation or improvement symptoms.

Table 4. Symptomatic Outcome by Treatment Group and Diagnosis

	UTI/US* Total	Improved	Vaginitis Total	Improved	Both Total	Improved
Nurse–protocol	16	16	49	47	3	3
Physician	23	22	35	34	7	7

*Urinary tract infection/urethral syndrome.

Similarly, only 2 of the 68 nurse–protocol patients reported no improvement. The 3 patients with vaginitis who did not improve were thought to have nonspecific vaginitis on the first visit and were later treated for monilia infection. One patient who had a urinary tract infection (treated by the physician) had an allergic reaction to sulfisoxazole.

Results of antibiotic treatment for urinary tract infection are shown in Table 5. Nine of the physicians' 15 culture-positive patients had repeat cultures one week after termination of treatment. Eight out of 9 cultures were sterile. Similarly, of the 14 positive cultures in the nurse-protocol patients group, 12 were recultured and 10 of these were sterile in three weeks.

Table 5. Culture Results of Antibiotic Treatment for Urinary Tract Infection

Patients	Positive before Treatment	Total Recultured	Culture Sterile 3 weeks
Physician	15	9	8
Nurse-protocol	14	12	10
Totals	29	21	18

This study supported the hypothesis that the nurse could accurately collect the relevant clinical data; and that, using the protocol, she could make appropriate diagnostic, therapeutic and disposition judgments. Thus the protocol was both efficient in conserving physician time and effective in delivering medical care. The outcome of an encounter would always appear to be the best criterion for its success or failure; however, for the complaints studied here, culture and and symptomatic outcome are not sufficient to validate protocol decisions because urinary tract symptoms, vaginitis symptoms, and bacteriuria can be self-limited. This particular study design permitted independent evaluation of both process and outcome.

Safety, one of our major considerations, was found to be adequate. Those patients who would have been sent home by the protocol rules without seeing a physician had no complications, at least as ascertained by a followup by concurrent physician estimation of the complexity of the problem. All potential complications were referred to the physicians and we anticipate that the protocol decision logic is conservative enough to continue this degree of safety with even larger numbers.

Similar kinds of results have been obtained with the validation studies of backache, upper respiratory infection, and headache. These results reinforce our concept that a nonphysician using materials that allow for intensive training in well-defined skills with definite rules for referral can perform as well as a physician.

Before discussing the implications of protocol usage in relation to the law, the final aspect of the protocol movement, use and barriers to use in practice, must be considered. There is growing acceptance of protocols in the United States. Validation studies are being published in the major medical journals. Requests for protocols have exceeded the supply, and a nationwide survey to determine the extent of usage in various situations is in progress. The major barriers to their use, which are being examined at the present time, fall into two major areas. One is that nurses who have had general nurse practitioner training in addition to working with protocols are motivated to make more and more independent decisions as their knowledge and skills develop. They are often anxious to go further than the protocol or to deviate from it, and they may find the protocol to be limiting. We have stressed repeatedly that a protocol represents minimum standards—a floor rather than a ceiling. Once the minimum workup has been done, insuring minimum quality of care, then other aspects of the workup can be added.

The second concern is that nurses, like physicians, often feel that the protocol workup calls for too much. It is said that the workup is too compulsive, too lengthy, too cumbersome. This criticism reflects the tension between exigencies of daily practice on one hand and the high quality workup of patient complaints on the other. For example, of all patients that present with headache to a family practice or general practice office only a vanishing small fraction will have stroke as a cause of headache. While headache is a common concomitant of stroke, most patients with stroke have signs or symptoms that are serious enough to take them right to the emergency room. However, there is no question that a few patients with stroke present initially with headache alone. Therefore we feel it incumbent to include some attributes to investigate the possibility of stroke causing headache. How far should we go? The doctor in practice might say that if a person doesn't look like he's having a stroke, ie no obvious paralysis or difficulty walking, that is good enough. However, because we are explicitly committing ourselves in print to sets of standards for practice for nonphysicians, we feel it necessary to be conservative and have required more than a casual look at a patient with only a remote possibility of a stroke. Nurses, like physicians, are anxious to be as efficient as possible and want to eliminate what they feel from their own experience is an unnecessary section on stroke. Many parallels to this example exist; practitioners are constantly "pruning" their workups according to their experience and their time constraints. The development at the Beth Israel Hospital of a single form allowing both the logic to be followed and the data to be recorded has been shown in preliminary time-motion studies not to slow down the practitioner's pace. Moreover, if a physician in a practice wishes to eliminate some attributes from the protocol this can be done quite easily and the attendant risks and benefits will be spelled out clearly. On the other hand, major modifications of the protocol, leading to different kinds of decisions and different kinds of outcomes, should probably be tested more formally (as in our trials). We feel that once the bulk of a protocol workup has been adequately tested in field trials with hundreds of patients, minor modifications and cutbacks can be done without harm to the patients.

Like standing orders, the protocol must constantly be changed and revised according to new discoveries in medical science. If a new diagnostic test eliminates a considerable part of a workup it should be incorporated into the protocol. If we adhere to the principle that a protocol should always represent, in the most parsimonious exacting form, the intellectual processes of the physician kept up-to-date, then it can be used as a safe and reliable instrument. There is no reason why a protocol should be fossilized like a medical textbook after three to four years of use.

The protocol relation to the law becomes clearer once the concepts of protocol use and practice, development and validation, and difficulties in use become known. If the protocols in fact represent what the doctor thinks and does, if the development of the protocols involves widespread peer review, if the protocols are validated in a way that allow them to have proven therapeutic efficacy, then the protocols can conceivably stand as analogs to standing orders. The protocols can ensure a minimum standard of quality of care based on current day standards for practice, and as such could have considerable legal support. To the extent that the protocol workups may also include the approval and support of local physicians in a community or in a health care unit, this approval would further strengthen their potential for approaching standing orders. In this regard it must be emphasized that it is the protocol, rather than the nurse, which recommends additional diagnostic tests, specific therapy, and disposition, ie whether the patient should be referred to the physician or sent home.

The role of protocols in relation to the law will necessarily be limited by their ability to account for all patient visits. It might be possible to cover a large fraction of patient visits with thoroughly tried and tested protocols, but the remaining fraction would not be covered by standardized and well-validated protocols. Locally-constructed protocols, not subject to as complete validation studies but incorporating local peer review, could supplement the well-tested protocol. In this way legal constraints operating for physicians could be similarly applied to nurses. The use of protocols may introduce a useful approach to normalizing the relationship between the law and the delegation of clinical tasks to nurses in the practice of primary care.

REFERENCES

1. A. Komaroff, G. Reiffen & H. Sherman, *Problem-Oriented Protocols for Physician-Extenders*, in APPLYING THE PROBLEM ORIENTED SYSTEM 186-96 (W. Hurst, H. Walker & N. Woody eds. 1973).
2. S. Greenfield, F. Bragg, D. McCraith, et. al., *An Upper Respiratory Complaint Protocol for Physician-Extenders*, 133 ARCH. INTERN. MED. 294-9 (1974).
3. A. Komaroff, W. Black, M. Flatley, et. al., *Protocols for Physician Assistants: Management of Diabetes and Hypertension*, 290 N. ENGL. J. MED. 307-12 (1974).
4. S. Greenfield, G. Friedland, S. Scifers, et. al., *Protocol Management of Dysuria, Frequency and Vaginal Discharge*, 81 ANNALS INTERN. MED. 452-57 (1974).
5. O. PETERSON, L. ANDREWS, R. SPAIN, ET AL., AN ANALYTICAL STUDY OF NORTH CAROLINA GENERAL PRACTICE (1956).
6. J. Dingle, *The Ills of Man*, 229 SCI. AM. 77-84 (1974).
7. S. Bain & W. Spaulding, *The Importance of Coding Presenting Symptoms*, CAN. MED. ASSOC. J. 97, 953 (October 14, 1967).
8. M. BUDD, B. REIFFEN, M. RODMAN, ET. AL., A PROGRAM FOR AN AMBULATORY CARE SERVICE, LINCOLN LABORATORY, MASSACHUSETTS INSTITUTE FOR TECHNOLOGY DOR-541 (January 27, 1969).
9. L. GOODSTINE, K. STREIFF & F. BRAGG, EVALUATION OF AIDE TRIAGE OF AMBULATORY PATIENTS, LINCOLN LABORATORY, MASSACHUSETTS INSTITUET FOR TECHNOLOGY AND BETH ISRAEL HOSPITAL ACP-20 (April 6, 1971).
10. COMMISSION ON CHRONIC ILLNESS, CHRONIC ILLNESS IN A LARGE CITY: THE BALTIMORE STUDY (1957).
11. H. Schonfeld, J. Heston & I. Falk, *Number of Physicians Required for Primary Medical Care*, 286 N. ENGL. J. MED. 571 (1972).
12. G. Goldberg, M. Grady & M. Budd, APPLICABILITY OF PROTOCOL MANAGEMENT OF CHRONIC DISEASE TO AN AGED POPULATION, ACP-7, LINCOLN LABORATORY, M.I.T. & BETH ISRAEL HOSPITAL (July 9, 1970).

13. NATIONAL DISEASE AND THERAPEUTIC INDEX, SPECIALTY PROFILE (Kozlow ed. 1970).
14. H. SHERMAN & A. KOMAROFF, PROGRESS REPORT 9A, ACP-II, LINCOLN LABORATORY, M.I.T. & BETH ISRAEL HOSPITAL (January 1, 1974).
15. W. Schwartz, G. Gorry, J. Kassirer, *et. al.*, *Decision Analysis and Clinical Judgment*, 55 AM. J. MED. 459-72 (1973).
16. S. Greenfield, H. Anderson, R. Winickoff, *et. al.*, Management of Low Back Pain by a Protocol and a Physician-Extender Clinical Research, 22: 378A, 1974.

ANITA BERWIND

7
The Nurse in the Coronary Care Unit

Nursing is often described as a dynamic discipline, implying that it is capable of growth and change. This has always been true of nursing, but the recent phenomenal expansion and diversification of nursing has occurred at a bewildering pace.

Considering the years that elapsed between the invention of the clinical thermometer and the assumption by nurses of the "medical act" of taking temperatures, and that prior to World War I use of the sphygmomanometer and stethoscope for taking blood pressures was considered too mysterious and complex a rite for nurses, recent advancement in the techniques held to be within the sphere and scope of nursing are nothing short of miraculous.

In a brief span of years nursing has moved from the use of simple instruments to the use of complex monitoring devices to extend observational ability and to other complicated electronic equipment as part of therapy. Several factors have influenced this tremendous acceleration of nursing practice: the explosion of knowledge in the science and technology of medicine, the relative shortage of doctors, and the shift of medical care from the home to the hospital, where the majority of professional nurses practice.

In the hospital acute care units, probably the most profound influence was the rapid innovation in medical science. New knowledge and techniques in the medical management of the patient with heart disease, for example, led to the development of the coronary care unit nurse. To understand how this one area of nursing practice evolved from new discoveries of medical science, let us trace briefly the development of the coronary care unit.

For nearly fifty years, medical scientists dreamed of finding a way either to prevent or to control coronary atherosclerosis, and concentrated their research efforts on the realization of this dream. But while they dreamed deaths due to myocardial infarction, the final insult of coronary atherosclerosis, mounted inexorably until, at the midpoint of the century, over 25 percent of those hospitalized with myocardial infarction died while hospitalized and another 50 percent of those afflicted died without ever reaching medical aid.[1,2(p 15)]

Researchers realized finally that the way to reduce the mortality from myocardial infarction was to leave discovery of the cause and prevention of coronary atherosclerosis for future study; current efforts were directed toward salvaging lives after the occurrance of the infarction. Attention was given to the study of the mechanism of death due to myocardial infarction.[2(p 3)]

It was discovered that anticoagulant therapy, which was the backbone of treatment for many years and was directed toward the prevention of thromboembolism, could not significantly reduce deaths from myocardial infarction because a relatively small number of these were due to embolism. Research revealed that the primary target of treatment should be arrhythmias, which accounted for nearly half the deaths.[2(p 6),3,4,5]

Close on the heels of this new understanding of the mechanics of death from coronary artery disease came two important discoveries that gave impetus to the efforts to prevent deaths due to fatal arrhythmias—the discovery of the ability to control a fibrillating heart by the direct application of an electric current across the myocardium[6,7,8(p 434)] and the discovery that adequate circulation could be maintained by directly massaging the heart.[8(p 435)]

Although helpful in demonstrating that deaths due to arrhythmia could be prevented, these two therapies never received wide, practical application because of the necessity of surgically exposing the heart to perform fibrillation and massage.[2(p 4),9] For such a maneuver to be successful, it would be necessary for a physician, preferably a surgeon, to stand at the patient's bedside with scalpel and defibrillator in hand when a potentially fatal arrhythmia occurred.[9] It also added insult to injury by requiring the opening of the chest wall in an already-dying patient. Electrical defibrillation, therefore, did not come into its own until a decade later, when new research demonstrated that the same effect on a fibrillating heart could be obtained by passing the current through the chest wall, thereby eliminating the need for surgical exposure of the heart.[10,11] But the need for a thoractomy in order to maintain circulation by direct cardiac massage until the defibrillator could be applied still remained.

The final enhancement of cardiac resuscitation was provided by the discovery that closed-chest cardiac massage acted just as effectively as internal massage in maintaining blood flow to the arrested heart.[9,12(p 25)] These two life-saving measures—closed cardiac massage and electrical stimulation of the myocardium—were synchronized in the correction of many complex cardiac arrhythmias and eventually became the crux of the campaign against death due to arrhythmia. Combined with mouth-to-mouth respirations, they came to comprise a system of resuscitation that should have been highly successful.

But the first trials with this new concept of resuscitation produced disappointing results. A mobile crash cart was equipped with a defibrillator and external pacemaker, and manned by a team of trained personnel who could be dispatched anywhere in the hospital in response to a distress call.[13] The survival rate among those for whom resuscitation was attempted under this system was discouragingly low.[14] The essential flaw in the system was the length of time between the discovery of the arrested patient, the sounding of the alarm, and the arrival of the team and equipment. It became evident that the critical factor for the success of cardiac resuscitation was time. Survival was rare if more than a relatively short period of time passed between the onset of cardiac arrest and the initiation of the life-saving measures.[11,12(p 27),9]

Since arrhythmias occurred so frequently and unpredictably in patients with myocardial infarction, and since time was clearly of the essence, it became evident that patients at risk from cardiac arrest should be grouped where both life-saving equipment and personnel specially trained in methods of cardiac resuscitation were readily available and, further, that some means of continuous monitoring should be devised.[12(p 29)] Fortunately, the development of electronic instruments to monitor cardiac rhythms had kept pace with the development and refinement of techniques of resuscitation. In fact, the concept of using electronic devices to monitor body systems had been familiar in medicine for some years; now it was necessary only to adapt the concept to coronary care and design a facility where patients who were potential victims of arrhythmias could be under constant surveillance and close to needed equipment. The coronary care unit was born.

Not long after the advent of the first coronary care units in the early 60s, nursing made its entrance into the world of coronary care. Even with optimal arrangements for prompt and effective resuscitation, the mortality rate for the patients treated in the coronary care unit and those treated in the general hospital wards remained the same.[15] Two critical factors produced these disappointing results. First, the focus of care on heroic resuscitative measures was misdirected. Studies showed that the emphasis of care should be on the prevention of arrest by early recognition of the minor arrhythmias that could lead to fatal electrical derangement of the cardiac rhythm.[2(p 6)] Second the units were not effective unless they were staffed by physicians—which was hardly feasible—or by personnel who could recognize and terminate arrhythmias when necessary in the absence of the physician.[15] Even when the focus of concern was changed from resuscitation of the arrested patient to prevention of arrest through prompt detection and termination of arrhythmias, if the units failed to delegate authority to perform life-saving emergency measures to the unit staff they remained virtually ineffective.[15]

The key to the success of the whole system was finally realized to be the nursing personnel, who kept the long vigils, who provided the routine care as well as the specialized tasks, who were skillful in identifying arrhythmias, and who were prepared to act promptly and independently in saving lives.[16] A whole new nursing role had been created, which was to have a profound effect on the image, practice, and preparation of nurses.

The new role of the coronary care nurse demanded that the nurse assume multiple responsibilities in the system of care, some of which overlapped with medical responsibilities; that she required unique new skills that were unknown to nursing; and that she possess knowledge that was still relatively new and unfamiliar even to medical science. The traditional training of nurses and organization of nursing practice was not designed to respond to rapid change and innovation in the nursing role, and the impact of the new nursing responsibilities were felt profoundly by the institutions of nursing education. Nurse education had to change its focus in order to prepare nurses who could collaborate with physicians instead of merely perform in a role subordinate to them.[30,17(p 8)]

The effects of the nurse's expanded role in coronary care are still influencing the image of modern nursing and the direction of nursing education, and cannot be fully assessed. This article deals primarily with the dramatic changes in the scope of nursing practice that have occurred since the nurse first established herself as a valuable member of the coronary care team. Once the nurse became recognized as the essential figure in the coronary care unit, the physician increasingly deferred to her in matters related to the technical details of the unit, and to her expertise and knowledge, collaborating with her in the best interest of the patient. This new collaboration and interdependence between medicine and nursing has led to increased delegation to the nurse of authority to act in the absence of the physician, and has made it difficult to determine where the doctor's function stops and the nurse's begins.

Nursing increasingly shares an enlarging core of theory and skills with medicine and, not surprisingly, the nurse more and more often performs tasks that traditionally were performed by the physician alone. With the assumption of new tasks, the nurse has also assumed the responsibility for her own actions. In an area such as the coronary care unit, it is impossible for the nurse to function on medical dictate alone. She needs the freedom and authority to plan and take action independently. This requires the delegation of authority to the nurse —which both the hospital administration and medical staff are often reluctant to do.

Since the coronary care unit was only effective if the nurse was given some leeway in which to act, there were only three alternatives open: continue to withhold authority from the nurse and let the expensive units function ineffectively; decline to establish a coronary care unit and deprive a community of the newest and most effective means of care; or establish some system of delegating authority to the nurse.

The first two alternatives were prohibited on economic and moral grounds, respectively. In most instances, the administration and medical staffs of each hospital formed a coordinating committee to govern the activity of the units. The committee was responsible for setting down standards of practice, requirements for training, and guidelines to keep close control of clinical practice within the unit. Policies established by the committee governed patient admission criteria, admission routines, delegation of authority by the attending physician to the physician staff of the coronary care unit, and visitation rights. Most important, the committee attempted to establish protocols that would provide the nurse with a legal umbrella.

The legal umbrella in the coronary care unit took the form of what might be called contingent orders or, more commonly, standing orders. In other words, to assure that the nurse could act with some confidence in the legality of her actions, every conceivable contingency that might occur in the unit is covered in advance by an order that governs the nurse's action. Routine standing orders often provide in detail for checking of vital signs, oxygen therapy, recording of fluid intake and output, attachment of monitoring electrodes, monitoring of the ambulatory patient, restriction of smoking, reading, phone calls, listening to the radio or watching television, diet and feeding techniques, activity (including progression from bed to chair and from bedpan to bathroom), shaving the patient, passive exercise, sedation, laxatives, analgesics, and instituting intravenous therapy.

Sometimes a standing order might be quite involved in order to assure that all bases are covered. For example, when ordering "stat" or routine diagnostic studies, the nurse might be confronted with the following:

A stat electrocardiogram is to be taken on every patient admitted to the unit unless the patient is being admitted from another hospital area where an electrocardiogram has been taken within the last four hours and the electrocardiogram accompanies the patient to the unit. Thereafter, a patient with an acute myocardial infarction will have daily electrocardiograms for the first four days after admission to the unit.

or

All patients suspected of having an acute myocardial infarction will have a determination of the LDH, SGOT, and CPK ordered daily for three days unless the results of the first studies are grossly abnormal and then this order should be discontinued and more frequent studies performed at the discretion of the physician.

Standing orders not only spell out functions that are a traditional part of nursing and rather elementary in nature, but, as indicated in the above examples, pave the way for the nurse to assume functions, ie, requesting diagnostic studies, that are a traditional part of medicine. They also move nursing into the gray areas of practice that are new to both professions, and thus are not strictly medical or nursing.

For example, in most coronary care units there are standing orders for a nurse to use certain medications to terminate arrhythmias that she identifies from the cardioscope, without contacting the physician. Most units also provide in their standing orders for the nurse to initiate cardiopulmonary resuscitative measures and to apply an external pacing device or defibrillator in an emergency in the absence of the physician.

Standing orders that generally relate to the routine care of the patient in the unit, such as those pertaining to diet, feeding, and activity, are basically instructions to the nurse about a patient who was diagnosed before admission to the unit, and their validity is generally thought to be secure: but standing orders that provide for measures in instances where the nurse must make the judgment of need, such as defibrillation in case of ventricular fibrillation, are held to be suspect. In these instances the nurse must diagnose, treat, and prescribe, and it has been axiomatic that the physician may not delegate the authority to diagnose, to treat, or to prescribe.[18]

Before pursuing the leak-proofness of standing orders as a legal umbrella, the objections that have been brought against standing orders on other grounds should be given some note. The new roles for nursing are not unanimously embraced by nursing leaders or other members of the profession. They realize that, historically, there is a tendency for the nursing profession to be swayed by the urgency of the situation; to assume tasks on the basis of expediency, and to let them fall into current practice without ever analyzing them in depth for their validity as part of nursing function. These nurses feel that, all too frequently, nursing allows the scope of practice to be defined by medical dictate or other outside pressure, thereby abdicating the professional responsibility for self-determination of the scope of nursing practice.

The determination of the boundaries of nursing practice should be a nursing decision that results from continuing reevaluation of the nature of nursing, the changing needs of the public it serves, and the most beneficial role for the nurse in the delivery of present and future health services. It is the responsibility of the nursing profession to accept or reject a function as either a part of nursing or outside of nursing, and to assume the responsibility of preparing its members for those functions that are deemed to be nursing functions. No function should be assumed by the profession through default, dictate, or exigency.[17(p 6)]

Careful research into the nurse's role in the coronary care unit indicates that it came about primarily as a result of default, dictate, *and* exigency, and not from careful analysis of the role by the nursing profession.[2(p 7)] Doctors staffed one of the original coronary care units that later served as the prototype for many other units, until they rebelled against the boredom and constant vigilance; then nurses, who are believed somehow different in temperament so that they readily withstand boring vigils, were assigned to replace the doctors. When it became obvious that the nurse's vigilance was not enough in the coronary care unit, it was conveniently reasoned that the same nurses, who throughout history were thought to be capable only of observing and reporting, could now not only detect a potentially fatal arrhythmia, but were capable also of terminating it with a complex electronic device—capable, that is, only in the event the physician did not arrive in the critical first two minutes. Virtually all the nurse's functions within the coronary care unit were determined by hospital administrators and medical staff, without deferrance to opinions or suggestions by nurses. Even the units in which the nurse is the primary practitioner were originally designed, often deplorably, by hospital administrators, physicians, engineers, and monitor salespeople, without input from the nurse.

Members of the profession who take a critical view of the nurse's new roles are not necessarily opposed to the roles per se, but they insist that we should understand and acknowledge our motives for what we do. We should not delude ourselves that our movement into new areas of practice is necessarily the result of our new-found self-determination and independence, but may be another instance in history when nursing has blindly allowed itself to be led down the primrose path. Also, discerning minds should question the validity of a profession that is moved toward change almost entirely by external forces rather than in response to the forces within. The same critical voices who question the expanded roles of the nurse raise doubts about the auspices under which these roles are performed, particularly that of standing orders. Is it feasible to routinize with standing orders a condition as unpredictable as myocardial infarction? Are standing orders not stultifying rather than stimulating to the nurse's role of decision-maker, since they often prescribe the nurse's function with such exactness that there is little need for inference or judgment? Can a role that can be so carefully outlined and prescribed require the expertise of a professional nurse? Couldn't it be as adequately performed by any person with a modicum of intelligence and a passable ability to read?

Although some nurses still hesitate and are reluctant to embrace the new areas of practice unequivocally as nursing, the majority of the profession has long since resolved the matter to its satisfaction simply by applying the creed that nursing is involved where there is illness to prevent and lives to save, and now have focused their energies and concern on establishing a legal basis for their new nursing roles.

The legality of the nurse's functions within the coronary care unit is dependent upon the legality of the standing orders by which the physician delegates functions to the nurse. As already stated, orders that relate to actions of nurses in caring for a patient with a previously diagnosed condition are viewed with less skepticism than those in which the nurse first must make an inference or judgment about the patient and then act. Such orders imply that the nurse cannot only diagnose but also treat emergencies and prescribe pharmacologic agents.[18]

The professional nurse has always been held responsible for critical thinking and decisive action both routinely and in emergencies. The function of critical thinking and decision making becomes more complex as the nurse's knowledge base in the sciences broadens and enlarges, increasing the alternatives for action.[19] What to *call* the critical thinking and judgments of the nurse, is actually the center of the current debate on the legality of some of her functions. Whether called judgment making, clinical inference, or diagnosis, the task has been shown by research to be an integral part of nursing practice.[18,19] Throughout nursing history, nurses have observed phenomena relative to the care of the patient and have made judgments for action based on multiple data sources.[20] The term diagnosis merely implies the cognitive or intellectual ability to appraise a situation, draw conclusions based on this appraisal, and plan actions based on the conclusions. This intellectual function has always been well within the boundaries of nursing.[21] Confusion arises because statutory law for for the licensure of nurses has commonly included a clause forbidding the nurse to diagnose, prescribe, or treat, without really defining the terms, providing guidelines for interpretation, or qualifying the statement in any way.

In practice, a distinction is made between the diagnostic functions of the physician and those of the nurse. The diagnostic function of the physician is directed toward determining the cause and most effective treatment of a disease; the nurse functions to identify symptoms and discover the means to alleviate them.[19,(p 25)] Using this interpretation as a guide, one could say that the nurse in the coronary care unit is not diagnosing, because the physician determines the patient's disease prior to admitting him to the unit; when the nurse identifies ventricular fibrillation in a patient she has merely identified a symptom of his disease, rather than making a basic diagnosis.

The course of action open to the members of each profession after a decision based on observation is made is the real core of distinction between the physician and the nurse. Traditionally, the nurse does not prescribe therapy; but she does all in her power, particularly in an emergency, to avoid complications or deterioration of the patient's condition—even taking, if necessary, actions which are normally those of the physician. Common law holds the nurse responsible for tentatively diagnosing a patient's condition in an emergency and taking whatever measures are necessary in the absence of medical help.[22] In fact, cases can be cited where the nurse was held liable because of a failure to diagnose and act.

The nurse's conduct in the coronary care unit has been defended on this basis of acting in an emergency. However, it is a weak defense. A cardiac arrest in the coronary care unit is anticipated, and preparations for resuscitation by the nurse in the absence of the physician are carefully made. It is at best a planned emergency. Furthermore, the exception made regarding the prohibition of diagnosis by statutory law is that the services rendered in an emergency be "gratuitous," and there are few nurses providing gratuitous services in the coronary care unit.

Although medicine and nursing may mutually recognize and accept certain standards of performance, this practice may or may not be upheld in the courts. Nursing gets its legal definition of scope and sphere from two sources: common law and statutory law. Common law is essentially judge-made law and can be more flexible and contemporary because it is unwritten. The courts are often guided by medical custom in identifying the nurse's functions, since these functions have traditionally been determined by medical practice.[22(p 89)] Increasingly, court decisions reflect the high level of responsibility the nurse has assumed in practice and to which she is now being held by society.

The nursing profession learns much about the public and legal view of the standards of nursing practice by being aware of the court decisions.[23(p314)] Often common law decisions are the first guides the nurse has to standards of practice in areas not defined by statutory law. Common law, using as its guide current and accepted standards of practice, is easier for a dynamic profession such as nursing to live with. But statutory law is often both inflexible and ambiguous. When statements are not qualified, terms defined, or guidelines offered, the intentions of the law can be confusing and the meaning may vary according to the interpretation. Present problems have developed because the irresistable force of change has met an immovable (or seemingly immovable) object—statutory law.

The statutes governing the practice of nursing generally attempt to define that practice, but do so in such a nebulous way that they are difficult to use as a guide to determine the legal functions of the nurse. Most of the statutes were written in broad terms to prevent them from being restrictive and allow for change, but this has produced only ambiguity.[22(p313)]

Although there has always been a shifting and realignment of functions between medicine and nursing, the transition is taking place at an increasingly faster pace to meet the demands for more and better health services in a more efficient and realistic way. It is necessary to build in regulations of functions that are now a part of nursing but were virtually unfamiliar even to medicine a short time ago.

Even though legal doctrine has not kept pace with the advances in nursing, the nurse should be aware of what is considered the boundaries of reasonable conduct for today's practice. When she advances into the vulnerable gray areas of practice, she should be prepared to be held to a level of knowledge of science and practice commensurate with the responsibilities she assumes and the actions she takes.[17(p6)] The growing body of judicial decisions reflect, though the statutes may not, the development and expansion of nursing practice and the standards expected of that practice. There is little doubt that nurses are functioning in roles that may be in violation of many state laws. Although no nurse has to date been prosecuted for assuming the new roles, there is justifiable concern among nurses because of the broad interpretations made of the standing orders that govern their practice. Nurses are concerned for themselves and for the public that nursing practice have adequate legal safeguards, and recognize their obligation to examine the new roles for justification as part of nursing practice and, if found justified, to fight for the legal sanctions necessary to protect the practitioner in these roles.

There appear to be at least three questions about the legality of the role of the nurse in the coronary care unit: Is she required to make diagnoses that are beyond the sphere of nursing? Is she performing medical acts outside the existence of an emergency situation? Is she functioning under an umbrella that is not legal—namely, standing orders?

That the profession realized its obligation to its members to provide support and to promote the legal foundation needed for practice is first evidenced by the development of joint statements to establish policy governing the procedures carried out by the nurse in the coronary care unit. Even before the advent of coronary care nursing, some state nursing associations approached medicine to develop joint statements on other functions of the nurse to provide some legal base for these functions.[24] Generally, joint statements have been felt to be adequate and would probably be accepted by the courts, but they are only policy statements and not law.[22,23(p 11)] The ideal answer is to change the law to reflect reality. Fortunately, the nursing associations in most states are continuing to battle to put the new nursing practice on sound legal footing, and there is a movement in almost every state to change existing law radically by amendment, or to rewrite completely the nurse practice acts, to assure the continued expansion of nursing within the law. This movement is welcomed by coronary care unit nurses.

REFERENCES

1. V. KEYLOUN & G. WILLIAMS, THE CORONARY CARE UNIT, 1 (1970).
2. L. Meltzer & J. Roderick, *The Development and Current Status of Coronary Care*, in TEXTBOOK OF CORONARY CARE (L. Meltzer & A. Dunning eds., 1972).
3. L. Meltzer & J. Kitchell, *The Incidence of Arryhthmias Associated with Myocardial Infarction*, in PROGRESSIVE CARDIOVASCULAR DISEASE 20 (1966).
4. H. Day & K. Averill, *Recorded Arrhythmias in an Acute Coronary Care Area*, 49 DIS. CHEST 115 (1966).
5. R. MacMillan, et. al., *Changing Perspectives in Coronary Care*, 20 AM. J. CARDIOL. 453 (1967).
6. D. Hooker, et. al., *Effects of Alternating Electrical Currents on the Heart*, 103 AM. J. PHYSIOL. 444 (1933).

7. C. Beck, et. al., *Ventricular Fibrillation of Long Duration Abolished by Electric Shock,* 135 J. AM. MED. ASSOC. 986 (1947).
8. C. Beck, et. al., *Fatal Heart Attack and Successful Defibrillation,* 161 J. AM. MED. ASSOC. (1956).
9. W. Kouwenhoven, et. al., *Closed-Chest Cardiac Massage,* 178 J. AM. MED. ASSOC. 1064 (1961).
10. B. Lown, et. al., *New Methods for Terminating Cardiac Arrhythmias,* 182 J. AM. MED. ASSOC. 548 (1962).
11. P. Zoll, et. al., *Termination of Ventricular Fibrillation in Man by Externally Applied Electric Countershock,* 254 NEW ENGL. J. MED. 730 (1956).
12. W. Minogue, et. al., *External Cardiac Massage,* 13 AM. J. CARDIOL. (1964).
13. H. Day, *A Cardiac Resuscitation Program,* 82 JOURNAL-LANCET 155-6 (1962).
14. H. Day, *Preliminary Studies of an Acute Coronary Care Area,* 83 JOURNAL-LANCET 55 (1963).
15. T. Killip & J. Kimball, *Treatment of Myocardial Infarction in a Coronary Care Unit,* 20 AM. J. CARDIOL. 464 (1967).
16. J. Epstein, *Objectives of Coronary Care Units,* in A SYMPOSIUM PRESENTED BY CEDAR-SINAI MEDICAL CENTER DEPARTMENT OF NURSING: AGGRESSIVE NURSING MANAGEMENT OF ACUTE MYOCARDIAL INFARCTION 13 (1968).
17. B. E. Anderson, *Legal Aspects of Nursing Care for Cardiac Patients,* 5 CARDIOVASC. NURS. (1969).
18. M. LESNIK & B. E. ANDERSON, NURSING PRACTICE AND THE LAW (1962).
19. K. Kelly, *Clinical Inference in Nursing,* 15 NURS. RES. 23 (1966).
20. F. NIGHTINGALE, NOTES ON NURSING: WHAT IT IS AND WHAT IT IS NOT (Facsimile of the 1859 edition, 1946).
21. K. Hammond, *Clinical Inference in Nursing.* 15 NURS. RES. 27 (1966).
22. S. WILLIG, THE NURSES' GUIDE TO THE LAW (1970).
23. B.J. Anderson, *Orderly Transfer of Procedural Responsibilities from Medical to Nursing Practice,* 5 NURS. CLIN. NORTH AM. (1970).
24. *See* California Nursing Association Joint Statements and PROCEEDINGS OF CNA MEDICAL-LEGAL INSTITUTE (1966).

LEONIDE L. MARTIN

8
View from the Firing Line: Family Nurse Practioner in California

Practicing as a family nurse practitioner (FNP) in California from 1973 to 1974 was an enlightening but hazardous experience. The major danger was posed by an outdated nurse practice act which, combined with a preemptive medical practice act, made extended role functions clearly illegal. Other occupational hazards confronting nurse practitioners included the process of role change and the many intricacies of the nurse-physician interface. In my experiences over the last year as an FNP in a community ambulatory care setting, I have encountered all these problems. This account discusses the real events and my perceptions of some underlying dynamics.

The Basic Issues

To my mind, nursing is now involved in a major battle. The primary issue is power. The cause for which the battle is pitched is greater nursing influence and control over the nature and delivery of health services. Our adversaries are predominantly medicine and health facilities administration. Certain segments in nursing are in the front lines and carry forth the fight; others are in supply lines and support the battle; yet others are in the adversaries' camp. It is an undeniably sexist conflict, for nurses are mainly women while physicians and health facilities administrators are mainly men. The opposing segments within nursing are mainly conditioned sexist women, effectively socialized in their own inferiority.

Underlying this power struggle are several pervasive and ancient issues. Whenever an argument arises about whether nurses should expand their functions or not, each of these issues can be identified if the particular items of contention are translated into principles. Take the issue of individual competence: Nurses (women) are not educated or competent enough to make critical evaluations and decisions. Physicians (men) spend many long, arduous years learning a particular process for collecting, analyzing, interpreting, and acting upon data related to the malfunction of the human body. Nurses, with their much shorter training period could not possibly make comparable evaluations and decisions. This is true to the extent that one's education prepares one for one's functions. Following this reasoning, if nursing education included information similar to medical education, then nurses would be competent to make such decisions. Contrary to popular myth, there is nothing magical about the practice of medicine. It is a systematic approach that can readily be learned.

Why, then, the general belief that nurses are not as smart as doctors? That only the doctor can give the definitive answer or make the final decision? Because of sexist attitudes. If women are innately inferior to men, then education cannot really bring them to the same plane. If high-level competence and the ability to make really critical evaluations and decisions are male characteristics, then no amount of preparation will give women these capabilities. This is the situation of nursing vis-a-vis medicine. Most nurses, most doctors, and most of the general population have been socialized to believe that the things women do (such as nursing) are of inferior worth and require lesser ability than the things men do. No wonder the opposition to an extended role for nursing, which requires a high degree of independence, judgment, responsibility, and skill overlapping into the physician's domain. Repeatedly one hears the question, "Can nurses really do these things?" Yes, they can and they do, with great competence. A woman's ability and intelligence is no less than a man's; with incapacitating attitudes removed, whatever she is educated to do she can perform effectively.

Self-actualization, or the achievement of full personhood, is another underlying issue. This, too, is permeated with sexism. Women (nurses) are only part people and have circumscribed, supportive, and subservient roles that allow those highly talented and important individuals in the society (men, doctors) to be released from mundane activities in order to achieve greater heights. After all, behind every successful man (doctor), there is a woman (nurse). How else could he enjoy a family, a home, and a career, if someone was not there to carry on with the minutiae of living and provide supports for his important high-level activities? People acting the subservient roles should ask little for themselves, least of all power and authority. Nurses and women are now questioning these premises and are increasingly less willing to live by them. Nurse practitioners are not accepting a sharply circumscribed and narrowly limited role. Our goal is to practice to the level of our abilities, without artificial (sexist) constraints. Self-actualization, here partly expressed in a respected and valued career, is seen as a woman's inalienable right.

Humanitarianism is another issue that I feel motivates this national movement toward extended nursing roles. The present health care system is glaringly inadequate in meeting all the health needs of the country's people. It denies equal access to care, and provides care of differing quality according to socioeconomic status. Physicians have been the controlling force in shaping the character of medical and health care now available. Their concerns have obviously been overly economic and egocentric. While one cannot deny the advances made in medical care (disease control and management), very little has been done for health maintenance and preventive care. People need to know how to live healthier and more satisfying lives, and how to avoid illness and injury as much as they need drugs, physical and electronic manipulations, and operations when they are sick. The nurse practitioner inculcates nursing's concern for prevention and promotion of health with the techniques for treatment of common illnesses. Social awareness and the desire to better distribute health and medical care, with less service to the economic goals of the practitioner, are integral to the movement to extend nursing and health personnel roles. Nurses have always been, in my opinion, greater humanists than doctors. Now they are fighting for the power to increase the humanism in medical and health care.

Democracy versus monopoly, as general principles, are critical issues. When viewed from a distance, the incredible medical monopoly over both the character of care and the functions of other health professions is appalling. I feel this could not have occurred except for the totally subservient and powerless position of women in this country during medicine's early years of development. Because nursing was then an exclusively female occupation, and because women were in effect the property of their husband or father, it was inevitable that the male-dominated group would completely overshadow the only competitors, a group composed solely of women. When one realizes that at the turn of the century women had few individual rights, no vote, unequal protection under the law, and a federal constitution devoted to the self-evident truth that "all *men* are created equal," nursing's inability to affect the medical monopoly becomes clear.

There is no justification now for that monopoly. Medical and health care have become so complex, and the body of knowledge so huge, that no one group can claim exclusive rights as the only legitimate decision-maker. Physical therapists and inhalation therapists probably know the indications and uses of their treatment modes better than most doctors; pharmacists know the use and effects of drugs in the greatest depth; psychiatric social workers understand best the dynamics of human behavior; other "paramedical" groups are the experts in their own disciplines. It is absurd that a general practitioner of medicine is licensed to perform brain surgery—but he is. The principle of a medical licensure that is all-inclusive for the in-group but excludes all out-groups is invalid, despite such steps as peer review and community standards to control medical practice.

Expanding nursing roles are eroding the power base of the medical monopoly. That many physicians are personally very threatened by this movement, is reflected in the repressive moves of their professional organizations and some incredible articles in medical publications. Economics, ego dynamics, and the personal need for power are undoubtedly involved in this threat. And, at the very deepest level, so is sexism, as expressed in a favorite misquote: "Scratch the surface of a doctor and you will find a man." If the socialization of men did not lead to a self-concept that requires women to be inferior, at least one part of nursing's battle would not need to be fought.

The Legal Bind

The terms of the battle to upgrade nursing have been couched in the language of the law. As licensed professionals, nurses are subject to nurse practice acts for the protection of the public. We are also subject, by exclusion, to medical practice acts. Each state has different language in its professional licensing acts, so functions and problems differ. In California, we had a nurse practice act dating from 1939, and a highly exclusive medical practice act. The nurse practice act stated:

The practice of nursing within the meaning of this chapter is the performing of professional services requiring technical skills and specific knowledge based on the principles of scientific medicine, such as are acquired by means of a prescribed course in an accredited school of nursing as defined herein, and practiced in conjunction with curative and preventive medicine as prescribed by a licensed physician and the application of such nursing procedures as involve understanding cause and effect in order to safeguard life and health of a patient and others.

This chapter confers no authority to practice medicine or surgery or to undertake the prevention, treatment or cure of disease, pain, injury, deformity, or mental or physical condition in violation of any provision of law.[1]

Although it appears that the nurse practice act allowed the nurse to do whatever was taught in the school of nursing, as long as it was practiced in conjunction with a physician and the nurse knew the cause and effect of her actions, the medical practice act carefully delineated what "violation of any provision of law" meant:

The physician's and surgeon's certificate authorizes the holder to use drugs or what are known as medical preparations in or upon human beings and to sever or penetrate the tissues of human beings and to use any and all other methods in the treatment of diseases, injuries, deformities, or other physical or mental conditions.

Any person, who practices or attempts to practice, or who advertises or holds himself out as practicing, any system or mode of treating the sick or afflicted in this State, or who diagnoses, treats, operates for, or prescribes for any ailment, blemish, deformity, disease, disfigurement, disorder, injury, or other mental or physical condition of any person, without having at the time of so doing a valid, unrevoked certificate as provided in this chapter, or without being authorized to perform such act pursuant to a certificate obtained in accordance with some other provision of law, is guilty of a misdemeanor.[2]

The concentration of power in the physician is abundantly clear in the wording of this statute. At first it may seem that the practice of nursing could be rather broadly interpreted (as long as the practice was authorized by a physician), because of the vagueness of the nurse practice act. However, the interpretations of the practice acts by the attorney general of California have consistently been conservative. The resulting restrictions on nursing practice will be described, as these are pertinent to the examples discussed.

When I began working as a family nurse practitioner, my role had not been clearly defined. I was employed by a new prepaid health care plan, partly funded by the US Department of Health, Education, and Welfare. Called a Health Services Network, this organization provided complete care for its enrolled population, and was based upon the health maintenance organization model. I was part of the professional staff of their first health center clinic. Most of the professional staff was drawn to the clinic for idealistic reasons: we wanted to pioneer an alternate method for delivery of health services, be more responsive to community and social needs, and develop extended roles for health care personnel. As the first FNP to come on staff, my job description was:

Family Nurse Practitioner—Duties and Responsibilities

Collects supplemental information for medical and social history. Performs a review and examination of anatomical and physiological systems—structural, neurological and metabolic functions.

Initiates requests for laboratory and radiological tests and studies as predefined by team procedures and protocols.

Provides health teaching and preventive health measures.

Monitors and manages the care of stabilized chronic conditions, under the preceptorship of the physician.

Provides care to uncomplicated pre- and postnatal patients.

Participates in family health care planning conferences on a regularly scheduled basis.

Provides counseling in nutrition, child-rearing patterns, family planning and family living.

Participates in the formulation of policies, procedures and protocols for health service delivery.

Maintains required medical records and forms in a complete and accurate manner.

Exercises independent judgment in the management and the delivery of service in accord with the predefined procedures and protocols.

Education and Qualifications

Minimum educational requirement is a Bachelor of Science degree in

Nursing; Master's degree preferred. Should be currently enrolled in, or have completed, an approved family nurse practitioner course. Must have a current California registered nurse's license. Supervised by the Medical Director.

With this job description for a guideline, and with an operational-type procedure manual, the clinic commenced seeing patients. In the beginning, there were no protocols for patient management. The provider staff was divided into two teams, each consisting of one physician (MD), one FNP, one licensed vocational nurse (LVN), one receptionist, and two to three clinical assistants. Other supportive services included in the clinic were radiology, laboratory, central supply, pharmacy, business office, appointments, medical records, transportation, child care, housekeeping, and maintenance. All interrelationships had to be worked out; there were no precedents or entrenched patterns; and we had no idea how well our organizational schema (Fig. 1) would work.

FNP functions included complete history and physical examinations, episodic care for common minor illnesses, long-term care for stabilized chronic illnesses, initial work-up and partial management of normal prenatal and postnatal patients, well-baby care, initial evaluation and triaging of any variety of health problems, family planning, and as much teaching and counseling as there was time for. Although there were guidelines in the procedure manual for which patients were to be seen by MDs and which by FNPs, in actual practice very little differentiation was made. One major reason for this was an inefficient and confused appointment system. With a mushrooming enrollee population, we became busy so fast that there was no time to work out roles and functions adequately. This resulted in considerable role confusion between MDs and FNPs, with the inevitable personality problems and ideational conflicts.

Early in our operations there were no guidelines regarding the prescribing of medications and ordering of lab tests. Outside consultations and procedures were also uncharted ground. Referral to and consultation with the team physician was largely at the FNPs discretion, with the dubious help of the nonspecific procedure manual. So the FNPs forged ahead, doing as much as we felt comfortable taking on. Needless to say, a multitude of problems arose from this laissez-faire situation. Some were not directly related to legalities, but will be included because they are so germane to the underlying issues in this battle for acceptance.

Who's the Boss?

Problems of authority quickly surfaced between FNPs and MDs. In our organizational structure, the medical director of the clinic was the supervisor of both the team MDs and FNPs. The team MDs assumed they were the immediate supervisors of the FNPs, but the FNPs saw themselves as colleagues to the team MDs and thus not directly accountable to them. Each MD and FNP had a separate office and schedule, with assigned clinical assistants. Each did his or her own charting, ordering of tests, prescription of medications and treatments, and follow-up. In-house prescriptions were either written by FNPs or called to the pharmacy. Early in this modus operandum, one of the MDs requested a copy of his team FNP's curriculum that pre-

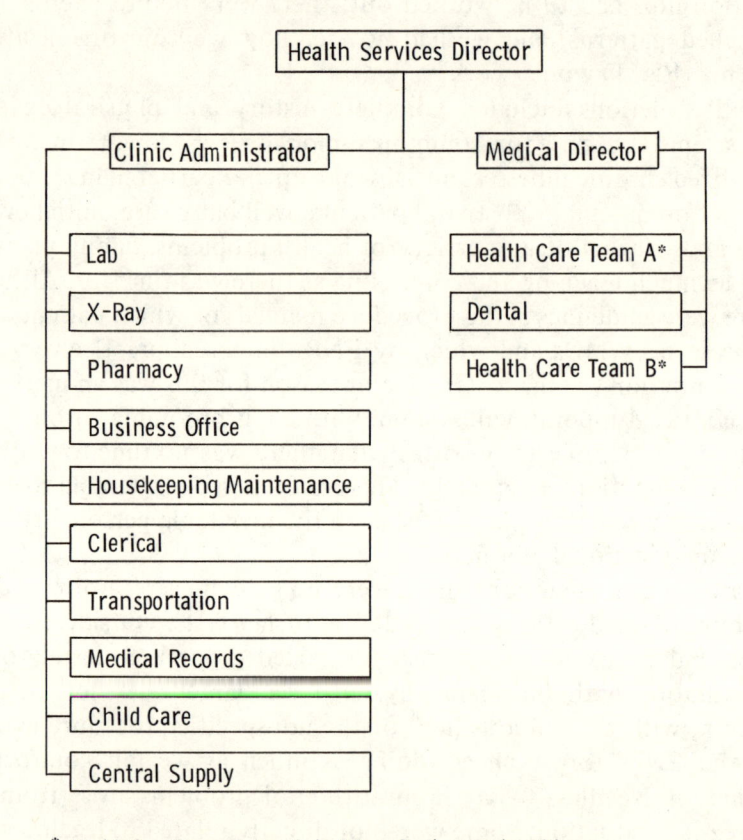

* Health Care Team consists of physician, family nurse practitioner, licensed vocational nurse, clinical assistants, and team receptionist.

Fig. 1. Initial table of organization of the health center clinic.

pared her to be a nurse practitioner. Although he said "I want to see what you can do," the interaction around this request was perceived as a demand for the FNP to show proof of qualifications. The FNPs felt questioning of qualifications was inappropriate, and really signified nonacceptance of extended nursing roles. Supposedly, the organization would not have recruited FNPs without basic philosophical support of extended nursing roles. Later we learned that budgetary considerations weighed more than philosophy—nurse practitioners were less expensive than physician's assistants.

Inevitably, there was a direct conflict about who was in charge of the team. One day when the team MD was heavily scheduled and there were numerous walk-ins, the FNP had planned time for hospital visits. The MD ordered her not to go, but to stay and help with walk-ins. The FNP felt her preplanned hospital visits were more important. In the ensuing argument, the medical director supported the MD. In a similar vein, during a heated meeting discussing this issue, another team MD addressed the topic of "FNPs wanting to practice independently." This clinic operated on a team concept, he noted, and had no place for someone who wished to be in independent practice. And, whatever the contributing circumstances, the MD was always the "head of the team" and must make the ultimate decisions. Another FNP responded that it was really an ego trip for the MDs to think that in every situation they were the appropriate persons to head the team. Surely there were some types of problems encountered by patients for which another professional or paraprofessional was more qualified to direct team effort. Taken aback, the physician mused "I really have to rethink that."

Another area presenting authority problems involved decisions about the best therapeutic approach in a given illness. Realizing that the clinic could not have a different style of management for each provider, we went to work on a set of protocols for the most common types of illnesses and health problems encountered, utilizing several sources and creating some original protocols. However, the protocols never were more than guidelines, and various providers did continue to use their preferred approaches. Conflicts arose during peer review meetings, when records were exchanged among FNPs and MDs for audit. Lengthy arguments would ensue about which was the preferred antibiotic for otitis media in children; whether to do routine sensitivities with urine cultures; whether adequate attention had been given to findings on the physical exam; the thoroughness of work-ups; adequacy of follow-up; and so forth. Sometimes these were good learning experiences, but at other times they were merely frustrating and disheartening. One FNP earned the nickname "the Judge" among the MDs because of her high standards of care and critical approach at peer review meetings.

Despite these conflicts, there generally was more cooperation than resistance. The FNPs usually were able to follow their best judgment in management—sometimes by openly disagreeing, sometimes by not consulting the MD, and sometimes by presenting data effectively. The medical director did try to set limits on the FNPs. He vacillated about requiring MDs' signatures on outside consultations and procedures, but this practice was never completely followed by the FNPs. The restrictions related to prescriptions and charting will be discussed later. In this battle over authority, the FNPs made significant progress after some months. Under a new health services director, the entire clinic structure was reorganized. Largely because of input from FNPs, there were separate medical and nursing departments in the clinic, with the FNPs immediately supervised by a nurse rather than a doctor (Fig. 2). The MDs continued to have difficulties, however, with the difference between making independent decisions and being in independent practice.

The Little Things That Count

The sensitized viewer may see discrimination in many ways. The FNPs were alert to discrimination on the basis of being women and and being extended-role nurses. Although these items may seem petty, they reflect attitudes that are pervasive and thus important. For example, a list of hospitalized patients was circulated daily to all clinic providers and outside consultants. At first the FNPs names were not among the providers to receive this list. After a telephone call this was corrected, but there was still a slight: all the physicians had "MD" after their names, but the nurses were listed by name only, no titles. A second slightly sarcastic telephone call remedied that. Some months later, when a new secretary took over the hospital list, behind the FNPs names was "PHN." Although also public health nurses (PHN), that title did not describe out present practice. Another telephone call was needed.

All nurses in extended roles must become alert to the "name game." How one is addressed is a mark of status and affects the quality of

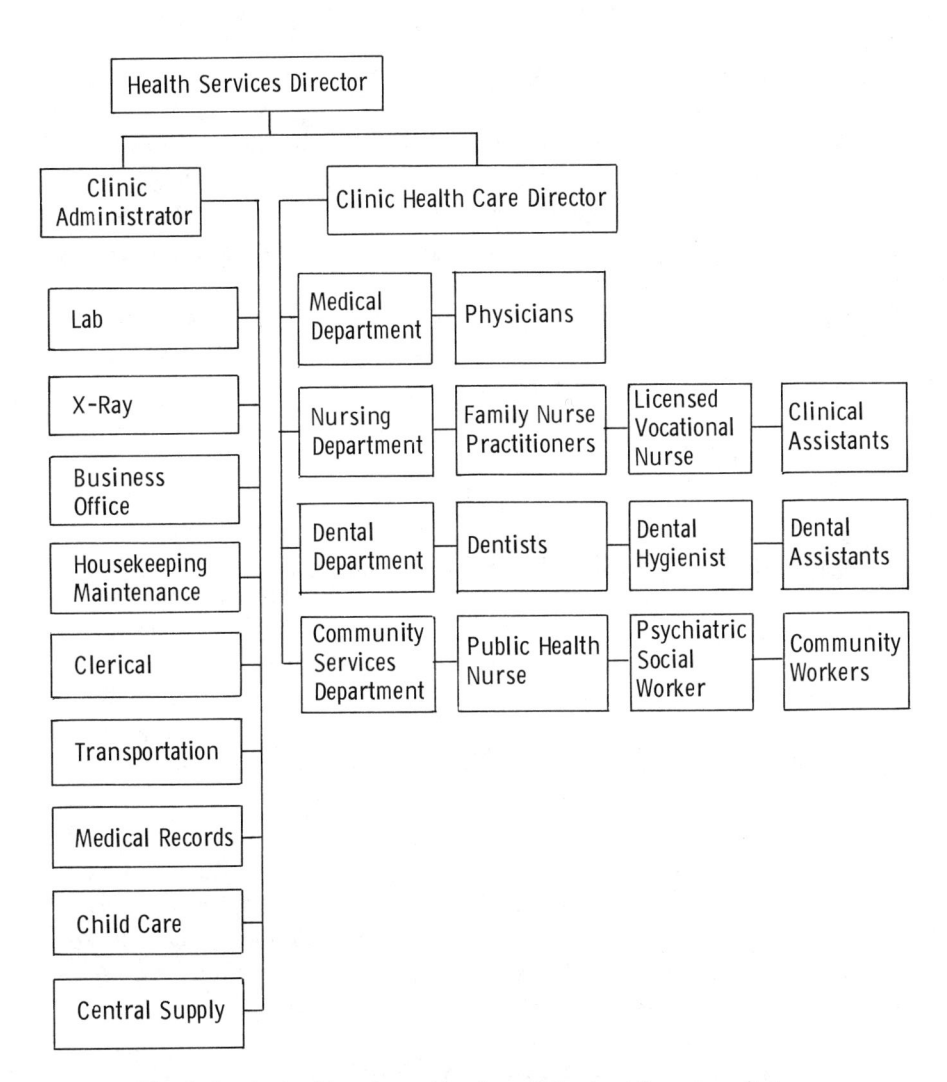

Fig. 2. Revised table of organization of the health center clinic.

interaction. From the beginning, most clinic staff were on a first name basis. The FNPs and MDs consistently addressed each other by first names in private. Before patients, if the MD was called Dr. the FNP was called Ms. At times, one of the older MDs reverted to calling the FNP by her first name before patients, no doubt a carry-over from his "girl" in his private office in previous years. We would point this out, and soon he was catching his slips and saying, "I guess if I call you by your first name to patients, you should call me by mine also." Sometimes this was indeed what we did.

Outside doctors had trouble with our titles. Consistently, the FNPs received reports from outside consultants addressed to "Dr. X" even though we clearly wrote the letters FNP behind our names. Telephone calls were no better. Few outside doctors seemed to comprehend nurses functioning in extended roles. In fact, one of our legal problems was a direct result of this. The FNPs were always very careful to introduce themselves as nurses to patients. Some few patients insisted on calling us Dr. despite repeated explanations, but most recognized and accepted us as nurses, calling us Ms. or by first names when this was comfortable. Because outside doctors felt the need to address reports to "Dr. X" the FNPs were required to write the team physician's name as well as their own on consultation forms.

Meetings provide a fertile ground for discrimination. Usually when there are both women and men involved, the females always get the coffee and take the minutes. At our clinic, the FNPs never took on the job of getting coffee or taking minutes. Soon it was established that getting coffee was a shared responsibility, and MDs and FNPs took turns at it. Minutes and agendas were handled in another way. For a while, the clinic administrator (a nurse and a woman) distributed agendas and took minutes. When she tired of that and ceased, a secretary began attending committee meetings.

All of this is not to say that the FNPs and MDs had a desexualized relationship—only that FNPs must constantly be alert to and resist sexual discrimination. As with any mixed group working closely together, a certain amount of sex-tinged humor is inevitable and probably beneficial. Among several providers, touching in the form of hugs, patting arms, hand holding, and cheek kissing developed in comfortable, mutual interchange. If touching is initiated only by the men, it is a sign of superior status. When initiated by either sex, it reflects a camaraderie born of equality.

Recently a new physician came on staff. Due to the need for more examining rooms, the team MDs and FNPs were sharing an office. The new doctor was discussing his employment forms with the clinic administrator in the shared office, while the team MD and FNP were at their desks. The clinic administrator was explaining how the new MD normally would have to go to the main administrative office (at a different location) to fill out the forms, but that an exception had been made to bring the forms to the health center. The new MD said, "I'm a physician, I should have these special privileges." The team MD could not resist interjecting some cynical humor, saying to the new MD, "You've got to watch saying things like that around here; we docs keep a low profile in this organization."

A Family Nurse Practitioner Is Not Half an MD

One of the chronic irritants to the FNPs was the staffing pattern, which equated FNPs as half an MD. In the initial grant funded by the Office of Economic Opportunities, a broad philosophy of health care and development of new health manpower guided recruitment of staff for the clinic. When OEO expired, the grant was transferred to the Department of Health, Education and Welfare (HEW) and monies provided only for "medical care." Through the ingenuity of a comptroller with a "cost-effective" credo, and assisted by reams of statistics, a ratio was worked out for provider staff: MDs must see 24 patients per day at 15 minute intervals, over 6 hours per day for 5 days per week. FNPs were programmed as half an MD: to see 12 patients per day at 30 minute intervals. This could be cost-effective because FNPs were paid less than half the salary of MDs. The 15 and 30 minutes were averages; if a visit took 45 minutes or an hour, other visits would have to take 5 to 10 minutes. If the provider ratio was kept at 3.4 MD equivalents per 1,755 patient visits per month, the clinic's operations could be cost-effective.

Were FNPs just thought to be slower than MDs, or were we supposedly doing different things with the patients in our 30 minutes? In actual practice, FNPs were seeing many more than 12 visits per day—in fact, were often booked almost as heavily as MDs. MDs were finding they had no time for anything but acute episodic care, and were dealing mainly with presenting symptoms. With a low-income population of enrollees and multiple-problem families, the providers felt in principle that a more flexible approach to scheduling was needed. Great frustration developed among FNPs and MDs alike, because we could not spend enough time to explore multiple problems in depth, plan and coordinate efforts to combat health problems due to social conditions, ignorance, poor hygiene and nutrition, and unhealthy life styles and coping patterns. Much of the illness we saw on an episodic basis stemmed from these factors.

The pace of work kept the providers scrambling just to get the patients seen. The persistent feeling was uneasiness over lack of thoroughness and follow-through. The blurred roles between FNP and MD only contributed to these frustrations, because we felt clearer definitions of functions could make the daily routines go more smoothly and our operations more efficient. No one who really knew about our roles had enough time free, however, to address him or herself to this problem.

The FNPs kept reiterating that we were not "half an MD." Although we certainly could do acute episodic care, our main thrust should be determining the health status of individuals and families, counseling, and health teaching for prevention and maintenance. We felt that conceptually there had been a failure to differentiate FNPs from physician's assistants, and the administration could only understand our roles in terms of our being "physician extenders." As long as the scheduling reflected the delivery of medical care, and FNPs were seen as half-MDs, efforts to meet the larger health maintenance needs would be thwarted.

Competence Notwithstanding

While in the throes of working out philosophies of care, smoothing operational snags, defining roles of personnel, and coping with a burgeoning population of enrollees with significant health/illness problems, the clinic was confronted with yet another difficulty—the legality of nurse practitioners. Acceptance of a prepaid health care plan seems to pose a real problem for community physicians in private practice. The clinic needed a certain amount of cooperation from local physicians, because we relied on them as outside consultants for specialty problems. In a special public relations effort, one FNP was taken by two clinic MDs to a luncheon meeting of the local family practice division of the California Medical Association. The hostility at that meeting could have been cut with a knife. The FNP and clinic MDs were quizzed extensively about the scope of FNP practice and medical surveillance. Dissatisfied with our answers, the family practice physicians' objections revolved around malpractice coverage, judgment in triaging (which they thought should be done at the highest level of preparation), and basic competence of FNPs ("What about the sore throat that isn't simple pharyngitis, but is a symptom of leukemia?")

It is especially ironic that this group's fears should crystallize around the possibility of a FNP missing a case of leukemia. In our clinic, there is much more routine blood screening than in a private office. It is also clear to those who have worked with nurse practitioners that our assessments tend to be more thorough than physicians', and that we tend to be more careful in decision-making, taking less for granted. The real fears relate to the basic issues mentioned earlier: economics, ego, power, and masculinity.

Following that ill-fated meeting, the clinic was informed there might be a complaint filed with the local California Medical Association office charging that we harbored persons who were practicing medicine without a license. Indeed, some months later two representatives from the Association visited the clinic administrator, but she was able to satisfy them regarding the adequacy of safeguards and physician supervision of FNPs. How this incident might be related to our more serious problems certainly invites speculation.

Having a contract with the State of California to provide care for persons on public assistance, the clinic was subject to review by a State Department of Health committee. For some obscure reason, the clinic was reviewed after only five months of operation. The first visit of the State Committee was veiled in secrecy by our administrative personnel. The clinic staff received fragments of information and disjointed "hallway" reports. Although no formal report was provided to the clinic staff, the conclusions filtered down that we generally were delivering good quality care. The State Committee was concerned, however, about the broad scope of FNP practice and required the following changes:

1. Medical records of procedures done by non-MDs should be countersigned and dated by *the ordering physician.*
2. Physicians should make notes on the chart regarding referrals and consultations.
3. Consultation reports and lab reports should be countersigned and dated by *the ordering physician.*
4. All in-clinic prescriptions must be signed by *the prescribing physician.* Copies of prescriptions should be included in the chart.

The language of these requirements implied that all diagnostic tests, procedures and treatments, medications, referrals, and consultations were to be ordered by the MD. In essence, the FNP was to act only on the direction of the MD. Once again, the issue of independent function, or "Who's the boss?" surfaced. The State Committee, with its conservative physicians and pharmacists, was requiring our administration to make certain that control was at all times in medical hands.

Although this was the first rumble of legal trouble, the FNPs had raised the issue three months before. We had requested a meeting with the clinic's lawyer and a top administrator. Being familiar with the nurse practice act, we did realize that our scope of practice fell outside its archaic protection. A new bill providing temporary legal coverage for nurses and other health personnel to learn extended roles had recently been passed (Assembly Bill 1503). The FNPs wanted to discuss applying for coverage under this legislation. In the meeting, more time was spent in wonderment and amazement over the things FNPs did than in dealing with possible legal problems. The FNPs came away from the meeting with a sense of management's disapproval of our doing what we were educated to do, but with no clear idea of what their official stand would be. We were never given a directive or formal report, but indirectly learned that the lawyer felt that the clinic could not qualify under this legislation because it was not an educational institution. He did not fully explore coverage through our nurse practitioner programs, which seemed possible under the law.

Out of this meeting came a new label for FNPs. In the grapevine of clinic gossip we were criticized for our "Watergate mentality." We were compared to the perpetrators of the Watergate breakin, in which agents of the (Republican) Committee for the Re-election of the President broke into the Democratic National Headquarters office in the Watergate Hotel in order to obtain campaign information that might be useful in advancing Richard Nixon's 1972 presidential bid. The analogy was that FNPs were willing to disregard the law in order to accomplish their goals, even as the Watergate burglars did. This made us seem to lack respect for the legal process, and hinted at "guilt by association" with criminals. A small war of memos resulted from the State Committee's first visit and the meeting with the lawyer.

TO: All Providers of This Health Center
FROM: Medical Director
SUBJECT: Prescriptions
1. Family Nurse Practitioners will review every patient's problem with the team

doctor who will sign all prescriptions according to our usual medical policies. No variations are to be tolerated.
2. A copy of each prescription will be filed in each patient's record.
3. Any infraction of the above threatens the medical licenses of the physicians of the group and subjects all of us to penalties of the medical practice act so that any deviation will lead to termination of employment.

A few days later this reply was circulated:

TO: Medical Director and All Providers of This Health Center
FROM: Family Nurse Practitioners
SUBJECT: Prescriptions, etc.

As Family Nurse Practitioners we are certainly aware of the problems surrounding prescription medications, and the potential dangers inherent for *all of our* licenses. In recognizing the need to adhere to "the letter of the law," we also recognize the inequities imposed by unjust laws whose intent to protect the consumer has become distorted into a means for assuring monopolistic control. We would also like to respond to certain allusions of "Watergate mentality" by pointing out the profound differences between violating personal liberties for political purposes, and opposing unjust and elitist laws in the finest American tradition of fighting to change statutes which deny the needs of the people.

We appreciate the need to respond to outside forces and pressures in a decisive way. If, however, we are indeed to realize ideals of extending health services through expanding roles, there must be more mutual respect for human sensitivities; especially in the selection of language. This, as well as confidence in each others' integrity and abilities.

Our internal need for cohesion, now at critical dimensions, would be better served by open communication and a reinforced sense of mutual regard as colleagues.

After the State Committee directive, providers followed the policy of having the MD sign all prescriptions after review of the case, and having the MD cosign all the FNPs' charts. The MD's name was put on all referrals and consultations, but diagnostic tests were still initiated by the FNP's name. Accomplishing this created some strain on clinic operations, but we did comply.

About four months later the State Committee made its second visit to review the clinic. Once again the staff was not involved in the meetings. Only administrators met with the State Committee, and there was little communication about the proceedings. Working daily at a breakneck pace, the providers had little time and energy left to seek information. During this same time, the funding agency (HEW) was also conducting an audit. This agency did interview providers as part of their review. Immediately following the visits by the State Committee and HEW, several organizational changes were instituted by the administration. Just in time to be one step behind these changes, the providers demanded a meeting with all key administrators to discuss our frustrations. In this meeting, we were presented with the new table of organization (Fig. 2) and promised a slow-down period to regroup our resources. The FNPs tried to push the issue of administrative support for nurse practitioners, but this could not adequately be dealt with due to lack of time.

Individually, however, FNPs were informed by a top administrator that something serious was brewing in the State Department of Health. He did not know if any action would be taken, but it was possible that a cease and desist or restraining order would be issued. Even an indictment for practicing medicine without a license was a remote possibility. He asked about coverage under AB 1503 through the FNPs' educational programs, but none of us had official notification of coverage. The administrator concluded that we were in trouble. He admonished us not to bemoan "water under the bridge," or why coverage under AB 1503 was not more thoroughly investigated when first brought up by the FNPs. His advice to us was to get ourselves covered under AB 1503 as soon as possible. It was unlikely that any FNPs would be terminated if the State took action and we were not covered, but neither could the administrator guarantee our positions.

Angry and concerned, the FNPs asked what had happened during the recent State Committee visit. We were told the Committee was most impressed with the work of FNPs, and that in fact the care we delivered was superior to that of the MDs, as reflected in problem-oriented records. Also, the Committee recognized that the clinic had conformed to all requirements set after the first visit. Competence notwithstanding, the Committee considered FNPs to be illegal according to current nurse and medical practice acts. When the administration had been asked, "Under what authority do your FNPs practice?" the answer was found wanting. Indeed, any arguments about competence, education, community standards, or joint statements were made irrelevant by opinions of the Attorney General and his office:

This office has always issued its opinions cautiously to avoid any precipitous expansion in the practice by non-physicians into the field of medicine as defined in Section 2141.

[In regard to unsupervised injections such as immunizations] The fact that the registered nurse may be fully trained and competent to perform the acts involved or by custom and practice does in fact perform these acts, is immaterial...[3]

[In regard to pelvic exams, pap smears, insertion of IUDs, and dispensing birth control pills] It is our opinion that under existing law paraprofessionals or paramedics cannot perform any of the described functions...since these functions clearly constitute the practice of medicine. The licensing provisions of registered and vocational nurses specifically preclude them from performing any functions which constitute the practice of medicine.

The fact that trainees have had training enabling them to practice competently, or the fact that they are performing such functions as part of their continuing supervised training, does not exculpate them or any physician who is aiding or supervising them in such practice. In the absence of exceptions such as those with respect to licensed and vocational nurses, permitting them to perform venipunctures, the [nurse] cannot perform acts which require a healing arts license under California law.

Thus...they would be unable to perform pelvic examinations, insert intrauterine devices, take pap smears, or dispense birth control medication....[Nurses] can perform only those duties which a valid state license permits them to do. Otherwise, [nurses] are prohibited from performing [these] currently defined duties since such tasks constitute the unlawful practice of medicine.[4]

This interpretation has been extended to include any type of physical examination, use of instruments, or other traditionally medical diagnostic aids. Any type of treatment of the sick and afflicted, whether physical or mental, was made by law the sole province of the physician. Only certain very limited acts might be delegated, under MD supervision, to nurses or paraprofessionals.

A few days after this meeting, the State Department of Health did send a letter requiring that the FNPs cease functioning in extended roles unless or until they were covered under AB 1503. The letter named the nurse practitioners, and required that their activities be restricted to the performance of those functions sanctioned by the nurse practice act. Effective immediately the restriction was to be in force until the clinic was notified that it had been lifted. This restriction was not officially a court order, but it was assumed with good cause that if the clinic did not obey, and restrict the FNPs accordingly, that legal action would be forthcoming.

One FNP was unable to practice for only one day. The others could not practice for three weeks, during which time arrangements were made for coverage under AB 1503. No FNP was terminated, but the upset at the clinic was considerable and the needs for explanation multiple. Under AB 1503, approved projects are exempt from the healing arts practices acts. The nurse practitioners so covered must be included in an approved program, must work under an approved physician preceptor, must participate in regular continuing education and must report back to their program.

AB 1503...authorizes the State Department of Health to approve experimental health manpower pilot projects sponsored by nonprofit educational institutions or nonprofit community hospitals or clinics for the purpose of developing new kinds and combinations of health care delivery systems. Authorizes, notwithstanding other provision of law, trainees under such programs, and under specified conditions, to perform specified health care services... .it is the intent of this legislation that existing healing arts licensure laws incorporate innovations developed in approved projects which are likely to improve the effectiveness of health care delivery systems.[5]

The Crisis of Confidence

The immediate legal crisis was over for the FNPs at the clinic. The fallout continued, however, with far-reaching effects. The entire operation was forced to face the issues of philosophy of care and the place of nurse practitioners in the organization. Was the clinic to provide medical care or health care? Were nurse practitioners to be used as "half a doctor," or should they provide a different kind of care? Should future staffing patterns call for more nurse practitioners? Could this operation be economically viable once federal support was ended? Would the price for solvency be assembly-line episodic care? If so, should nurse practitioners continue to be part of such a system?

The conflict between the hard realities of the budget versus the providers' ideals continued. Despite organizational changes, the alienation between professional providers and the administration resulted in several key providers leaving, myself included. As new people are recruited, the complexion of the clinic staff will change, with the final outcome uncertain. Still, the FNPs feel strongly that we have an important place in prepaid health care plans. To get health care translated into budget and personnel is the momentous task that must be accomplished. It will also be necessary to structure scheduling and operations in a way to provide the time and supports for FNPs to deal effectively with multiple-problem families, undertake real family care, and do the essential counseling and teaching necessary for making an impact on long-standing social problems.

Whether or how these questions will be answered carries the key to the future of this clinic. If creative answers can be found, such programs could become role models for profound changes in the health care delivery system of this country. If the answers are mediocre or standard, this program will become just another bandaid in the stopgap process of symptomatic treatment.

The New Legal Question

During the year in which these events were occurring, the California Nurses' Association was conducting a campaign to revise the outdated 1939 Nurse Practice Act. As if by providence, all events came to a head about the same time. Only one week after the clinic received the order to restrict the functions of nurse practitioners, the California legislature passed the new Nurse Practice Act in the form of Assembly Bill 3124. This bill redefined the practice of nursing to include the planning and performance of various direct and indirect patient care, and acts of basic health care, testing, and prevention procedures. It also modified the section prohibiting nurses from practicing medicine.[6]

Of most significance to nurse practitioners was the section which included as part of nursing practice the assessment of illness, differentiation of normal and abnormal characteristics, and implementation of reporting, referral, or standardized procedures or changes in treatment regimens in accordance with standardized procedures. These "standardized procedures" are policies or protocols developed through collaboration among administrators and health professionals, including physicians and nurses. "Organized health care systems" may develop their own policies and protocols, which in certain settings, such as ambulatory care clinics, may be subject to guidelines determined by the Board of Medical Examiners and the Board of Nursing Education and Nurse Registration.[7]

Obviously, the new legal question is: How much will "standardized procedures" cover? To some observers, the new nursing act can be very broadly interpreted to cover almost everything nurse practitioners do. As long as the practice setting has protocols for nurse practitioner functions, then such functions would be within the scope of the nurse practice act. Another view holds that "standardized procedures" will be narrowly interpreted, and will exclude most physical diagnosis and nursing management of illnesses. If the guidelines developed by the Boards of Nursing and Medicine are restrictive, then at least in ambulatory care settings most of what nurse practitioners do will not be covered. With this question unanswered and the legal situation still very tenuous, even after January 1, 1975 when the new nurse practice act comes into effect, it is quite possible that the meaning of "standardized procedures" will be tested in the courts.

In effect, AB 1503 is serving as the nurse practitioner practice act in California. In my clinic, the administration decided all nurse practitioners must be covered through AB 1503 to be employed, even after the new nurse practice act became effective. This was basically an economic decision. They wanted to avoid any possible court costs or loss of state or federal money. It is hoped that when AB 1503 terminates the legal status of nurse practitioners under the nurse practice act will be clarified, or other legislation passed. This attitude, of course, makes employment of out-of-state nurse practitioners very problematic, as well as those graduates in California whose program has not applied under AB 1503 with preceptorship and continuing education provisions.

The Lessons of Experience

From my encounters as a family nurse practitioner, several conclusions can be drawn. Outdated nurse practice acts must be changed to encompass extended role functions, and medical practice acts altered to recognize the realities of today's health care delivery scene. Nurse practitioners must recognize the significance of their changing roles as nurses, as women, and as symbols of change in the medical and health care delivery power pyramid. Nursing should ally with the feminist movement, because our battle is essentially the same—that the full human rights and potentials of all people be realized.

Nurse practitioners should seek out creative organizations or be prepared to fight for organizational change. Administrative support is very important if new roles are to be pioneered. As individuals, the administrators must stand behind innovation, be willing to think in new ways, and be courageous enough to take a different approach to the budget. Nurse practitioners should not undertake changing the organization without multiple supports and a clear understanding of the agonizing process of change.

As an individual, the nurse practitioner must constantly question standard operating procedures as well as her own habit patterns. Sexism and nursing inferiority are so deeply ingrained that it will take innumerable individual efforts and many years to fully effect the needed social change. However, the nurse practitioner can, to the best of her ability, personally refuse to play the doctor–nurse or male–female game. She can demand a greater voice in the decision-making process of her organization as it effects her functions and the quality of care delivered. And above all, the nurse practitioner needs the time to think, to plan, and to integrate this new role. Given adequate time, physical diagnosis skills and medical knowledge can be properly combined with a nursing orientation toward prevention and maintenance, so the full meaning of "health care" can be realized.

REFERENCES

1. STATE OF CALIFORNIA, DEPARTMENT OF CONSUMER AFFAIRS, BUSINESS AND PROFESSIONS CODE, §§ 2725, 2726, Nursing Practice Act.
2. STATE OF CALIFORNIA, DEPARTMENT OF CONSUMER AFFAIRS, BUSINESS AND PROFESSIONS CODE, §§ 2137 and 2141, Medical Practice Act.
3. CV 72 OP. EVELLE J. YOUNGER ATT'Y GEN. 187 (California, February 15, 1973).
4. California, Evelle J. Younger, Attorney General, Indexed Letter of Louis C. Castro, Deputy Attorney General, October 4, 1972.
5. STATE OF CALIFORNIA, HEALTH AND SAFETY CODE, Chap. 2, Part 1, Division 1, Article 18, Legislative Counsel's Digest of AB 1503.
6. Assembly Bill No. 3124, introduced by Assemblyman Duffy, February 13, 1974, *an act to amend* §§ 2725, 2726 of the BUSINESS AND PROFESSIONS CODE relating to nurses.
7. California Nurses' Association, Government Relations Department, unofficial version of results of two bills amending the Nurse Practice Act, AB 3124 & AB 2789 (June 25, 1974).

CORINE L. HATTON

9
The Mental Health Clinical Nurse Specialist in Private Practice

One of the first new "evolving roles" for nurses was the clinical nurse specialist. In some parts of the country, and in different institutions, this nurse is variously called nurse clinician or clinical nurse. However, for the benefit of this paper the term clinical nurse specialist will be used to encompass all these various titles.

Actually, the specialist was the first new clinical role for nurses dating as far back as the early 1960s. This role became necessary benurses complained that in order to advance in the hierarchy of any institution they had to take administrative posts, drawing them away from patients. This situation often left the patients without optimum nursing care, and the nurses frustrated about pushing paper and attending committee meetings. Several schools of nursing then decided to write graduate curriculums that would include clinical specialities. Upon graduation the nurses would function as specialists to a group of patients and their families, as well as teach and consult with staff nurses. In short, they were nurses who had the opportunity to function more responsibly and autonomously, by virtue of their clinical education and experience, without leaving the patient. The objective of these specialists was to enhance and increase the quality of nursing care delivered.

Usually the specialist has a master's degree in nursing, is concerned primarily with nursing care, staff development, and often research. I say that *usually* the specialist has a master's degree. There are several nurses functioning as specialists without master's degrees. However, the ANA Congress for nursing practice at the ANA Convention in June 1974 presented a definition of the clinical nurse specialist that stated she must have a master's degree to be called a specialist.

Specialists have had to contend with various problems about identification of their roles and accountability within the bureaucracy. Generally, the problems for those of us in psychiatry and mental health have been fewer than for our colleagues in medical–surgical, maternal–child health nursing, etc. Someone once told me that this is because psychiatric nurses have historically been deviants and rabble rousers, so specialists were just following a general trend.

I won't argue the point, but I think there is a more obvious and definitive reason. The entire practice of psychiatry is probably more "unabsolute" than the rest of medical practice. Therefore, there has never been, and still isn't, as definite a demarcation of roles in the practice of psychiatry. Often, psychiatrists, psychologists, nurses, and social workers are using similar if not identical treatment modalities and see patients individually and in groups. This is especially true in community mental health centers, where many of us see individual clients and conduct group therapy sessions. All kinds of disciplines work together, and we are usually called consultants and often use the same treatment modalities. The same kind of expertise is expected from everyone; similarly, everyone is treated the same way.

Another major reason that nurses in mental health nursing have probably had it easier is that people are not as hung up on who is "in charge" of the patient. It has been my experience that more collaboration between physician (or therapist) and nurse occurs in mental health than in the other areas of clinical practice. Again, maybe this is because the field is relatively young, searching, stretching, and has not become as established as other areas of practice.

A few years ago I functioned as a clinical specialist in the mental health unit of a large general hospital in a large southwestern city. I encountered no major obstacles from psychiatrists or other disciplines while I was establishing my new role. They and the other staff viewed me as someone with expertise in my field and looked to me to offer guidelines about nursing care, especially with difficult management problems. I rarely "carried" my own patients in private practice; however, I consulted on almost every admitted patient with both physicians and the other nursing staff. I was a co-therapist with a psychologist on one of his outpatient groups and was paid separately by him.

Thus far I have been discussing the clinical nurse specialist in mental health as they exist within the institutional system. But what happens when they wish to go outside the institution and set up their own private practice as therapists? What are the obstacles? What are the legal problems? In order to answer these questions thoroughly it seems appropriate to examine the historical background of the clinical nurse specialist in private practice.

One of the first major questions was whether psychiatric nurses should be doing psychotherapy at all; and if so, would she be giving up her role as a nurse? In an article in 1962, J.A. Schmahl confronted psychiatric nurses by saying that "in the competition for autonomy and prestige and in fear of being plunged into therapeutic nihilism, everyone ie, psychiatrists, psychologists, social workers, and now psychiatric nurses—is scrambling to practice psychotherapy."[1] Ms. Schmahl further stated that many aspects of psychotherapy become involved in psychiatric nursing; however, "psychotherapy is an autonomous specialty, as is nursing, and I believe it is impossible for the psychiatric nurse to become a practicing psychotherapist and at the same time retain her identity as a nurse—in attempting to do so, she becomes a kind of two-headed creature who is neither nurse nor therapist and thereby relegates herself to the position of second class citizen."[1] For the next four or five years this controversy raged and was the source of various discussions and published articles.[2-6]

In the meantime, institutes of higher education were putting greater emphasis on psychotherapy in their graduate nursing programs and nurses were beginning to function as psychotherapists in greater numbers. There seemed to be no question now that nurses could and would function as therapists. In 1972, *Perspectives in Psychiatric Care* published a thorough and succinct article on this topic and the author, Terrence Calnen, concluded that "because of their improved education, their ongoing contact with the patient, and their capacity to intervene in his interpersonal conduct and manipulate his environment, psychiatric nurses have joined other professionals as therapists."[7]

If the question of their capability was no longer a major obstacle, then the logical next problem was: is their practice legal? In 1969, Marcia Stachyra urged the nursing profession to "begin legislative reform which will explicitly sanction qualified nurses doing psychotherapy."[8] She identified major areas to consider, has been continually promoting certification programs, and in 1973 again urged the national organization to develop a certification program for clinical specialists in mental health.[9] She warned that "certification by a professional association does not legally prevent uncertified persons from performing the functions, since professional associations do not have legal regulatory power. Nonetheless, certification is a beginning step toward self-regulation."[9]

One state that moved ahead with its own certification program was New Jersey. In 1972 the New Jersey Society of Certified Clinical Specialists in Psychiatric Nursing, under the Division of Mental Health Nursing of the States Nurses Association, certified 49 psychiatric nurses as charter members of the society. Standards were set and certification was a reality in the state of New Jersey.[10] And it does appear that certification on a national level will soon become a reality also.

The ANA Council of Advanced Practitioners of Psychiatric and Mental Health Nursing held its first meeting at the ANA Convention in June, 1974. There are now 300 members and council officers were elected. Their first major task will be to work on specialist certification standards, examinations, etc.[11] There is no doubt that such certification will identify to the public qualified practitioners who meet the standards as psychotherapists as identified in other disciplines. This has been long coming and is badly needed.

Along with these events at the national level, states are updating their nurse practice acts so that they meet the realities of the day. The California legislature just recently passed a revision of our nurse practice act. This will do much to add legal sanction to the role of those clinical specialists who wish to set up a private practice. The section in the revised act that states that the "practice of nursing includes direct and indirect patient care services that insure the safety, comfort, personal hygiene and protection of patients; and the performance of disease prevention and restorative measures" is, to my mind, a direct sanction for private practice in mental health.

Several clinical nurse specialists are in private practice (fee for service) here in California. Some of them, who set up their practices years ago, obtained a Marriage, Family, and Child Counselor license that is issued by the Board of Behavioral Science Examiners. A few years ago it was relatively easy to get such a license if you could show a master's degree in psychologic or sociologic science. Now the license is more difficult to obtain, and an examination is required. Many nurses have become discouraged because their applications were turned down. Nurses have also desired to be licensed and certified by their own professional group.

In the meantime, nurses in private practice carry regular malpractice insurance through their own nursing association or other sources. Most of them have a consultant (psychologist or psychiatrist) that they see on a regular basis to discuss cases. To my knowledge they have never had any legal problems and seem to be able to establish their practices with relative ease. There was a recent article in the *American Journal of Nursing* that identified a large number of nurses who started independent practices, delineating their problems and costs and giving advice for others.[12] There are several illuminating and interesting ideas in the article, but one point that struck me was that of a nurse who felt she had fewer legal pressures in private practice then when she was practicing in an institution. She finds "the ability to assure authority commensurate with responsibility exposes her to far less legal pressure."[12]

It would be my recommendation that a nurse get into a group practice with a physician, psychologist, social worker, etc. and work as part of a team. That would seem a comprehensive and encompassing way to practice. I think HMOs are an avenue through which clinical specialists could move into a health care delivery system that would utilize their talents as well as offering challenges. My obvious bias is in group practice and collaborative roles for all health disciplines.

Although we have moved far since the early 1960s, there are still several problems and questions. In conclusion I would like to pose some of them for reflection and further consideration for the future.

Do clinical specialists or practitioners see private or group practice as a means of gaining more status or prestige? Are all the people opening private practices (be they in mental health or other clinical areas) really concerned about preventive health care, maintenance health, etc., and living up to these ideals, or it is merely a way of feeling that they have "made it" as an independent profession? This issue and question concerns me very much. It is not an accusatory remark or question—rather a concern to which I think our profession needs to address itself.

I think we should arrive at a basic and advanced level of education necessary for these specializations. As it now stands, we are confusing to ourselves let alone the general public. It seems to me specialization is meaningful only at the graduate level. There is now some thinking that clinical nurse specialists in mental health should be differentiated from nurse psychotherapists. Gertrud Ujhely (one of the pioneers in private practice) wrote recently that "we shall have to differentiate the nurse psychotherapist from nurses in general and from the clinical specialist in psychiatric nursing in particular."[13] She states that a psychotherapist undergoes rigorous training, supervision, and personal analysis, and this may be in conflict with what the clinical nurse specialist is educated and trained to be or, even further, might be antithetical to her theoretical beliefs about practice. She says further, "I have the feeling that the reason we are not proceeding any faster with clinical specialist certification has to do with this conflict. I think we may well need two kinds of certification—one for clinical specialists in mental health—psychiatric nursing, and one for the clinical specialist who wants to practice psychotherapy."[13] I believe this issue will continue to emerge as the ANA Council for Advanced Practitioners in Mental Health and Psychiatric Nursing does its work in getting certification to be a reality. I believe this is a worthwhile argument because it will have a tendency to strengthen everyone's practice.

There is a general trend among psychiatric nurses to feel that "we must get out of hospitals and into the community." Now I have no desire to tell people where they must practice. Surely many people are being seen these days outside the hospital walls. However, if we all abandon the hospitals who, may I ask, will be left to take care of patients? And if another discipline or less trained nursing personnel take over, where does that leave patients and nurses? Let's face it—right now there is not a demand for nurse therapists, but there is an enormous demand for quality, conscientious, and concerned nursing care. Patients are crying desparately to be heard—they are shocked if they get taken care of by a RN for a whole day, but they desire that kind of strength and reassurance that an RN can give.

REFERENCES

1. J.A. Schmahl, *The Psychiatric Nurse and Psychotherapy*, 10 NURS. OUTLOOK 460–5 (July 1962).
2. C.R. Hartman, *The Role Fusion of Psychiatric Nursing with Psychiatry*, 7 PSYCHIATR. OPINION 7 (October 1971).
3. J. Churchill, *An Issue: Nurses and Psychotherapy*, 5 PERSPECT. PSYCHIATR. CARE 4 at 160-2 (1967).
4. *The Nurse as a Therapist v. Her Role in the Medical Model,* and *Psychiatric*

Nurse v. Mental Health Worker, 6 PERSPECT. PSYCHIATR. CARE 6 at 271-2, 288-9 (1968).
5. J.S. Hays, *The Psychiatric Nurse as Sociotherapist,* 62 AM. J. NURS. 64-7 (June 1962).
6. M.S. Zaslove, J.T. Ungerleider & M. Fuller, *The Importance of the Psychiatric Nurse: Views of Physicians, Patients, and Nurses,* 125 AM. J. PSYCHIATRY 482-6 (October 1968).
7. T. Calnen, *Whose Agents?: A Re-evaluation of the Role of the Psychiatric Nurse in the Therapeutic Community,* 10 PERSPECT. PSYCHIATR. CARE 5 at 211-9 (1972).
8. M. Stachyra, *Nurses, Psychotherapy, and the Law,* 7 PERSPECT. PSYCHIATR. CARE 5 at 200-13 (1969).
9. M. Stachyra, *Self-Regulation through Certification,* 11 PERSPECT. PSYCHIATR. CARE 4 at 148-54 (1973).
10. S. Rouslin, *On Certification of the Clinical Specialists in Psychiatric Nursing,* 10 PERSPECT. PSYCHIATR. CARE 5 at 201 (editorial, 1972).
11. *Report of Convention,* AM. J. NURS. 1272 (July 1974).
12. B. Agree, *Beginning an Independent Nursing Practice,* AM. J. NURS. 636-42 (April 1974).
13. G. Ujhely, *The Nurse as Psychotherapist: What Are the Issues,* 11 PERSPECT. PSYCHIATR. CARE 4 at 155-60 (1973).

PATRICIA J. McCLURE

10
Nurses in Private Practice

In isolated parts of the country it is not unusual to find a nurse practicing alone. With no physician readily available, the nurse takes on the responsibility of providing nursing care for the people in the community. In 1971, M. Lucille Kinlein hung out her shingle in an area where physician services were adequate.[1] That was the first recorded instance of a nurse in an urban area who practiced on a fee-for-service basis and was responsible only to herself and her patients, not to a doctor or an organization, for the care she gave. Since that time an increasing number of nurses have also opened their practices, either alone or in groups with other nurses.

The reasons the nurses gave for taking that step centered primarily around the frustrations of trying to work within an institutional framework, and, for many of them, a desire to work in a more expanded role.[1-7] The nurses felt that institutional work required that too much time and energy be used to keep the organization running, and too little was left for working directly with patients. There was a feeling of powerlessness resulting from their lack of influence on policies that governed nursing care delivery and from having to give nursing care within the confines of a rigid structure.

Several of the nurses noted that, at the present time, it is difficult for many people to enter the health care system because the point of entry is through the physicians, many of whom are too busy to accept more patients. To some extent, this problem could be relieved by providing entry through nurses. As early as 1969, Charles Lewis forsaw the possibility of nurses serving this function by going into private practice and using physician services as a backup.[8]

There are also some sociologic factors that have influenced the movement toward private practice. The first private nursing practices started in the early 1970s—about the same time the feminist movement toward more independence and recognition of women as individuals made a strong surge forward. Because the nursing profession is made up primarily of women, the status of nurses as professionals closely paralleled that of other women in our society. As women demanded their legal and cultural equality they began to reach out more into areas that had been thought of primarily as a man's area—such as opening an independent business or practice. At the same time, nursing was rejecting its image as "assisting" the medical profession, and asserting its position as a group of professionals capable of making independent decisions for which they were willing to be held accountable. The frustration of not being able to do this within the institutional framework probably contributed to some nurses' desire to work outside that restrictive structure.

Although in the past physicians have tended to come from the higher social classes and nurses from the middle and working classes, this is less true today.[9,10] It can be observed that nursing students from upper middle and upper class backgrounds are becoming more prevalent. Many physicians are not aware of this change and continue to relate to nurses as social, as well as professional, subordinates, which leads to a feeling of discomfort and anger in the nurses. This may be another factor in the nurses' desire to work less closely with physicians.

The Expanded Role

The expanded role many of the nurses were seeking could well be defined in the terms formulated by a committee of the Wisconsin Nurses Association:

The expanded role refers to enlargement of one's role in utilizing all aspects of problem-solving processes: delineation of the field of the problem, assessing and implementing care, and evaluating outcomes. The result is a qualitative change in the nurse's delivery of patient care services.

Role expansion is based on theory, utilizing natural and behavioral sciences which give direction to nursing action. Knowledge and skill are applied to decision-making, as well as to performance.

A nurse functioning in an expanded role acts on knowledge that reflects theory eg, determining the need for a pap smear and dealing constructively with the behavioral factors which inhibit the patient from taking the recommended action.

The nurse assumes or shares responsibility for the health care services delivered to the patient. Plans and goals are established by the nurse or in consultation with other health care professionals.[11]

Nurses in private practice have expressed satisfaction about having full authority over their practices and assuming all the responsibility for the quality of the care they give. Their acceptance of that responsibility has earned them respect from many other professionals who treat them as equals.

The Patterns of Practice

Most of the nurses in private practice follow the patterns established by some of the first solo and group practices. In Maryland, M. Lucille Kinlein sees patients in her office or in their homes. After talking to the patient she takes a health history and does a partial physical exam before formulating a plan for assisting in implementation of a medical regimen. On following visits she will check on progress and discuss ways to solve problems that may have come up. If indicated, she will recommend over-the-counter drugs and initiate laboratory tests on blood and urine. Ms. Kinlein will contact the patient's physician if the patient approves. She gets few referrals from physicians but her patients and friends spread the word.[7]

In New York, Charles Koltz, Jr. sees most of his patients in their homes after receiving a referral from their physician or public health aide. Most of his patients are chronically ill and the services he offers closely follow those of visiting nurse services, helping to carry out a medical regimen and monitoring the patient's progress during the illness.[6]

A group nursing practice was started in New York by Jocelyn Greenidge, Ann Zimmern, and Mary Kohnke. Their services are similar to those of most community nursing agencies, but an important difference lies in the organization. Community Nurse Practitioners was formed as a partnership, which increases the commitment of the group as a whole and of the individual members. This commitment would be less likely in the case of an agency. The nurses also have the potential for getting increased financial satisfaction, as 25 percent of the profits are divided equally among the partners and the remaining 75 percent is divided on a prorated basis, depending on the input of each partner.[4]

Nursing Consultants, Inc., was formed by Rita Rafferty and Jean Carner in Rhode Island. The corporation was to provide primarily consultative, counseling, and educational services that would assist patients, physicians, and institutions with their nursing care problems. They were particularly interested in developing care programs for the patient discharged from the hospital to his home, but needing continuing care. They also offered health care courses to nonprofessionals in the community and continuing education for people in the health field.[3] Because it was undercapitalized, the practice is now defunct.[2]

Creative Health Services, Inc., of Denver, Colorado is composed of 16 nurses who are all equal partners in the corporation. Most of the nurses have master's degrees; because of the differences in their interests and backgrounds, the range of services is extensive. In addition to services offered by the previously discussed practices, Creative Health Services provides complete histories and physical exams on children and adults; health maintence services (eg, pap smears, breast exams, birth control exams and counseling); pre- and postpartum care and abortion counseling; mental health services for individuals and groups; teaching health and safety, sex education; inservice for professionals and para professionals; industrial services; etc.[12]

A survey of nurse practitioners from various parts of the country disclosed very few nurses in private practice who had completed a nurse practitioner program.[13] This is probably because intrinsic job satisfaction is high for nurse practitioners.[14] They find their jobs challenging and rewarding because they are encouraged to use a greater percentage of their skills in working with patients. This is particularly true for those who follow a caseload of patients over an extended period of time.

Nurse practitioners state that they prefer to work closely with physicians for several reasons. They need the legal protection the physician can provide, because they work in the areas of diagnosis and treatment, which have been designated as medical practice by law in most states and can legally be done only under a physician's supervision. By working closely with a physician who treats the nurse as a colleague as she learns and practices, most nurse practitioners achieve the prestige, challenge, and opportunities for creativity that the nurses in private practice are seeking while performing the more traditional nursing functions.

The Future of Private Practice

Although the number of private practices is increasing now, there are a number of factors that tend to inhibit this growth. First of all, there are the difficulties associated with running a business: balancing books, paying rent and taxes, hiring help, etc., involved business knowledge that many nurses do not have and/or do not want to have. If their practice is not large enough to support ancillary help, nurses will find themselves functioning in secretarial and housekeeping roles as well as nursing. Most nurses find it much easier to let someone else worry about the mechanics of making the practice run so that they can concentrate on patient care.

Second, many do not want to accept the financial risk. In addition to the initial expense involved in establishing the business, the nurse most support the practice as it slowly grows to the point where it can be self-supporting. The nurses in private practice would find the financial going easier if health insurance companies, Medicare, and Medicaid would cover their fees. However, the government agencies and most insurance companies will not cover nursing fees unless the service has been ordered by a physician. North Carolina, however, has recently passed a law ordering insurance companies to make third party payments directly to nurses. New York is in the process of considering a similar law, so this may not remain as an inhibiting factor indefinitely.

Some of the sociologic conflicts that contributed to the movement to private practice are likely to be resolved. The same pressures have slowly brought about changes within some institutions. Nurse practice acts have been liberalized in some areas, and new roles have evolved that have made it possible for some of the rewards of private practice to be gained within the institutional structure, thus reducing the desire of nurses to leave.

The final, but possibly most important, reason is legal. Institutions and physicians who employ nurses offer them some legal protection under the *respondeat superior* law, which states that an employer is responsible for the wrongful acts of his employee, in certain cases, so that both can be sued by an injured person.[15] Consequently, for their own protection, most employers set up strictly defines limits within which nurses can practice. By working within these limits, many nurses feel that their chances of getting into trouble for practicing outside the legal definition of nursing is minimized.

A nurse in private practice would not fall under the *respondeat superior* law, but would be an independent contractor, subject to the control of the person with whom she has a contract only as to the result of the work and not as to the method by which the result is obtained.[15] Consequently, if a nurse in private practice were to be sued for her actions, she alone would be responsible. Knowing this would make some nurses more hesitant to expand their roles to practice within less strictly defined limits. However, some nurses in private practice, like Ms. Kinlein, state that they felt more legal pressure while practicing as extensions of physicians than as private practitioners. She feels less legal pressure now that she has authority commensurate with responsibility.[2]

Group nursing practice is more likely to survive than solo nursing practice. In areas where there are enough professionals to permit it, even medicine is leaning toward group practices, many of them multidisciplinary. There is too much knowledge in the health field today for any one person to be a generalist who "knows everything." Health professionals need input from each other to provide comprehensive care to their patients.

In conclusion, it can be seen that even though nurse and medical practice acts frequently do have a restrictive influence on the scope of nursing practice, as practice changes the laws also change in response to the many factors in society that have initiated the pressures for change.

REFERENCES

1. M.L. Kinlein, *Independent Nurse Practitioner*, 20 NURS. OUTLOOK 22-4 (January 1972).
2. B. Agree, *Beginning an Independent Nursing Practice*, 74 AM. J. NURS. 636-42 (April 1974).
3. R. Rafferty & J. Carner, *Nursing Consultants, Inc.—A Corporation*, 21 NURS. OUTLOOK 232-5 (April 1973).
4. J. Greenidge, A. Zimmern, & M. Kohnke, *Community Nurse Practitioners— A Partnership*, 21 NURS. OUTLOOK 228-31 (April 1973).

5. C. Koltz, Personal Correspondence (October 29, 1973).
6. V. Sheward, *A New Long Island Concept: Independent Nurse*, Newsday, August 13, 1973 at 11A.
7. A. Robinson & M.L. Kinlein, *Independent Nurse-Practitioner*, 35 RN 40-4 (January 1972).
8. C. Lewis, The Team Is in the Doctor's Bag, paper presented at the meeting of the National League for Nursing in Detroit (May 21, 1969).
9. E. Rosinski, *Social Classes of Medical Students*, 193 J. AM. MED. ASSOC. 89 (July 12, 1965).
10. C. HUGHES, ET AL, TWENTY THOUSAND NURSES TELL THEIR STORY (1958).
11. Wisconsin Nurses Association Ad Hoc Committee to Define and Promote the Extended and/or Expanded Role of the Nurse in the State of Wisconsin.
12. F. Lang, Personal Correspondence (June 12, 1974).
13. Personal Correspondence (May 1974).
14. B. Bullough, *Is the Nurse Practitioner Role a Source of Increased Work Satisfaction?* 23 NURS. RES. 25 (January-February 1974).
15. H. CREIGHTON, LAW EVERY NURSE SHOULD KNOW (1957).

Section III

NEW NURSE PRACTICE ACTS AND OTHER APPROACHES TO THE LEGAL PROTECTION OF NURSES AND PATIENTS

LUCIE YOUNG KELLY

11
Institutional Licensure

Continuing criticisms of health care focus primarily on fragmentation of services, high cost, and poor utilization and maldistribution of health manpower. Small wonder, then, that conditions which affect these factors are being examined, with individual licensure of the health occupations coming under particular scrutiny, and institutional licensure being widely touted as an alternative. The proponents of institutional licensure see it as a remedy to the shortcomings cited above.

At the same time, professions which fought for mandatory licensure are now taking a look at existing licensing laws and concluding, sometimes reluctantly, that even those which were models at one time are not meeting the needs of today. Rapid proliferation of other health manpower groups with their inevitable thrust toward licensure, sometimes before educational standards, qualifications, and job responsibilities are firmly set, give further impetus to reexamination of personnel licensure.

Reflecting this trend, both the American Medical Association and the American Hospital Association in 1970 adopted resolutions calling for a nationwide moratorium on licensure of any additional categories of health personnel.[1(p 8),2(p 82)] They were joined in this stance by the American Public Health Association, the American Nurses'

Copyright September 1973, The American Journal of Nursing Company. Reprinted with permission from *Nursing Outlook*.

Association, the National League for Nursing, and others. In June, 1971, a HEW report on *Licensure and Related Health Personnel Credentialing* reiterated this viewpoint, recommending a two-year moratorium by all states.[3(p 73)] The report also recommended that "the concept of extending institutional licensure—to include the regulation of health personnel beyond the traditional facility licensure—has important potential as a supplement or alternative to existing forms of individual licensure. Demonstration projects should be initiated as soon as practicable."[3(p 77)]

What Is Institutional Licensure?

Institutional licensure has existed generally for almost 30 years, but has usually been related to facilities rather than personnel and concerned mostly with such matters as structural integrity, sanitation, and fire safety. In some cases there are also minimal standards of square footage per bed and minimal nursing staff requirements. The current issue—one that concerns, or should concern, all nurses—is whether personnel credentialing or licensing should be a part of the institution's responsibility under the general aegis of the state licensing authority.

There are a number of interpretations of just what institutional licensing means and how it would be implemented. Lawrence Miike, an HEW physician-lawyer, considers it "instructive to view institutional licensure not as a developed concept, but more appropriately as a convenient descriptive term applied to the concept of a unified health delivery system. . . ."[4] He adds that the "Hershey model" has become synonymous with institutional licensure to many people and has led to some confusion.

Nathan Hershey, professor of health law at the University of Pittsburgh, has indeed criticized individual licensure for years in speeches and articles. He advocates, instead, that institutionally-based health workers be regulated by that institution within bounds established by state institutional licensing bodies. His oft quoted statement is:

Because the provision of services is becoming more and more institution-based, individual licensing of practitioners might be legitimately replaced by investing health services institutions and agencies with the responsibility for regulating the provision of services, within bounds established by the state institutional licensing bodies.

The state licensing agency could establish, with the advice of experts in the health care field, job descriptions for various hospital positions, and establish qualifications in terms of education and experience for individuals who would hold these posts. Administrators certainly recognize the fact that although a professional nurse is licensed, her license does not automatically indicate which positions within the hospital she is qualified to fill. Individuals, because of their personal attainments, are selected to fill specific posts. Educational qualifications, based on both formal and inservice programs, along with prior job experience, determine if and how personnel should be employed.[5(p 73)]

Hershey further suggests the development of a job description classification similar to civil service classification. Personnel categories could be stated in terms of levels and grades along with descriptive job titles. Under such a system, the individual's education and work experience would be taken into consideration by the employing institution for the individual's placement in a grade; basic qualifications for the position, expressed in terms of education and experience, would be set by the state's hospital licensing agency.

Thus, a professional nurse returning to work after 10 or 15 years, Hershey indicates, might be placed in a nurse aide or practical nurse position, moving on to a higher grade when she "regained her skills and became familiar with professional and technological advances through inservice programs."[5(p 74)] Hershey is rather evasive as to the place of the physician in this new credentialing picture, implying that the current practice of hospital staff review is really a pioneer effort along the same lines.

A somewhat different concept is offered by the American Hospital Association. While the final recommendation of the AHA Special Committee on Licensure stated only that institutional licensure should be expanded to include use of personnel, a later AHA statement—one relating to Health Care Corporations, a part of AHA's Ameriplan—is more specific. This policy statement sees health care corporations as having specific responsibility for quality and effective delivery of care by all providers, including physicians.[6]

Variations on the Theme

Those involved in hospital administration have suggested still other concepts. McAdams, for instance, suggests that most of Hershey's proposed structure be kept intact, but that either the Joint Commismission on Accreditation of Hospitals or some new private body, instead of the state, be responsible for setting basic qualifications of health personnel and, presumably, policing for compliance.[7]

Lloyd offers still another interpretation of the term institutional licensure. He proposes that all present licensing statutes be repealed and that there be substituted medical, dental, nursing, medical technology, medical therapy, and "institutional" licensure. Each license would recognize only general skills, and an individual could change or upgrade into another category. Medicine would cover (besides physicians) optometrists, podiatrists, pharmacists, and nurses performing medical functions. In this proposal, institutional licensure would be for those personnel directly involved in the operation of institutions: hospital and nursing home administrators, for instance, medical record librarians, hospital dietitians, and medical social workers. He suggests, however, that all should have national certification for specialties and group identity.[8] Such certification, it should be pointed out, is usually considered the prerogative of the professional association.

Lloyd's concept is not dissimilar to a New Jersey Hospital Association proposal which raised the possibility of one license in each of six areas: medicine, dentistry, nursing, medical technology, medical therapy, and "institutional licensure."[9]

A further variation is presented in the Illinois Hospital Association's "White Paper," which recommends that: "Licensed hospitals should be privileged to utilize the services of competent health care personnel without reference to whether they are individually licensed or whether they are reimbursed by the hospital for these services."[10] Whether or not an individual is "qualified" to do a job, the association maintains, is more important than whether or not he is licensed. It advocates that present licensure acts be amended so as to exclude practitioners working in a licensed hospital.

Roemer, a health law expert who has suggested 20 options for improvement of the licensure situation, considers institutional licensure worth experimentation. She also suggests the licensure of health teams in an organized employment setting, in which the head of the team would be licensed as an individual and authorized to supervise certain kinds of unlicensed personnel working on his team, provided specified criteria of good patient care were met. Although she admits to some administrative and legal constraints to this plan, she sees it as protecting the public because it "distinguishes between health practitioners to whom the public has direct access and personnel working in an organized setting."[11]

The American Medical Association, in a 1970 review of licensure problems and possible alternatives, interpreted institutional licensure as exempting independent practitioners such as physicians, but affecting "dependent" practitioners such as nurses, physical therapists, and medical technologists. The report noted that the "concept of employer accountability for personnel working under that employer's supervision or direction seems to be workable for the physician as well as for the health care institution." A number of problems were foreseen, however, and support for institutional licensure was not among the final recommendations in the report.[1(p 4)] Furthermore, in its most recent action, the AMA at its June 1973 convention passed a resolution opposing the extension of institutional licensure in lieu of individual licensure to physicians and nurses. Representatives from nursing organizations and from the National League for Nursing spoke in support of the AMA resolution.

What's Wrong With Individual Licensure?

In every defense of institutional licensure, and often in the proposals requesting funds for experimentation with this approach, the evils of individual licensure are cited. While there is justification for some of the complaints, there is little recognition of actions that have been taken to remedy the faults. Evolving changes (which are indeed often slow in evolving) are brushed off as too little and too late. Edward Forgotson, a physician–lawyer who directed a study of licensure for the National Advisory Commission on Health Manpower, enumerates some of the key criticisms of individual licensing.

1. Most licensure laws for the health professions do not mandate continuing education requirements to prevent educational obsolescence. Therefore, the minimal standards of safety, theoretically guaranteed by granting the initial license, may no longer be met by some (perhaps many) practitioners.
2. Educational innovations in the health professions may be stifled by the rigidity of statutorily specified courses and curricular requirements. Changing these requirements to make them responsive to the rapid informational and technological explosion is a diffi-

cult and time-consuming process, and the result is the possibility that existing minimal standards may lag behind the practice realities.
3. Definitions of the area of practice are generally not specific, so that allocation of tasks is often determined by legal decisions or interpretations by lay people. On the other hand, some limitations of practice—ones that are not in tune with changing health care needs—*are* delineated.
4. Most licensing boards are composed of members of the particular profession (or, in some cases, the professional superior of that group), without representation of competent lay members or of allied health professions. This is seen as allowing these professionals to control the kind and number of individuals who may enter their field, with the possibility of shutting out other health workers climbing the occupational ladder and also limiting the number of practitioners for economic reasons. Moreover, the members of a one-profession board may lack overall knowledge of total expertise in the health care field, so that the scope of functions which could be delegated to other workers is not clearly determined. This creates the possibility that others capable of performing a particular activity may be prevented from doing so by another profession's licensing law.[12]

In addition to these generally reiterated criticisms, the HEW report also points to the lack of geographic mobility for some health professionals, who may be licensed in one state but barred from another unless a second license is obtained.[3(p 43)] And, of course, not all health occupations are licensed; of the 32 that are, only 10 are licensed in every state.*

The licensure problems of one health occupation, however, are not necessarily the same as those of all the others. Nursing, for instance, permits licensure by endorsement in all states, thus reducing the geographic mobility problem. Yet, because the majority of all kinds of health workers function in institutional settings, the various weaknesses of all health occupations' licensing laws appear to be the basis for whatever enthusiasm exists for institutional licensure. There are

---

*The ten health occupations licensed in all states are: physicians, osteopaths, professional and practical nurses, physical therapists, optometrists, podiatrists, dentists, dental hygienists, and pharmacists.[3(p 136)]

consistent accusations that formal credentialing accentuates the manpower shortage, maldistribution, and cost, as well as preventing career mobility.

Actions and Reactions

Organized nursing's reaction to the recent surge toward institutional licensure culminated in a strong resolution approved by the ANA House of Delegates in 1972. The resolution reaffirmed commitment to individual licensing and individual accountability as an essential of safe, high quality care and promised opposition to any efforts intended to shift this responsibility from individual to institution. Institutional licensure, ANA pointed out, would vest in the employing agency the major responsibility for defining the scope of nursing practice, long held to be the profession's prerogative and responsibility. (This reasoning applies equally to other professions.) In addition, ANA saw the wide variation among institutions as preventing, instead of improving, geographic mobility of health practitioners.[13]

Shortly thereafter, the executive committee of the National League for Nursing Board of Directors reaffirmed that organization's 1971 position in favor of separate nurse licensure. Its 1972 statement stated that it was "unalterably opposed to the concept of extending institutional licensure to include the regulation of nursing personnel."[14] Similar resolutions opposing institutional licensure have come from the National Association for Practical Nurse Education and Service and the National Federation of Licensed Practical Nurses. The board of the Association of Operating Room Nurses has also taken a stand against institutional licensure, as has the Nurses Association of the American College of Obstetricians and Gynecologists.

In early 1973, the National Commission for the Study of Nursing and Nursing Education also reiterated its position that the public was best protected by individual nurse licensure.[15]

Until relatively recently, nurses have listened to Hershey's statements on licensure and read his articles without, as a whole, realizing the implications of institutional licensure for the future of the nursing profession, or becoming aroused to any opposition or reaction. Some nursing leaders, though, have recognized the weakness of many current nurse practice laws in light of social, technological, and scientific progress as well as the obvious needs of a faltering health delivery system, and have set about making those laws more responsive to current needs and demands. Outstanding examples are the Idaho, New York, Washington, and Arizona revised practice acts, which make provision for an expanded nursing role.

Legislation relating to nurse licensure is also being planned, introduced, or acted upon in other states. Major emphasis is on a broader definition of nursing practice, provisions for mandatory continuing education for relicensure, reorganization of the licensing board to include lay members and/or allied health professionals, and provisions for equivalency and proficiency examinations.

Unfortunately, not all of these changes are understood and supported—much less initiated—by many nurses. They cling idealistically to the illusion that all nurses will voluntarily continue their learning, but can provide no evidence to this effect. They maintain firmly that they are practicing legally, but have never read their own practice law. They resist any kind of public or allied professional participation in determining their practice and isolate themselves from the knowledge of other health professionals' practice, but talk glibly of the health team. They live in a world of we and they, where no self-analysis is necessary because "We're okay, but they...." And then they find, too late, that "they"—those others, non-nurses—have acted to change the law controlling nursing practice. Will this be the case with institutional licensure?

The Current Scene

Legislators, like other critics, have some tendency to view individual licensure as a union shop or guild mechanism whose main concern is protection of its members and not the public. They see such licensing as an attempt to control quantity rather than quality, as self-preservation rather than health preservation. They threaten, or offer, to change the laws to make them more flexible and to correct some of their shortcomings. In many instances, state nursing associations—either through fear or conviction—are working cooperatively with these legislators and other disciplines to institute changes. On the other hand, one of the most overt attempts to force through such changes without consultation with nurses (or, for that matter, with other concerned health professionals) and to initiate a form of institutional licensure was the plan proposed by Governor Sargent in Massachusetts.

His proposal would have abolished the Board of Registration in Nursing, along with other health professions' licensing boards, and would have assigned their regulatory functions to a new Health Systems Regulation Administration. Nurses would have had almost no input in any way. Additional legislation was proposed to provide that anyone employed in a licensed or approved health care facility could provide nursing services, so long as such services were provided "under the supervision of a registered nurse or licensed practical nurse."[16]

Of major importance would have been the quality of nursing care under such loose and perhaps unenforceable conditions, as well as the question of how both Massachusetts nurses and those from other states wishing to practice in Massachusetts would have been licensed. Strong protests by the nurses of Massachusetts and other states, however, including a series of resolutions passed at the 1973 NLN convention, aroused the interest of the public and legislators. As a result, the Governor has submitted a revised plan that has the support of the nursing organizations.

As is often the case, the degree of federal funding has an impact on the implementation of concepts of health care delivery. At the same time that Illinois' governor signed into law a bill that retains individual licensure, for instance, a proposal to explore institutional licensure submitted by the Illinois Hospital Association was funded for a year by HEW and began in June, 1972. Although this project purports to study only unlicensed personnel, the fact that nurses are responsible for the nursing regimen, as well as for seeing that the medical regimen is carried out, mandated nursing participation by the Illinois Nurses Association.[17]

It was made clear that this participation did not in any way negate the association's commitment to individual licensure, but it was expected that INA would have the opportunity to contribute significant nursing input to the project. When this did not materialize, and when neither INA nor the Illinois Medical Society were ever given the opportunity to review the continuation proposal for HEW, both organizations withdrew from the project. The project has nevertheless been refunded for another year (through June 1974), with plans to put a credentialing model to work in mid-fall.

The Hospital Educational and Research Foundation of Pennsylvania, an arm of the Hospital Association of Pennsylvania, has also developed a grant request related to institutional licensure. The foundation proposes a 3-year demonstration project, involving 6 to 12 health care institutions, "to examine an alternative method of regulating health personnel." The project would include, among other things, a plan for selection and utilization of hospital personnel regardless of existing licensure regulations.[18] It, too, has recently been funded by HEW, and it is reported that a number of other states are also contemplating experimentation with institutional licensure.

Risks, Dangers, Threats

Nurses are often reassured that institutional licensure would not include or affect them or their practice. But it is difficult to see how institutional licensure would *not* affect them, when others would decide upon the duties of other nursing personnel whom nurses, presumably, would supervise. It is also unrealistic for nurses to expect to be exempted when many of the tasks once considered in the realm of professional nursing have even now been assigned to others with less preparation when this is expedient. And sometimes the assignment has been made by someone in nursing administration. The classic tale of a practical nurse in charge of a nursing unit after 3 P.M., under the "supervision" of an RN on another floor or in another building, is not fantasy.

Whether that LPN has had special preparation for those assigned responsibilities—whether she has the knowledge, or just the external skills, to carry them out—cannot be answered with a consistent yes. (Still, it is this external manifestation of activity, not the quality, which is observed by non-nurses doing job analyses.) Today there are nurses who protest that kind of staffing. But what kind of protest to such a situation could be made under institutional licensure? There is no guarantee that an RN would even need to supervise from any distance. Will this improve patient safety?

If there is any thought that hospitals would not be inclined to take the risks involved in institutional licensure, consider the evening or night supervisor who currently dispenses needed medications from the locked pharmacy, thus practicing pharmacy. Institutional licensure might make this act legal, but will it be any safer? There are those who say that nurses have helped to bring institutional licensure on themselves, for it is just such acts that allow proponents of institutional licensure to say that current hospital practices are no different, though less legal, than they would be under such a licensing approach.

One advantage cited for institutional licensure is that job descriptions and classifications, combined with inservice training or other experiences and education, would allow health practitioners to move from one classification to another within this field. But is this new? This plan has already been adopted by some of the more progressive hospitals. More to the point is to determine whether all hospitals would be willing to initiate the expensive and extensive educational, evaluative, and supervisory programs necessary to fulfill the basic tenets of institutional licensure.

This raises the specter of a return to an apprentice system. Probably a hospital's own personnel would be used as teacher–proctors. Who then would do their job? How would they be compensated? How long would a "student" be expected to function in his current position with the current salary while he "practices" his new role? And with what kind of supervision? What kind of testing program for each level? Testing by whom? With what kind of standards? While such sliding positions might cut manpower costs, might they not also indenture the worker instead of freeing him to new mobility?

Problems of criteria are obvious. If 50 states cannot now agree on criteria for individual licensure, why would institutional licensure be any different? Add to this the thousands of profit and nonprofit hospitals with bed capacity ranging from the tens to the thousands, in rural areas and urban, with administrators and other key personnel prepared in widely varied ways, and a state of confusion, diversity, and parochialism becomes an overwhelming probability. Moreover, the disadvantages to those health professions that have fought to attain, maintain, and raise standards may be disastrous to patient welfare. Nurses, particularly, who are just beginning to fulfill their potential for total health care, proudly accountable to the patient and not to an administrative hierarchy or a physician for their professional acts, may find themselves relegated to increasing technical tasks, substituting for a more expensive physician. Will this save the patient money, or cost him optimum health?

The most recent publication on institutional licensure written by Hershey and a colleague makes it clear that under this proposed system an institution would have the power to determine the specific tasks and functions of each job and indicate the skill and proficiency levels required, regardless of the employee's licensure, certification, or education.[19] Control could be almost complete, since the guidelines to be developed by the state institutional licensing agency are intended to be general.

Moreover, while the state licensing agency would be empowered to review the institution's utilization and supervision of health personnel to determine whether employees are performing functions for which they are qualified, how realistic could such an evaluation be? What army of inspectors knowledgeable in all the subcategories of health care can be recruited, employed, and dispersed to check the hundreds of thousands employed in these multiple subcategories—not only hospitals, but all other institutions providing health services to the public, such as nursing homes, physician's offices, clinics, and, as Hershey says, "et cetera"? It is doubtful whether the patient's safety will be guaranteed, but it is not doubtful that it will cost him, as a taxpayer, more to maintain this bureaucratic state structure than any existing licensing boards, which are often self-supporting.

A final question remains concerning those health professionals providing care outside the walls of a "health institution." Is the possibility of independent practice eliminated? Or will multiple systems of certification, individual, and institutional licensure add to the confusion?

Alternatives

The HEW report warns that institutional licensure should not be regarded as a panacea for the present licensing problem, but rather as significant in its recognition of foreseeable trends in the organization of health care delivery patterns. While the report suggests that institutional licensure would encourage a health team approach and provide a regulatory framework for systematic development of new kinds of personnel in organizational settings, the operational difficulties of interhospital and interstate mobility, the impact of unionism, and the possibility of exclusion rather than use of qualified personnel are also noted.[3(pp 68–77)]

Health law experts recognize that there are other solutions to the problems of individual licensure. Among them are peer certification, uniform licensure code, amendment of medical practice acts to allow delegation of tasks by physicians to allied health personnel, encouragement of educational equivalency measures and proficiency testing, encouragement for updating of knowledge of all health care personnel, and encouragement of action to include representation of other than the professional being licensed on state licensing boards.[1(pp 3–8),2(pp 125-7)]

A possible alternative to a national uniform licensing code (which would present many of the same problems as current state licensure, including reluctance to substitute a national for a state code) is development of a model code which could be adapted by each state. National examinations would be developed for those occupations which do not now have them. Roemer and Forgotson also suggest that standards could be set and mobility assured through national health insurance and/or Medicare laws.

It is of some interest to note that HEW's Bureau of Health Manpower Education has granted a contract to the Institute of Public Administration in Washington, D.C., to explore the feasibility of a national system of certification. This system is conceived as an umbrella system at the national (not federal) level, which could provide coordination and direction of certification practices for selected health occupations through voluntary participation. Such a system would enable the establishment of common policies and practices and determination of the desirability of extending certification to new occupational groups and specialties.[20]

Where Does Responsibility Lie?

Nurses tend to sit back and look to their organizations to act. Currently the ANA and NLN have taken action on, or are studying, the issues of open curriculum, mandatory continuing education for relicensure, and certification. State associations are almost all studying their nurse practice acts. All these activities are related to institutional licensure. However, individual nurses must also look at these issues and develop a clear understanding of what is involved.

There is no question but that nursing has been slow in responding with positive action to justifiable criticisms, often maintaining a head-in-the-sand or a stolid acceptance of the status quo position. Some of these criticisms, like those related to upward mobility, have been tied to the licensure issue but are basic to other social trends; they could easily have been anticipated, and better, quicker action taken. Other criticisms related to the fragmentation of care by the continuing undisciplined proliferation of assistants, aides, and specialists find nursing as guilty as any other health profession.

Miike states that the reasons that the institutional licensure concept was proposed in the first place were better regulation of quality, more freedom for innovation in delegation of patient-care tasks, particularly in the training and use of new categories of health professionals, and greater geographic and career mobility.[4]

None of these concerns belongs exclusively to any one health discipline. It is entirely possible, therefore, that they cannot be resolved by any one health discipline. The two-year moratorium on licensing new health personnel is over, according to the calendar, but the problems that instigated the moratorium are *not* over; they continue. Even if individual licensure is improved, what of the unlicensed worker? Has the geometric increase of numbers improved patient care? Is there another answer? Resolution of the problems posed could well result in helping to resolve some of the other problems of health care delivery. And, if some one must take the lead in initiating cooperative action, can it not be nursing?

REFERENCES

1. American Medical Association, Council on Health Manpower, Licensure of Health Occupations (mimeographed, December 1970).
2. American Hospital Association, *Statement on Licensure of Health Care Personnel*, 45 HOSPITALS (March 16, 1971).
3. U.S. DEPARTMENT OF HEALTH, EDUCATION AND WELFARE, PUBLICATION NO. (HSM) 72-11, REPORT ON LICENSURE AND RELATED HEALTH PERSONNEL CREDENTIALING (1971).
4. L. Miike, Institutional Licensure: An Experimental Model, Not a Solution (Paper presented at New Jersey League for Nursing Symposium on Institutional Licensure: What It Means to You, mimeographed, February 27, 1973).
5. N. Hershey, *Alternative to Mandatory Licensure of Health Professionals*, 50 HOSP. PROG. (March 1969).
6. AMERICAN HOSPITAL ASSOCIATION, SPECIAL COMMITTEE ON PROVISION OF HEALTH SERVICE, POLICY STATEMENT 9 (1971).
7. D. McAdams, *Institution-based Licensure System May Help Solve the Licensure Dilemma*, 50 HOSP. PROG. 52 (July 1969).
8. J.J. Lloyd, *Arguments for State Regulation of Health Professions*, 51 HOSP. PROG. 71 (March 1970).
9. L. Miike, What Is Institutional Licensure? 8 (Paper presented at N.L.N. Forum for Nursing Administrators of the West, Seattle, Washington, March 14, 1973).
10. Illinois Hospital Association, Hospitals, Manpower, Licensure and the 1970's. p. 5 (mimeographed, November 1971).
11. R. Roemer, *Legal Regulation on Health Manpower in the 1970's: Needs, Objectives, Options, Constraints, and Their Trade-Offs*, 86 H.S.M.H.A. HEALTH REP. 1062 (December 1971).
12. E. Forgotson, Licensure, Accreditation and Certification as Assurances of High Quality Health Care (Paper presented at National Health Forum meeting, Los Angeles, March 1968).
13. American Nurses' Association, *Resolution on Institutional Licensure*, 72 AM. J. NURS. 1106 (June 1972).

14. National League for Nursing, Resolution Opposing the Extension of Institutional Licensure to the Regulation of Nursing Personnel (Mimeographed, June 21, 1972).
15. *Institutional Licensure Opposed by NCSNNE,* 72 AM. J. NURS. 701 (April 1973).
16. Massachusetts Nurses' Association (personal communication).
17. Illinois Nurses' Association, Statement Regarding Participation in the Project Credentialing Health Personnel by Licensed Hospitals (mimeographed, 1972).
18. L. Miike, Institutional Licensure (paper presented at National League for Nursing Convention, Minneapolis, Minn., May 9, 1973).
19. N. HERSHEY & W. WHEELER, HEALTH PERSONNEL REGULATION IN THE PUBLIC INTEREST. QUESTIONS AND ANSWERS ON INSTITUTIONAL LICENSURE 13-14 (California Hospital Association, 1973).
20. U.S. National Institutes of Health Press Release (February 26, 1973).

Addendum

In the spring of 1974, a follow-up report on the 1971 HEW report on licensure was published (dated June 1973).[1] It presented a general overview of state activities in the various aspects of licensure and manpower credentialing, including institutional licensure. In the foreword, Dr. Charles Edwards, then Assistant Secretary for Health, recommended an extension of the moratorium on licensing of new health personnel through the end of calendar year 1975, citing the need for more time "to assess properly some of the new directions that have been taken by State legislatures, licensing boards, professional organizations, and the educational community with respect to the credentialing of health manpower."[1,p v] He also reiterated that the examination of health manpower credentialing would continue to be a significant departmental activity.

The section on institutional licensure was extremely brief, probably because there were as yet no meaningful reports from the two funded projects in Illinois and Pennsylvania. Moreover, the strong objections to the concept by various professional groups were recognized: the denial of individual licensure to emerging professions; the threat to presently licensed groups; the danger involved in laymen wielding ultimate authority in clinical situations; and the possibility that institutional licensure would be geared primarily to administrative convenience.[1,p 47]

However, the idea that institutional licensure was just a concept, a developing experimental model, was again put forth, and the need to test the concept was emphasized. Of particular significance was the statement that health care delivery today is already a form of institutional licensure, with actual scopes of duties restricted by prescribed competency levels through such modalities as certification, hospital staff regulation, and even voluntary specialization within allied health fields. Demonstration projects in institutional licensure were seen as one means of documenting the extent of the de facto situation. Perhaps, as a reassurance to objecting health professions, the report added:

Documentation of such practices does not necessarily mean that formalizing the structure will improve the system. Before that is done, such change would have to be justified by showing that it is of greater value than accommodating the present licensing system to such practices; moreover, it would have to be demonstrated that it would function more effectively than the de facto situation.[1](p 48-49)

One such funded project in Illinois terminated in 1974. The findings concluded that although certain aspects of institutional licensure were theoretically feasible, the concept was not practical in terms of the needed resources and potential cost of an effective program. The computerized data showed that the majority of the seventeen hospitals studied could agree on the majority of the job descriptions of the unlicensed personnel employed; nevertheless, implementation of a whole system, with legal responsibility, could be an overwhelming task.

No aspect of implementation was attempted in this project, but there was some assumption that this logical next step might be carried out in Pennsylvania. However, halfway through the second year of that project, (at the end of 1974) no hospitals had yet been selected to participate in such an experiment. Some preliminary studies with with x-ray and laboratory personnel had been done in one hospital with no fanfare, but the results were not published. The project director had, however, drafted legislation which would authorize suspension of existing licensure laws for experimental purposes, which had been a suggested action in the original project proposal. When flooded by protests from nurses and others, a statement was issued by HERF that this proposed legislation was intended only to protect the participants in the experimental situation from violating the licensure laws of other health professionals and was actually very similar to a California law already in existence.

Whether or not the law referred to is indeed California's own version of institutional licensure is still being debated. The original intent of AB1503 was to allow nurse practitioners to continue to function after the California Medical Board has issued a cease and desist order. In essence, the law states that, for purposes of experimentation in health delivery systems, "a select number of publicly evaluated health manpower pilot projects should be exempt from the healing arts practice acts." (Thus nurse practitioners could not be accused of violating the medical practice act as they practiced in their expanded roles.) Safeguards for the public were written into the law, and the state department of health was given the responsibility of designating experimental programs. Actually, implementation of the law was a bit unwieldly since nurse practitioners were forced to maintain trainee status under the supposed supervision of an educational program even though they had completed the program and were employed in a variety of settings. Moreover, after passage of a new nursing practice act which did legalize expanded practice, the law continued to operate, presumably to cover the expanded role of the medical auxiliaries and dental auxiliaries, as well as maternal-child care, pharmacy, and mental health personnel which were among the designated programs which could be approved for experimentation. It is not unlikely that this law will remain on the books, with an unknown effect on the health care delivery system.

In other states, there have been some overt attempts to legislate institutional licensure, which were kept in committee or killed, primarily through the efforts of organized nursing. Indirect approaches, such as attempts to consolidate or eliminate the licensure boards of the various health occupations have also been defeated, but their struggles have made clear to nurses the need to be knowledgeable about the many actions currently focused on licensure and health manpower credentialing. This new awareness has manifested itself in considerable positive action on the part of nursing: the success of nurses in some twenty states in updating their nursing practice acts for relevance to current needs; the swing toward mandatory continuing education for relicensure, supported by the ANA House of Delegates at the 1974 convention; the increasing emphasis on peer evaluation, certification for outstanding practice, and implementation of standards of practice. It is through such actions that nursing, as the largest group of health professionals can demonstrate their accountability to the consumer, the most meaningful deterrent to institutional licensure.

REFERENCE

1. H. Cohen & L. Miike. Developments in Health Manpower Licensure: A Follow-up to the 1971 Report on Licensure and Related Health Personnel Credentialing. Washington, D.C.; U.S. Department of Health, Education and Welfare, (1973), p. v, 47–49.

BONNIE BULLOUGH

12
The Third Phase in Nursing Licensure: The Current Nurse Practice Acts

Although the primary focus of this paper will be the current changes in the nurse practice acts that are occuring to accomodate an expanding nursing role, an overview of some of the other features of contemporary codes is also included to give a more comprehensive picture of the laws regulating nursing. There are nurse practice acts, or collections of laws regulating nursing, included in the codes of all fifty states, Washington, D.C., Puerto Rico, Guam, and the Virgin Islands. In spite of the fact that each of these states and territories enacted or amended its own statute, there are many commonalities among the laws and only a few significant differences. Moreover, as was indicated in the historical review of the development of the nurse practice acts in the first section (Chap. 1), it is possible to trace trends in licensure, so that once a given provision is included in the laws of a significant number of states it is likely to spread to most of the others.

All the jurisdictions delegate the task of administering the laws to appointed boards. These boards of nursing or nurse examiners are responsible for drawing up the detailed regulations for accrediting schools of nursing, examining candidates, issuing licenses to qualified applicants, and disciplining people who violate laws or regulations that relate to the practice of nursing. Although there is some state-to-state variation in the percentage of provisions legislated and the percentage left to board regulations, the trend seems to be in the more flexible direction of leaving more of the details open to regulations.

For example, most of the state codes now simply indicate that the candidate for nursing licensure must have graduated from an accredited nursing school; the characteristics of the curriculum and the management of the school are left to regulations, rather than being spelled out in the law. In an earlier era, many of the laws called for specific theoretical or clinical content. Although the majority of the acts still require high school graduation and a good character for registration, some of the new revisions allow the boards to specify even these basic criteria.

The interstate similarities in the laws and regulations, plus the use of state board pool examinations, makes the movement of registered nurses between states relatively easy. Registration in a second state is ordinarily possible without the necessity of repeating board examinations. Some nurses who move retain their original license, and some 15 percent of the registered nurses are included on the rolls of two or more states.[1(p47)] The situation for practical nurses who decide to move is more mixed. The standards for licensure still vary more from state to state, and 25 percent of the group currently in practice were originally licensed by waiver rather than by examination.[1(p156)] This is because the licensure acts are more recent, and new acts tend to include provisions for coverage by waiver of the practitioners already in the field. As the older practical nurses retire, and the standards become more uniform, interstate movement will undoubtedly become easier.

The earlier problem of outsiders dominating nursing boards no longer exists (see Table 1). The most common pattern is a board made up completely of registered nurses; the second most common pattern is a board made up of registered and practical nurses, with the registered nurses in numerical superiority. Although there are often educational or geographic stipulations for the board members, it seems apparent that the profession has a significant voice in its own regulation.[2] Moreover, the professional associations also have power: in many of the states, members of the boards are selected by the governor from lists of candidates provided by the state nurses' association. In a few states, the language of the law emphasizes the influence of the voluntary associations in an even more decisive manner. For example, the South Carolina State Board of Nursing is composed of six members:

The South Carolina State Nurses' Association shall be entitled to two representatives on the Board, who shall be members of the South Carolina State Nurses'

Table 1. Patterns of Membership on State Boards of Nursing

Registered Nurses Only (3-7 Members)	Registered and Practical Nurses (5-15 Members)	Other Patterns of Membership (6-13 Members)
Alaska	Alabama	*Nurses and Physicians*
Arizona	Delaware	Louisiana (RN)
Arkansas	Florida	Mississippi (RN & LPN)
Connecticut	Hawaii	*Nurses, Physicians, and Administrators*
Georgia	Illinois	
Idaho	Indiana	
Iowa	Maryland	North Carolina (RN)
Kansas	Missouri	South Carolina (RN & LPN)
Kentucky	Nebraska	Tennessee (RN & LPN)
Maine	New Mexico	*Nurses and Consumers*
Montana	New York	Colorado (RN)
New Hampshire	Ohio	Minnesota (RN)
New Jersey	Oklahoma	Nevada (RN & LPN)
North Dakota	Oregon	South Dakota (RN & LPN)
Texas	Utah	Vermont (RN & LPN)
West Virginia	Virginia	Washington (RN)
Wyoming		*Other*
Guam		California (RN)
Puerto Rico		Massachusetts (RN & LPN)
Virgin Islands		Michigan (RN & LPN)
Washington D.C.		Pennsylvania (RN)
Rhode Island		Wisconsin (RN)

Association. . . . The South Carolina Medical Association shall be entitled to two representatives on the Board. . . . The South Carolina Hospital Association shall be entitled to one representative on the Board who shall be a registered nurse. One member shall be a licensed practical nurse, who shall be a member of the South Carolina Federation of Licensed Practical Nurses, Inc.[3]

Only seven states besides South Carolina have physicians sitting on their nursing boards; in all but two of these, Mississippi and Louisiana, there are also other non-nurse members.[4,5] The North Carolina, Tennessee, and Wisconsin boards include physicians and hospital administrators, but do not specify that the administrators must be nurses (as does South Carolina).[6,7,8] In California, one physician and two consumers are included on the board.[9] The Massachusetts board is the most heterogeneous, with physicians, hospital administrators and public members all included.[10] In all these cases nurses outnumber physicians—which was not always the case in the early years of the twentieth century. Moreover, as can be seen from Table 1, physician members tend to serve on the larger boards, where their voices merge with other community representatives. However, it may also be noted in passing that although there are a few medical boards with consumer or state official members, no nurse representatives are called for in any of the medical practice acts. The tide of paternalism apparently does not flow in both directions.

Unfortunately, registered nurses might well be accused of a similar sort of paternalism regarding practical nurses. Thirty-eight boards are combined registered and practical nursing boards; in nine jurisdictions a separate subcommittee or similar structure handles practical nursing licensure; in seven states regulation of the two levels of nurses is completely separate. Registered nurses dominate all the combined boards and most of the semiautonomous units. There are in fact eleven boards that are responsible for practical nurse regulation which as yet include no practical nurses. Only on the seven separate boards are the practical nurses in the dominant position in their own regulation. Apparently registered nurses do not see any lack of justice in this situation; nor are they cognizant of the parallels between their struggles for autonomy, vis-à-vis the medical profession and the struggles of the practical nurses against them. In a statement issued in 1974, the Model Practice Act Committee of the Congress of Nursing Practice of the ANA recommended that there be only one board of nursing in each state to regulate the affairs of both levels of nursing; since registered nurses constitute the largest number of health professionals and are responsible for supervision and teaching of other nursing personnel, it was recommended they have numerical superiority on the combined boards.[11]

The new trend in board membership is the inclusion of one or more public members who are neither state officials nor health professionals. Eight states have pioneered in this direction: California, Colorado, Minnesota, Nevada, South Dakota, Vermont, Washington, and Massachusetts.[9,10,12-17] Nursing members who have served with the new consumer members report that they are a welcome addition; they force the professionals to clarify their assumptions and are often a source of support in the community.[18] This trend can be expected to grow because of the legitimate criticisms that have been raised about the control of professional licensure by the professions.[19]

The goal of mandatory licensure, considered so important 30 years ago, has been achieved for registered nurses in all jurisdictions except

Georgia and Washington, D.C., and for practical nurses in 37 jurisdictions. However, any feeling of accomplishment over mandatory licensure must necessarily be tempered with a certain amount of scepticism because of the many exemptions written into the codes. Gratuitous and emergency services are allowed in almost all states. In many jurisdictions, members of church groups operating within the tenets of their religion can give nursing care without licensure. In some states the list of people who are allowed to nurse outside the law is long. For example, Nebraska allows the three exemptions listed above plus nursing by domestic servants, friends, nursemaids, auxiliary nursing workers, nurses from outside the state who are accompanying patients, out-of-state and Canadian nurses awaiting registration, new graduates, student nurses, federal employees, and nurses attending graduate school.[20] Also exempted in one or more states are people who administer home remedies, other health professionals, physicians' office employees, and attendants who work in prisons or other state institutions. Obviously the mandatory provisions written into the state acts have not been overwhelmingly restrictive towards non-nurses.

Facilitating Role Expansion for Registered Nurses

As the profession and the state legislatures turn their attention to current needs for revision, most of the changes are in the direction of lessening the restrictions on nurses themselves, including most notably the prohibitions against diagnosis and treatment, which were added to nurse practice acts during the second phase of nursing licensure. Such disclaimers were particularly popular after 1955, when the American Nurses' Association advocated such a statement in its model definition of professional nursing.[21] As indicated in Table 2, 20 states have revised their nurse practice acts since 1971 to facilitate role expansion for registered nurses. In 15 other jurisdictions there is some ambiguity about the nurse's right to diagnose and treat patients, but no actual disclaimer exists in the nursing law. All the medical practice acts in these jurisdictions claim treatment as a medical function, but many do not mention diagnosis as an exclusive medical prerogative. Moreover, several of these states have recently added exemptions for workers who carry out delegated medical functions, including physicians assistants and sometimes nurses. In 18 jurisdictions the nurse practice acts still clearly forbid diagnosis

Table 2. The Legitimization of an Expanded Nursing Role in State Nurse Practice Acts

Recent Amendments Facilitate Role Expansion		Diagnosis and Treatment Not Forbidden	Diagnosis and Treatment Prohibited Without Exceptions
Alaska	1974	Connecticut	Alabama
Arizona	1973	Florida	Arkansas
California	1974	Georgia	Delaware
Colorado	1974	Iowa	Hawaii
Idaho	1971	Massachusetts	Illinois
Indiana	1974	Missouri	Kansas
Maine	1974	Nebraska	Kentucky
Maryland	1974	North Dakota	Louisiana
Minnesota	1974	Rhode Island	Michigan
Mississippi	1974	Virginia	Montana
Nevada	1973	West Virginia	New Mexico
New Hampshire	1974	Wisconsin	Ohio
New Jersey	1974	Wyoming	Oklahoma
New York	1972	Washington D.C.	South Carolina
North Carolina	1974	Virgin Islands	Texas
Oregon	1973		Utah
Pennsylvania	1974		Guam
South Dakota	1972		Puerto Rico
Tennessee	1972		
Vermont	1974		
Washington	1973		

Totals

54 acts analyzed in the table.
21 jurisdictions have recently added provisions which facilitate role expansion.
15 jurisdictions have not added new provisions, but the nurse practice act does not mention or prohibit diagnosis and treatment.
18 jurisdictions prohibit the nurse from diagnosing and treating.

and treatment, but many of these states are actively considering revision, so the situation can be expected to change rapidly.[22]

The first state to change its nurse practice act in this new direction was Idaho. In 1971 the legislature inserted the following clause after the prohibition against diagnosis and treatment:

except as may be authorized by rules and regulations jointly promulgated by the Idaho state board of medicine and the Idaho board of nursing which shall be implemented by the Idaho board of nursing.[23]

Following the passage of the amendment, the combined boards met and adopted such regulations. Nurses seeking to expand their activities to include acts of medical diagnosis or treatment are required to submit evidence to their agency that they have had the necessary special education. Then a committee or committees made up of nurses and physicians or dentists in the facility concerned must draw up standard policies and procedures under which the nurses with expanded functions will work. Certain special rules have also been made to supplement the agency protocols. Nurses giving anesthesia must be certified by the American Association of Nurse Anesthetists, and nurses who write prescriptions for controlled substances have to be registered with the US Bureau of Narcotics and Dangerous Drugs.[24]

The Idaho pattern for establishing new nursing roles using guidelines drawn up by boards has been used in 13 states, although there is some variation in the boards named. As indicated in Table 3, six other states followed the Idaho lead and specified the two boards of medicine and nursing: Alaska, California, Indiana, New Hampshire, North Carolina, and Pennsylvania (see Table 2).[25-30] The Arizona, Maryland, and Washington boards of nursing are assigned the regulatory responsibility, but they are directed to authorize only those functions for nurses recognized by both professions as properly belonging to nursing.[31-33] The Oregon Board of nursing carries the task alone without any statutory obligation for consulting with medicine.[34] The guidelines in Maine are to be jointly promulgated by the boards of nursing, medicine, and osteopathy; but they apply only to educational programs for the new roles rather than to the roles themselves.[35] The California guidelines are also limited; they will apply only to nurses in ambulatory care settings not connected to hospitals, and their promulgation is only permitted rather than mandated by law.

Most of the guidelines are administered by the boards of nursing, although three boards work together in Maine to certify educational programs. In North Carolina part of the revisions are in the medical practice act, and the medical board carries the administrative responsibility for the guidelines. The regulatory responsibility will be jointly carried by the boards of medicine and nursing in Virginia, which is not included in Table 3 because it is a medical practice act revision with no changes in the nursing statutes.[36] The experience of North Carolina and Virginia demonstrates one of the problems of medical practice act revisions for expanding the nursing role: the regulatory functions then tend to fall to medicine.

The second major approach has been simply to expand the basic definition of professional nursing to include more autonomous

Table 3. Approaches Used in Recent Revisions of State Nurse Practice Acts to Facilitate Role Expansion for Registered Nurses

States	Board Guidelines	Administered by	Definition of RN Expanded	Delegation by MD Increased	Agency Protocols
Alaska	two boards*	nursing			
Arizona	nursing	nursing	x		
California	two boards	nursing	x		x
Colorado			x		
Idaho	two boards	nursing			x
Indiana	nursing†	nursing	x		
Maine	three boards‡	three boards		x	
Maryland	nursing	nursing	x		
Minnesota			x		
Mississippi	nursing and health§	nursing			
Nevada	nursing	nursing			
New Hampshire	two boards	nursing			
New Jersey			x		
New York			x		
North Carolina¶	two boards	medicine		x	
Oregon	nursing	nursing	x		
Pennsylvania	two boards	nursing	x		
South Dakota				x	
Tennessee			x		x
Vermont			x		
Washington	nursing	nursing	x		

*Boards of nursing and medicine.
†Nursing board, alone or in collaboration with medical board.
‡Board of osteopathy also mentioned.
§Board of Nursing and Health.
¶Provisions for board regulation are in the North Carolina medical practice act, but the nursing act was also changed. Revision in Virginia is in the medical act only.

functions, particularly in the area of diagnosis and treatment. The first state to use this approach was New York, which in 1972 revised its definition of professional nursing:

The practice of the profession of nursing as a registered professional nurse is defined as diagnosing and treating human responses to actual or potential health problems through such services as case-finding, health teaching, health counseling, and provision of care supportive to or restorative of life and well-being and executing medical regimens prescribed by a licensed or otherwise legally authorized physician or dentist. A nursing regimen shall be consistent with and shall not vary any existing medical regimen.[37]

This basic approach seems sound and may eventually emerge as the dominant one, either in combination with regulatory mechanisms or as the sole mechanism. Eleven other states besides New York have expanded their definitions of registered nurses: Arizona, California, Colorado, Indiana, Maryland, Minnesota, Oregon, Pennsylvania, Tennessee, Vermont, and Washington.[9,17,27,30-32,34,38-41] A few of these states merely removed the prohibitions to diagnosis and treatment, while others now spell out the nursing role in more detail and include a broader scope of functions than was previously enumerated. Unfortunately, the use of the New York statute as a model may have created less than clear statements in some of the acts, since in addition to the basic definition of nursing quoted above the New York statute also includes a definition of the term diagnosing:

Diagnosing in the context of nursing practice means that identification of and discrimination between physical and psychosocial signs and symptoms essential to the effective execution and management of a nursing regime. Such diagnostic privilege is distinct from a medical diagnosis.[42]

This language suggests that the act of diagnosis is somehow different when performed by a nurse rather than by a physician, but lacks clarity in actually operationalizing that difference. Members of a nursing in-group who are familiar with the argument that the nursing diagnosis should be psychosocial rather than physical might well understand the language, but to the uninitiated the wording suggests that when nurses examine patients they place the signs and symptoms in two piles (one physical and one psychosocial); physicians presumably are allowed to be cognizant of the essential interplay between the psyche and the soma. This seems a peculiar way to distinguish a nursing from a medical diagnosis, particularly in light of the fact that the nursing educational system has for many years stressed the importance of the interplay between the biologic and psychosocial factors in illness, while medicine has been less interested in this phenomenon. In spite of this apparent unclarity five states—Colorado, New Jersey, Oregon, Pennsylvania, and Washington—have used this definition of diagnosis, and several other states mention a nursing diagnosis or a nursing regime.

Probably the reality of the situation is that the cognitive process used by nurses and physicians in diagnosing and planning a treatment regime would be quite similar, although the two types of practitioners might well give priority to different patient problems—with nurses attending more to the social and psychological signs, symptoms, and treatment modalities. This generalization would hold only part of the time and would be influenced by the practitioner's specialty and the patient's needs. For example, the coronary care nurses must necessarily be continuously aware of the physiological state of the patient; a psychiatrist must focus on the social and psychological problems presented by the patient.

Nurses generally seek more consultation and advice from physicians and other members of the health team than physicians seek, but even this does not neatly distinguish the nursing diagnosis and treatment plan from the medical one. There are also many humble physicians who seek consultation when needed. The point is that while there certainly are differences in the diagnostic and treatment process carried out by nurses and by physicians, there are also significant similarities. The overlap makes clear definitions difficult, and any differentiation will probably become even more problematic as nurses gain in skill and confidence in the future. Probably the only operational definition of a nursing diagnosis and care plan that would hold up over time and empirical study would be a diagnosis and care plan done by a nurse, as distinguished from one done by a physician.

In spite of these difficulties the attempts to differentiate the two types of approaches may well be a reasonable political expediency. Although the original bill to amend the New York nurse practice act included some notion of nursing process that different from a medical process, the original language did not stress the differences.[43,44] That bill was vetoed in 1971 because of medical opposition, and in his veto message the governor explained that the definition failed to differentiate between medicine and nursing. In 1972 the New York State Medical Association dropped its opposition, and the bill was again passed and was signed into law. The further differentiation of the medical v. the nursing approach through the addition of the concept of the nursing regime seemed to have helped in this effort, although the vigorous campaign carried out by the nurses of the state in support of the bill cannot be overlooked as perhaps the more significant factor.[45]

The 1972 Tennessee amendment to the nurse practice act carries the approach of delineating a separate medical and nursing process to its simplest level. The disclaimer to diagnostic and treatment functions was merely amended by adding the word "medical," so that the code now indicates that "the foregoing shall not be deemed to include acts of medical diagnosis or the development of a medical plan and therapeutics for a patient."[40] Apparently, Tennessee nurses are now able to carry out a nursing diagnosis and develop a nursing care plan; all they are restricted from doing is calling it medical. A 1974 statement by the Board of Nursing supports this interpretation by indicating that the nurse practice act does not now prohibit registered nurses from expanding their role.[46]

By a very careful use of words, the California legislature managed to expand the definition of registered nursing without invoking the concept of a nursing diagnosis or treatment regime:

The practice of nursing within the meaning of this chapter means those functions helping people cope with difficulties in daily living which are associated with their actual or potential health or illness problems or the treatment thereof which require a substantial amount of scientific knowledge or technical skill, and includes all of the following:

(a) Direct and indirect patient care services that insure the safety, comfort, personal hygiene, and protection of patients; and the performance of disease prevention and restorative measures.

(b) Direct and indirect patient care services, including but not limited to, the administration of medications and therapeutic agents, necessary to implement a treatment, disease prevention, or rehabilitative regimen prescribed by a physician, dentist, or podiatrist.

(c) The performance, according to standardized procedures, of basic health care, testing, and prevention procedures, including, but not limited to, skin tests, immunization techniques, and the withdrawal of human blood from veins and arteries.

(d) Observation of signs and symptoms of illness, reactions to treatment, general behavior, or general physical condition, and (1) determination of whether such signs, symptoms, reactions, behavior, or general appearance exhibit abnormal characteristics; and (2) implementation, based on observed abnormalities, of appropriate reporting, or referral, or standardized procedures, or changes in treatment regimen in accordance with standardized procedures, or the initiation of emergency procedures.[9]

Notice that the emotionally tinged word "diagnosis" is not invoked in this definition, so there is no need to explain it away. Rather, a definition of diagnosis is substituted for the word in section (d). Of course, this supports the idea that there is a certain amount of gamesmanship involved in the construction of the new definitions, but that may well be one of the current political realities. It will be a better day when nurses cannot only make their full potential contribution to patient care, but also can openly admit that contribution. The careful tone of the new definitions suggest that the day is approaching, but has not yet arrived.

Treatment functions in the California act are facilitated by the use of standardized procedures or protocols. This approach also has been sanctioned by the two boards in Idaho, and in Tennessee the Board of Nursing (without statutory obligation to do so) has indicated that registered nurses who manage the medical aspects of patient care will need to use protocols jointly developed by the nurses and physicians in their agencies.[47] This mechanism, which is explained by Greenfield (Section II Chap. 2), will undoubtedly be used more frequently in the future. It is congruent with what already has happened in the acute care settings as the use of standing orders has increased; although they have been criticized as a "cookbook approach," the protocols do much to help to specify treatment techniques and make them more amenable to empirical study of their efficacy.

A fourth approach to legislation is exemplified by the nurse practice acts of Maine and South Dakota, which allow individual physicians to delegate the right to diagnose and treat.[48] The Maine statute indicates that the practice of professional nursing includes:

diagnosis or prescription of therapeutic or corrective measures when such services are delegated by a physician to a registered nurse who has completed the necessary additional educational programs.[35]

Even before the current phase in nursing licensure there were state medical practice acts, including those of Arizona, Colorado, Florida, Kansas and Oklahoma, which gave physicians broad powers to delegate medical acts to other workers.[49,50] As a consequence of the development of physician's assistants, fourteen other states have passed delegatory statutes in recent years. Arkansas, Connecticut, Georgia, Hawaii, Idaho, Maine, Maryland, Michigan, New Jersey, Tennessee, North Carolina, and Utah now provide exemptions to the medical practice acts for other workers when they act under physician supervision.[51] Some of these statutes allow the physician to decide to whom he is to delegate; others name specific categories, such as physician's assistants or nurses. The Arizona statute, which predates the current movement, indicates that "any person acting at the direction of. . . a doctor of medicine" is exempt from the prohibitions in the medical practice act.[57] The more recent Connecticut statute follows the trend toward more specificity and indicates that the following are exempt from the provisions of the medical practice act:

any person rendering service as a physician's trained assistant, a registered nurse, or a licensed practical nurse if such service is rendered under the supervision, control and responsibility of a licensed physician.[3]

It may be possible for nurses to use the delegatory provisions of the Maine and South Dakota nurse practice acts, or the provisions of the several delegatory statutes that have been added to medical practice acts, to sanction some expanded functions, although there is some question as to their usefulness for this purpose. An expansion of the physician's right to delegate received support from officials of the Department of Health, Education and Welfare, who called for a moratorium on the development of laws to sanction new types of health workers but approved this approach.[54] It has been used as a major mechanism for giving legal coverage to physician's assistants.

This may well be a reasonable approach for physician's assistants, who have no basic license of their own except in Colorado.[55] Obviously, they need legal coverage; moreover, their role is more circumscribed and their numbers are not formidable. With only approximately 1000 physician's assistants in practice, their direct supervision is not an overwhelming task for physicians.[56] However, even for physician's assistants the general delegatory statutes have some disadvantages. Winston Dean points out that this type of law fails to provide the physician with adequate guidelines to determine the activities he can safely delegate, and the educational and other qualifications the assistant should possess in order to practice safely.[57] Because of these problems, nineteen states have chosen to establish some sort of regulatory mechanism for physician's assistants, and have most commonly assigned this responsibility to the medical boards.[51]

The nursing situation is different. Nurses already have a basic license. Their role expansion is taking place in varying degrees, so there is no single new nursing occupation. In the early days of the current revolution some people predicted that a new level of practitioner would develop between medicine and nursing with an identity discrete from either of the other professions. Some authorities still hold this view and believe that not all nurses should be taught the techniques of diagnosis.[58] But the movement has not worked out so neatly. Rather, a large group of nurses seem to be in the process of expanding their role to a modest degree. In either the in-patient or ambulatory settings, they are taking on a few new functions or admitting more readily to the old functions that called for judgment. Some of the members of this group have acquired new knowledge through formal classes, but more have learned the new skills from the physicians with whom they work; or have enlarged their knowledge through reading the nursing journals, which have shifted their focus to include more information about diagnosis and treatment. The old nurse practice acts, which described nursing in a purely dependent and noncognitive way, are out of date for these people; but they are in no way members of any new occupational group. They are nurses who need and deserve better nurse practice acts.

On the other hand there is a smaller group of nurses, numbering perhaps about 10,000 (which is ten times the size of the physician's assistant group but still small relative to the total group of approximately 800,000 employed nurses), who have taken on new titles in ambulatory or critical care.[59,1] These nurses have moved further into what was formerly considered medicine's territory, and their need either for physician supervision or legal sanction is greater. Few of these practitioners need to have all their practice supervised by physicians, because most of them still carry out significant nursing responsibilities. Physicians should not and cannot supervise everything that nurses do and still have any time for direct patient contact, which is what physicians are trained for. The new laws of Maryland and Minnesota clearly specify that all nursing care is not to be supervised by physicians. The Maryland statute indicates that:

The practice of nursing includes both independent nursing functions and delegated medical functions, and may be performed autonomously or in collaboration with other health team members, or may be delegated by the registered nurse to other nursing personnel.[32]

In a similar view, the Washington statute indicates that "the registered nurse is directly accountable and responsible to the individual consumer for the quality of nursing care rendered."[60] These laws interpret nursing function in a broader manner than do the physician delegatory statutes.

Although the mechanisms outlined here probably will cover most nurses in expanded roles, there are two groups that have been concerned about their legal status and have sought special licensure: the nurse-midwives and the anesthetists. Modern nurse-midwifery in the United States started in 1921 at the Maternity Center Association in New York City,[61] but had a limited following for many years because of the opposition of organized medicine. Much of this opposition was aimed at lay midwifes, but it also touched nurse–midwives. Early in American history lay midwives were accepted throughout the country, but the trend throughout most of the twentieth century has been to terminate the statutes sanctioning their practice and turn maternity care over to physicians. Countering this trend has been the recent more rapid growth in the number of nurse–midwives who have taken a special refresher course and passed the certification examination. The American College of Nurse–Midwives reports that there are approximately 1500 certified members of their group, which the College defines as:

a registered nurse who by virtue of added knowledge and skill gained through an organized program of study and clinical experience recognized by the American College of Nurse-Midwives has extended the limits of her practice into the area of management of care of mothers and babies through the maternity cycle so long as progress meets criteria accepted as normal.[62]

The legal status of midwives varies. In 19 jurisdictions nurse midwifery is recognized either in the laws or the regulations. Four states require certification by the College as a prerequisite to practice. In the Virgin Islands there is even a separate midwifery board. In 22 jurisdictions their status is ambiguous, with some permissive regulations; but nurse–midwives are not differentiated from the lay midwives of an earlier era. In 13 jurisdictions the law is definitely prohibitive or restrictive.[61]

Nurse anesthestists are in a somewhat similar situation. Although they have been a recognized specialty throughout the country, there has been considerable discussion about their legality because they often carry out diagnostic and treatment functions. With 208 schools of anesthesia graduating approximately 800 anesthetists a year, they play a significant role in the operating and delivery rooms of the country.[63] Only four states specifically mention anesthetists in the nurse practice acts, but probably the new expanded definitions of nursing will solve their legal problems so that further special legislation will not be needed. Their situation differs somewhat from that of midwives, who may still need special legislation in some states;

laws were passed prohibiting the practice of midwifery, but not prohibiting anesthetists from practicing.

To summarize the recent legislation: provisions have been added to 21 nurse practice acts and one medical practice act to facilitate role expansion for registered nurses. This represents a significant trend to expand the scope of practice of registered nurses and is expected to continue as other jurisdictions revise their nurse practice acts. A variety of mechanisms are being used, including board regulations, expanded definitions of nursing, standing orders, and some specialty legislation that has been passed to regulate nurse-midwives and anesthetists. The best approach seems to be a combination of methods, including an expansion of the basic definition of the registered nurse and some type of regulatory mechanism to guide the practice and specify the educational needs of those nurses whose role expansion in the areas of diagnosis and treatment is significant.

The revisions are best accomplished in those portions of the state codes that are considered nursing sections, rather than in the medical sections—unless regulation by medicine is desired by nurses. Moreover, it is easier for nurses to ask for and achieve nurse practice act revision than medical practice act revision. Medical practice act revisions that increase the delegatory power of physicians do not seem to be a particularly desirable approach for sanctioning increased responsibility and accountability of nurses, who are already licensed to carry out delegated medical tasks.

The movement to expand the scope of function of nurses is probably related to other trends in the laws regulating nursing, including less domination of nursing boards by medicine and a beginning trend towards more consumer power in regulation.

REFERENCES

1. AMERICAN NURSES' ASSOCIATION FACTS ABOUT NURSING, 72-73 (1974).
2. R. de Tornyay, *State Board Member.* 69 AM. J. NURS. 570 2 (March 1969).
3. SOUTH CAROLINA CODE § 56-961.
4. MISSISSIPPI CODE, § 73-15-9.
5. LOUISIANA REVISED STATUTES, § 90-159.
6. NORTH CAROLINA GENERAL STATUTES, § 90-159.
7. TENNESSEE CODE, § 63-732.
8. WISCONSIN STATUTES, § 15.403.
9. CALIFORNIA BUSINESS AND PROFESSIONS CODE, § 6-1-2702.
10. MASSACHUSETTS GENERAL LAWS, § 13-13.

The Third Phase in Nursing Licensure

11. American Nurses Association, Congress for Nursing Practice, Model Practice Act Committee, Authority and Composition of Boards of Nursing (May 1974).
12. COLORADO REVISED STATUTES, § 97-1-4.
13. MINNESOTA STATUTES, § 148.181.
14. NEVADA REVISED STATUTES, § 632.020.
15. Letter from Margaret E. Cashman in behalf of the South Dakota State Board of Nursing indicates that two consumer members were added to the board in 1974 by executive order.
16. VERMONT STATUTES, title 26, ch. 24, § 1553.
17. WASHINGTON REVISED CODE, § 18.88.060.
18. AMERICAN NURSES' ASSOCIATION, LICENSURE AND CREDENTIALING; PROCEEDINGS OF THE A.N.A. CONFERENCE FOR MEMBERS AND PROFESSIONAL EMPLOYEES OF STATE BOARDS OF NURSING AND A.N.A. ADVISORY COUNCIL, 1972 at 23-31 (1974).
19. U.S. DEPARTMENT OF HEALTH EDUCATION AND WELFARE, PUBLICATION NO. (HSM) 72-11, REPORT ON LICENSURE AND RELATED HEALTH PERSONNEL CREDENTIALING, 1-6 (June 1971).
20. NEBRASKA REVISED STATUTES, § 71-1,132.06.
21. *A.N.A. Board Approves a Definition of Nursing Practice,* 55.AM.J.NURS. 1474 (December 1955).
22. L. Kelly, *Nursing Practice Acts,* 7 AM. J. NURS. 1310-19 (January 1974).
23. IDAHO CODE, § 54-1413.
24. Minimum Standards, Rules and Regulations for Nurse Practitioners (Expanding Role) and Guidelines for Nurses Writing Prescriptions, Jointly Promulgated by the Idaho State Board of Nursing and the Idaho State Board of Medicine as Authorized by § 54-1413 (e), IDAHO CODE.
25. ALASKA STATUTES, § 08.68.410.
26. CALIFORNIA BUSINESS AND PROFESSIONS CODE, § 2725.
27. INDIANA CODE, § 25-23-1-1.
28. NEW HAMPSHIRE REVISED STATUTES, 326-A:2.
29. NORTH CAROLINA GENERAL STATUTES, § 90-158. The joint committee of the two boards is established in medical practice act, GENERAL STATUTES, § 90-18 (14).
30. The General Assembly of Pennsylvania, House Bill No. 129 (1973), *amending* P.L. 317, No 69, § 2.
31. ARIZONA REVISED STATUTES, § 32.1601.
32. MARYLAND CODE, article 43, § 291.
33. WASHINGTON REVISED CODE, § 18.88.030.
34. OREGON REVISED STATUTES, § 678-410.
35. MAINE REVISED STATUTES, title 32, ch. 31, § 2102.
36. VIRGINIA CODE, § 54-275.
37. NEW YORK STATE EDUCATION LAW, title 8, article 139, § 6902.
38. COLORADO REVISED STATUTES, ch. 97, article 1, 2.
39. MINNESOTA STATUTES, ch. 148, § 148.171.
40. TENNESSEE CODE ANNOTATED, § 63-740.
41. VERMONT STATUTES, title 26, ch. 24, § 1552.
42. NEW YORK STATE EDUCATION LAW, op title 8, article 139, § 6901.
43. *Independence of Nursing Function Affirmed by New York State Legislature,* 7 AM. J. NURS. 1901-2 (June 1971).
44. V. Driscoll, *Liberating Nursing Practice,* 20 NURS. OUTLOOK 24-8 (January 1972).

45. T.M. Schorr, *Where the Action Is,* 72 AM. J. NURS. 671 (April 1972).
46. *Rules and Regulations of the Tennessee Board of Nursing Concerning Licensure and Education of Register Nurses,* NURS. RN 34-9.
47. TENNESSEE RULES AND REGULATION
48. SOUTH DAKOTA SESSION LAWS, ch. 101, § 27.09.
49. M.S. Fish, *Nursing Vis-A-Vis Medicine. A Proposal for Legislation,* in AMERICAN NURSES' ASSOCIATION, LICENSURE AND CREDENTIALING; PROCEEDINGS OF THE A.N.A. CONFERENCE FOR MEMBERS AND PROFESSIONAL EMPLOYEES OF STATE BOARDS OF NURSING AND A.N.A. ADVISORY COUNCIL, 1972 at 14-22 (1974).
50. E. H. Forgotson, R. Roemer, R. Newman & J. L. Cook, *Licensure of Physicians,* in REPORT OF THE NATIONAL ADVISORY COMMISSION ON HEALTH MANPOWER, VOL. II, 294 (1967).
51. AMERICAN MEDICAL ASSOCIATION, EDUCATIONAL PROGRAMS FOR THE PHYSICIAN'S ASSISTANT 9 (September 1973). The list was updated by the addition of Tennessee.
52. ARIZONA REVISED STATUTES, 32-1421 (6).
53. CONNECTICUT GENERAL STATUTES, ch. 370, title 20-9.
54. L. MIIKE & H. COHEN, U.S. DEPARTMENT OF HEALTH, EDUCATION AND WELFARE PUB. NO. (HRA) 74-3101, DEVELOPMENTS IN HEALTH MANPOWER LICENSURE AND RELATED HEALTH PERSONNEL CREDENTIALING 4-5 (June 1973).
55. W.J. Curran, *New Paramedical Personnel-to License or Not to License?* 282 NEW ENGL. J. MED. 1085-6 (May 7, 1970).
56. AMERICAN MEDICAL ASSOCIATION, ACCREDITED EDUCATIONAL PROGRAMS FOR THE ASSISTANT TO THE PRIMARY CARE PHYSICIAN (March 1974).
57. W.J. Dean, *State Legislation for Physician's Assistants; A Review and Analysis,* 88 HEALTH SERV. REP. 3-12 (January 1973).
58. J.E. Lynaugh & B. Bates, *Physical Diagnosis: A Skill for All Nurses?* 74 AM. J. NURS. 58-9 (January 1974).
59. Personal Communication from Pearl Dunkley, Executive Director, American Nurses' Association, to the National Health Law Program, U.C.L.A. (August 23, 1974).
60. WASHINGTON REVISED CODE, § 18.88.010.
61. L. Olsen, *The Expanded Role of the Nurse in Maternity Practice,* 9 NURS. CLIN. NORTH AM. 459-66 (September 1974).
62. AMERICAN COLLEGE OF NURSE-MIDWIVES, FUNCTION, STANDARDS AND QUALIFICATIONS (1966).
63. B. TIGHE, INSTITUTE FOR THE STUDY OF HEALTH AND SOCIETY, REVIEW OF TRAINING PROGRAMS AND UTILIZATION OF PARAPROFESSIONALS IN MEDICINE AND DENTISTRY 34-5 (1972).

DONNA F. VER STEEG

13
The Political Process, or, The Power and the Glory

There is supposedly an old Chinese saying that goes, "I curse you. May you live in a time of great change." I'm inclined to think that nursing in the seventies is, in this sense, twice honored. Both as a profession among professions, and as a grouping consisting predominantly of members of the female sex, we are living through a period of great change. These two identities have significant implications for the manner in which we participate in the political process that marks the changes. The implications of being female, of being a professional, and of having our practice controlled by laws are elaborated elsewhere in this volume. In this paper we shall consider the power and the glory of the political process as it applies to all citizens and professions; but we will illustrate it with examples from ongoing research in health manpower legislation. Insofar as this can be construed as a "how-to" paper, we shall include some comments on the particular problems of women and of nurses in politics, also drawn from ongoing research.

Although professions exist because of a mandate from society to perform certain functions, and many professions operate under legislative sanctions, there is a tendency among the rank and file

Portions of this paper first appeared in Ver Steeg, The Physician's Assistant: Interorganizational Influence on the Creation of a New Occupation (Dissertation filed with University Microfilms, Ann Arbor, Michigan 78106, © 1973. Donna Lorraine Frank Ver Steeg).

members to forget this fact. There was a time when it was not considered very "professional" to be involved in the political process. Professionals were somehow removed from the everyday world in which such decisions are made. This is an innocence which can no longer be excused. All kinds of decisions about areas of practice, distribution of resources, eligibility for care, etc., that were once the province of the professional alone, have been taken over by society, in the form of its legislators. The legislators must be informed, and it is the responsibility of the professions to do the informing.

We sometimes have the feeling that laws are unchangeable. They are not. The purpose of a system of laws is to express the collective interests and beliefs of society. These interests and beliefs change; eventually, the laws must change. When the laws on the books are too far out of step with the wishes of society, they frequently are not enforced. This is a dangerous situation because it breeds disrespect for the law. A credibility gap develops. A law ignored for "good reasons" is frequently followed by a law ignored for reasons of convenience; finally, good laws are ignored because one has grown used to the ignoring. We have such a situation in the health care delivery system in the United States, and it is not good. A serious credibility gap has developed between our medical and nursing practice acts and our medical and nursing practice, not only in California but elsewhere in the country. In some states nurses have succeeded in effecting changes in the practice acts to bring them into line with current practice. This has come about because nurses have marshalled their forces, and have amassed enough power to influence legislators to change the law.

Because no law can ever answer all claims equally well, those groups which amass the most power tend to be most favored. In a pluralistic society this is only to be expected. It is therefore vital that concerned professionals learn how power is acquired and how it can be used. The exercise of political power has become a professional responsibility. Nurses need to address this responsibility. To do this they not only must understand power, they must learn to be comfortable with its existence and to feel good about their exercise of it.

An Analysis of Power

Power has been defined and analyzed in a number of ways, depending not only upon the academic discipline of the writer but also upon the problems to be analyzed. For purposes of this paper we draw most heavily upon the work of Nuttall, Scheuch, and Gordon and of Eckstein.[1,2] Power and influence are sometimes used interchangeably and sometimes distinguished from each other. In this paper they are used interchangeably.

Power can be real or only perceived as real. If we analyze power using these two dimensions, we can postulate four main categories. If an organized group has both real power and is perceived as having power, its power is *manifest*. If the organization has no power and is perceived as having no power, its power is *absent*. Between these two extremes are the two mixed categories, which must be of greatest concern to us. One is *reputational* power, which exists where an organization is perceived as having power when it actually does not. This is a very important category, particularly because we find that organizations with reputational power try to avoid change. They try to prevent decisions from being made that will reveal that they have less power than people perceive them to have. Closely related is the situation that exists when a manifestly powerful organization has only a limited amount of power to "spend." The organization is aware that when this power is gone it cannot easily be replaced. Such an organization will be reluctant to see decisions made that will use up the manifest power it has, reducing it to powerlessness for other more pressing decisions. Such organizations typically try to exert their influence by threatening to use power, hoping that their reputations for strength will prevent anyone from challenging them.

The final category includes those organizations that have real power but are not perceived as having power. Such organizations may be unaware themselves of how much power they have. Such organizations are said to have *potential* power. Obviously, it is to the advantage of adversary organizations to encourage this ignorance. History is full of stories of organizations and men who were misled by an apparent lack of power or failed to appreciate the dangers of "arousing the sleeping giant." Sociologists are fond of studying the havoc that can arise in work situations when workers far down the hierarchy discover how much potential power they really have. Unfortunately, such discoveries usually lead to "illegal working arrangements," which operate to the detriment of the clients of such groups. Ideally, such discoveries should lead to a realignment of decision-making processes, which can be exercised openly and in a legal and accountable fashion. The client then has the opportunity to demand good services and has some recourse if quality is not received.

How does a group go about assessing its own or another organization's power? For political purposes, the most important assets are size, information base, professional expertise, physical resources (such as time and money), and the personal attributes of the members. In the discussion that follows, it is important to remember that an organization or group may be very deficient in one or more of these areas and still be very powerful because of its strength in other areas.

Size

The organization that has more members has more potential votes. If such an organization can demonstrate that its voters are interested and will show up on election day, the power of that organization is enhanced. Several years ago, an attempt was made to change the California Nurse Practice Act without the informed participation of the mass of California nurses. For a variety of reasons, the bill was not acceptable. A massive letter-writing campaign resulted against the bill. There are a lot of nurses in California. There is not a single legislator who can afford to ignore a visible nurse constituency that is agreed on how he should vote and is prepared to back up its beliefs at election time. The bill was defeated. The same is true of other states. The constituency must be visible and it must be united for size to have an impact.

Information Base

An informed membership that understands the importance of verified information is a tremendous asset to an organization. Conversely, a membership that reacts to rumors with gut-level responses can sabotage itself without any help from an outside force. An organization that obtains and distributes information accurately and rapidly, so that its members can respond effectively, can be very powerful. This is a two-way responsibility. It is equally important for the membership to assist in obtaining accurate information and forwarding it to a central place. Not every opponent fights clean. In the political arena the use of innuendo, half truths, and, occasionally, total misrepresentation of the facts is not uncommon. These tactics can be harmful. It is important that members have access to the true situation. It is especially important that members recognize their own responsibility for verifying what they hear. It is important to remember that the prestige of the source does not automatically guarantee its veracity.

Another kind of information is political know-how and political know-who. There are rules for playing the political game. Understanding those rules is essential if an organized group wishes to have an impact on the political process. One of the more important ways of having access to this game is through the employment of lobbyists. Organizations that cannot employ lobbyists must depend upon volunteer efforts on the part of their membership to keep them informed of the day-to-day—sometimes minute-to-minute—changes that can go on in the legislative process. Ideally, an organization has both volunteers and lobbyists working in close harmony to get the message of the organization to the people who need to have it and to keep track of the activities of the other organizations whose interests may be different. A bill may undergo radical changes as it proceeds through hearings and discussions on the floor of the legislative bodies. There is no substitute for informed vigilance. A good lobbyist knows the system, knows the legislators and their staffs, and is known by them as a reliable source of information about the wishes of his or her employing constituency.

It is not required that all members of an organization agree with the party line of the organization. It is important that dissident members who wish to be heard in the legislative halls make their dissatisfaction known to their organization and to whoever is monitoring legislation. It is possible for an organization to operate effectively in a situation of informed disagreement. However, dissent that the organization is unaware of in advance can be publicly embarrassing—it can confuse the legislators. Members must be aware that such activities weaken the organization for the day when those same members will be in agreement and want the organization to be strong.

Professional Expertise

In one sense professional expertise is another form of information base. It is, however, a special kind not equally available to all groups. We have tended, in nursing, to be so preoccupied with our search for academic respectability and an exclusive knowledge base that we forget how much special expertise we do have. In our search for the forest we have lost sight of the trees. A theory of nursing has two important functions in the political process. One is to help shape a meaningful redefinition of nursing for a new practice act. I believe that in California we are making very good progress in that area. The other function is to provide that sense of self-awareness or self-respect that the individual nurse needs to have when she offers her services in assisting in the development of legislation in her particular area of expertise. General agreement on what nursing is all about and well-executed and well-documented research in the areas of practice in which nurses are involved are necessary. We have that kind of expertise. We have the knowledge that arises from it. We need to have the self-confidence required to share such knowledge and to cite it when appropriate. One of the more important outcomes of the many arguments about nurse practitioners has been a more careful delineation of what nursing is all about in its separate as well as its overlapping responsibilities.

Nurses in the United States have a long history of working in organized health care settings. They have carried considerable responsibility for making those organizations function. As such organizations come under increasing government control, knowledgeable nurses need to be involved in helping design these controls. Without the professional input of nurses and other members of the health care team, is ample historical evidence shows that quality of care is ignored and cost of care becomes preeminent.

Physical Resources

Such things as money, available time, an organized means of communication such as a journal or newsletter, members in influential positions, prestige, and geographic propinquity are all physical resources. Money may come from assessments, dues, the individual contributions of members, support from other groups with similar interests, etc. On occasion, money has come in the form of grants to underwrite needed research or the support of consultants. As nurses have improved their financial standing in relation to other professions, they have become more able to contribute in this manner. Political action costs money. Newsletters cost money, travel costs money, telephones and offices cost money, and salaries of staff cost money.

As nurses become better known as qualified experts, and as they become known to legislators and the other members of government, they increase their chances of becoming members of influential groups. In California, Michigan, and other states, the legislatures are turning more and more to advisory groups to assist in developing solutions to difficult problems. Nurse members of such groups have an important opportunity to promote nursing goals for better health care. Increased participation by nurses in the decision-making bodies of their local governments, the academic institutions, and the health care institutions where they work develops another avenue to increased visibility and increased opportunity to affect the political process.

Prestige enhances the credibility of the group. Prestige can come from a legitimacy and special privilege that spring from recognized knowledge and technical competence. Prestige is more likely to guarantee news coverage. Where a prestigious group is in opposition to a less prestigious group, the less prestigious group may have to use extraordinary measures to be heard. There are times when informational access to the media is so unequally available that a news blackout may be essential to a fair settlement of the issues. Such was the case in the 1974 nurses' strike in San Francisco. Nurses insisted that their primary concerns were adequate staffing and the qualifications of personnel in specialized units. Further, they pledged full coverage for emergency units and critically ill patients during the strike. The news media concentrated on economic issues and on the statements of various individuals who claimed (erroneously) that emergency care was not being provided. Only after a federal mediator arrived on the scene and imposed a news blackout did the negotiation sessions proceed to a settlement satisfactory to the nursing profession.

There are other aspects of prestige that may work to the disadvantage of nurses. There is a tendency among groups with little power to depend on a collective equality that precludes the development of "stars." In such a group, those who excel may be seen as a threat to other members who lack the same qualifications. Nursing has for a variety of reasons been one of those groups. Efforts to upgrade the professional status of nursing as a whole have, in the past, led to unfortunately-worded statements that have served to divide (and to risk being conquered by interests outside nursing). There is a broad spectrum of talents within the nursing profession to meet the broad spectrum of needs that nursing must fulfill if it is to be a responsible part of the health care team. Prestigeful members should be cultivated, not castigated. Less prestigious members need also to be honored for their own particular contributions to the professions.

Availability of and flexibility in the use of time are critical power assets. So long as nurses are employed in settings that do not allow for flexible working arrangements, nurses will be handicapped in the political process. Public hearings are not held at the convenience of hospitals and other agencies. We still have nursing supervisors who view using days off to attend political meetings as basically sinful, and probably subversive. Nurses need to be secure in their right to the free use of their own time.

Time has another dimension. In a society in which the decision-making powers are dispersed, time is required to reach decisions. The politically naive have a tendency to expect miracles. No group is powerful enough to impose its wishes without some sort of agreement with other groups. This requires time and a great deal of patience. If a favored program fails to get through one way, there is always another approach, another session, a new legislature, a new governor, or a new president. Stories about the passage of each of the new practice acts point up the importance of patience. At one time in the many behind-the-scenes discussions that led up to the passage of the California act, a group decision was made to be kind, courteous, patient—and fierce. Patience is sometimes mistaken for passivity. Patience can mean an implacable determination; this is the sense in which it is a political asset.

A power asset not always fully appreciated is geographic propinquity. Are you in the right place at the right time? There is a certain value to be gained from attending the right meetings and being seen attending them. Part of this comes from demonstrating that you care enough to show up. Showing up consistently earns a reputation for faithfulness and concern, and is even better. Also, you become familiar with the other people who attend meetings—able to recognize them on sight, familiar with who talks to whom, etc. Eventually, opportunities arise for you to introduce yourself to these people. One acquaintanceship leads to another, so that eventually you find yourself in a position to meet and talk with individuals who might not otherwise give you the time of day. There is a lot of vouching-for in the political arena: a screening process that should not be abused but of which you certainly should take advantage.

Personal Attributes

Members who speak for their group are more apt to be effective if they display intelligence, style, and attractiveness. This does not mean physical beauty, although being handsome does not hurt. A certain physical and psychologic presence that demonstrates that the individual knows who she or he is and is comfortable with that fact is necessary. Such an individual handles himself/herself well in a variety of settings, and does not consistently require the assistance of other participants to "rescue" him/her. Unfortunately, this requires a knowledge base of skills that many women do not possess. For example, the public world of airplanes, hotel desks, and restaurants was not designed for women traveling alone or even in pairs. It was designed for men. This situation is changing rapidly (and for the good), but I expect that the remnants will be around for many years. Many women simply do not know how to buy plane tickets, how to register at a hotel, how to rent a car, or how gracefully to avoid having their meals paid for by others. The psychic costs to a woman traveling to a political meeting are high. She arrives with a psychic deficit. Married women particularly are at a disadvantage. It is difficult for anyone to maintain poise and attention to the purpose of a meeting when she is being quizzed for the umpteenth time about who is caring for her children and what her husband says about her being away from home. Such questions sometimes reach the point of absurdity. On one occasion this author had to be in two distant but adjacent cities on a Saturday morning and a Sunday evening. In rapid succession she was chided for (1) being away from home so much, and (2) wasting money by spending the intervening evening and day with her family. Epstein has reported that women are denied participation in some decision-making processes because they may not appropriately appear at or do not choose to participate in otherwise all-male functions.[3] The rationale offered by Epstein's informants is that the men would feel uncomfortable telling jokes meant only for masculine ears. This taboo is lessening, partly because men are becoming more comfortable with the presence of peer-level women at such times, and partly, I suspect, because women are recognizing that this self-imposed restriction works to their disadvantage. It should be noted that the etiquette of such encounters has not yet become widely accepted; nor are all individuals yet comfortable or even knowledgeable about what such etiquette might include. There is a fine line between a business or political meeting and a social encounter between people who happen to be of both sexes. Etiquette only develops through practice. There must be a mutual willingness to try. The simple solution would be for men nurses to assume political tasks, as has been done in other female occupations—but this has other ramifications which make it inappropriate.

It is especially useful for individual members of organizations to make themselves known to their individual legislators. This may be done through letters on important issues about which the member has an informed opinion or in support of some action the legislator has already taken. It can also be done by visiting the staff and perhaps the legislator personally. An avenue that nurses are beginning to use is active participation in election campaigns. Other professional groups have used this approach for a considerable length of time. Nurses need to expand their activities in this area. Again, a coordinated effort is needed, so that the efforts of individual members are in concert rather than in opposition. As noted earlier in this paper, the individual member should seek and is entitled to expect the support of the organization in supplying up-to-date information, hidden problems, etc. Armed with such information and his own expertise, the individual is in a much better position to present an intelligent picture to those in positions of power.

Other assets can be included under personal attributes. Social skills, administrative skills, willingness to work closely together with other members of the organization, having the "right" value system, having gone to the "right" school—all these are assets of political power that are peculiar to the individual member. This is a matter of some concern to a professional group such as nurses, most of whose members do not come to the profession via the university where other professions (including politicians) receive their education. There is a disadvantage in educating professional-level people in isolation from the other members of their team. One might wish, in an egalitarian society, that such things were not important, but they are. People feel more comfortable working with others who speak the same "language" and are familiar with the same rules for behavior. Such skills can be learned, and need to be learned if the individual lacking them wishes to participate on an equal footing with others on the political scene. Many organizations provide an informal training program for their members, assuring that those who have the inclination will have the chance to develop political skills. Nurses have been lax in this area. The alternative is to restrict access to positions of power to those who come to the organizations with these attributes—an unpalatable and destructive alternative that will not and should not receive the support of the membership.

The Political Process

Dahl has described political skill as "the ability to gain more influence than others, using the same resources."[4] With this in mind, let us now move to a discussion of how the legitimation of political decisions takes place in public performances and how the power assets already described can be used.

The process by which laws and organizational policies are constructed and implemented is designed to enhance the belief that "the will of the people" is being expressed. In point of fact, the people are rarely united in a single will. In a pluralistic society, legislators and leaders of large organizations are faced with the constant knowledge that whatever decision they make will render some portion of their constituency happy and another portion less happy, perhaps even furious. As with any social institution where strain exists, mechanisms evolve to reduce the strain. Gans, drawing on the work of Goffman, has characterized one such mechanism as being the development of two forms of government—the actual and the performing.[5,6] Using the language of the theater, a distinction is made between the backstage arena in which the supporting work, the basic decisions, the direction, the selection and casting of the performers, and the ultimate shaping go on, and the stage on which the play is presented to the audience. Those who are aware of the backstage activities and who are privy to the ultimate goals of the performance are "wise." Those who see only the play itself, even as participants, and have no backstage knowledge are termed "naive." Such an analogy might imply that the public performance is a sham and of no value except to dupe the public. This is not the case. Such performances fulfill an important function. Gans has suggested and research has confirmed that these performances are designed to establish a set of reasons or justifications for whatever the actual (backstage) government has decided is to be done. As will be noted later, the performances do not always succeed. Therein lies another opportunity for the use of power.

The initial and exploratory discussions between a governmental agency and an involved professional group regarding new laws or regulations are not usually public. They take the form rather of luncheon meetings, "hearings by invitation," office conferences, and corridor or telephone discussions. Eckstein cites a number of such instances, as do Gans, Dahl, Epstein, and Redman.[2-5,7] By the time a public performance—an open meeting or a formal hearing—is held, it can be assumed that the issues are fairly well-delineated. The chairman and leading participants have a clear view of what it is that they wish to establish by such a performance. The "wise" participants who appear to report or testify are also well versed in the process. A successful performance at such a meeting or hearing will lead to the results desired by those responsible for scheduling the meeting.

Because such a performance requires an audience, there is an element of risk involved: sometimes the performance "goes bad" or is spoiled. At the government level there are statutory ways of dealing with a spoiled performance.* In a professional organization, a spoiled performance must be handled carefully to insure preservation of the solidarity of the group. The mark of a skilled moderator is being able to sense when a performance is going bad and to decide the best way to deal with it. Several options exist: (1) The subject may be redefined as outside the purview of the group and be abandoned; (2) The performance may be terminated in as seemly a manner as possible and the matter referred back for further study; or (3) The "purpose" of the performance may be redefined (a) from the establishment of a position to "exploratory," giving it an interim quality that establishes the need for another later "final" performance; (b) from establishing a position to "tension release," in which those with deviant positions are given a further opportunity to present their own performance. It is probable that once a performance of this nature is begun, it must be continued until such an hour that all of the deviant positions are heard or their proponents have given up from fatigue and gone home. At that point the performance can be concluded with some motion (eg, to refer back to committee for further discussion) that preserves the appearance of solidarity of the group as a whole. Alternatively, a speech giving recognition to

---

*California Administrative Procedures Act (1969), Section 11425, states: On the date and at the time and place designated in the notice the state agency shall afford any interested person or his duly authorized representative, or both, the opportunity to present statements, arguments, or contentions in writing with or without opportunity to present the same orally. The state shall consider all relevant matter presented to it before adopting, amending or repealing any regulation.

In any hearing under this section the state agency or its duly authorized representative shall have authority to administer oaths or affirmations *and may continue or postpone such hearing from time to time to such time and at such place as it shall determine.* [italics added]

the differing concerns of the assembled members can be made, followed by a reminder of their higher responsibility to the common good. On occasion a recess can be ordered (assuming the spoilage occurs early in the day). Misunderstandings can be rectified and recalcitrant performers can be reasoned with privately.*

The importance of such public performances, properly presented, is in their utility as uncertainty absorption points.† A position stated, a fact testified to in such a performance becomes a citable event. It can later be used as established evidence to bolster some other performance.

The successful management of such performances requires a good deal of skill and organizational support. Not only the moderator (chairman) and the principal actors, but selected members of the audience must possess essential political and organizational skills if the performance is to be a valid one. Where the performance is a symposium or other public program outside the usual framework of *Roberts Rules of Order,* the burden on knowledgeable participants is even greater because the nature of the audience is less predictable.

A performance can be spoiled in a variety of ways. The most commonly observed is the introduction of evidence contrary to that accepted as valid. One must distinguish here between the scheduled discrediting that occurs during testimony, question and answer periods, etc. It is often possible to trace the origins of scheduled discrediting. A private investigation is made of a set of facts being advanced by an opponent. The results are reported back; not long after, loaded questions are asked at a performance. (This may not lead to discrediting if satisfactory answers to the loaded questions can be found.) Unscheduled discrediting is more likely to be done by naive performers—naive in the sense of not being an informed and/or planned part of the performance.

In the development of a political performance certain choices must be made about the facts to use to establish a formal basis for decision. These decisions cause what is seen by naive performers as errors of

---

*Merton discussed the genesis of such processes in his comments on the efforts made by groups to regularize the behavior of nonconforming members.[8]

†The concept of the "uncertainty absorption point" was developed by March and Simon to describe a specific location in a decision-making system.[9] This is the point at which a relatively diffuse group of data is reduced to an organized summation, which is thereafter used in place of the less clearly delineated and less concrete sounding data from which it was developed.

omission or commission. In their concern that the "whole" truth or the "real" truth be presented, naive or dissident performers may succeed in introducing to public view matters of which everyone is aware but have agreed privately to suppress. Whether this is "good" or "bad" depends on the intent of those scheduling the performance and the intent of those who cause the discrediting.

On one occasion observed by the author, a meeting was held to draft a resolution. A dissident member of the group engaged in *sotto voce* comments during the performance, expressing dissatisfaction with the proposed decisions. A naive performer who really favored the proposed decisions actually succeeded in discrediting the entire performance by responding to the dissident comments (also *sotto voce*). This illicit dialogue raised issues that made it politically impossible for the other members to reach a decision that all could support. A new performance had to be scheduled. At this second and successful meeting two differences were notable: (1) those who engaged in the *sotto voce* comments were not present, and (2) a fresh set of facts were presented to support the decision, which was then formally agreed to.

A second example concerns a public meeting during which a performer was challenged by a member of the audience about the validity of some information. The situation was eventually retrieved by a second performer who brought the escalating verbal exchange to an end with an appropriate statement. Closure was provided by a third performer, who promised that an investigation of the conflicting facts presented from the audience would be made.

A great deal can be done politically at a public performance without even being a public participant. One can "use" other people's plays to meet one's own goals. At one large gathering, a small group was heard complaining about what they felt to be the small amount accomplished. "It is just all a lot of talk." Conversation with members of this group revealed that they were unaware of the importance of informal contacts to be made in the corridors, the bar, the coffee shop, etc. Such encounters by performers with "the public" are sometimes cited by these performers as evidence in later public performances to support some official action.

An important aspect of symposiums and workshop meetings is that although the agenda may be fixed, it is essential to the credibility of the performance that there be at least an appearance of full participation by the entire group. This can be very anxiety-producing even for the skilled moderator. One of these was heard to remark of a participant, "He's got a hidden agenda, but I can't figure out what it is." A skilled participant with a hidden agenda of his own can "take over" from a less skilled moderator and reshape the entire focus of the session. This is particularly easy if the participant has greater occupational or other prestige (such as expertise) that gives him higher status than the moderator. Anyone who has attended a professional convention can recall occasions when a renowned and senior person—be he member of the audience or one of a group of panelists—has taken over and dominated the remainder of the session. It should be noted that on some occasions this domination is an agreed-upon arrangement that precludes the emergence of a different outside person as dominating member.

Moderators of workshops and symposiums may maintain control by trying to avoid recognizing members of the audience whom they suspect of wanting to make a negative contribution. When the majority of the audience is in sympathy with the aims of the moderator, this can be done fairly nicely and with finesse. Where the audience is not in complete sympathy it may side with the suspected deviant, forcing his or her recognition by subtle, and not so subtle, means. This is a case where being attractive, attired in proper establishment dress, and well-spoken can be a distinct advantage to the person seeking recognition. Being a sympathetic figure is a useful ploy where it is fairly certain that the audience will be swung to the side of the individual seeking recognition. It can also be a dangerous ploy if one's efforts backfire. In more sophisticated groups, such an intruder may be listened to in silence, after which the meeting continues as though the speech had never been made. Regardless of the intent of the intruder, his message is more likely to be heard if it is cast in terms that at least appear to fall within the "rules of the game." "You've explained the problem very well," said one such intruder, "but [my constituency] has some particular problems." How, he went on, was he to explain the actions of the group to the people back home? He was then able to present "new facts" in a manner that was "within the rules" for that particular gathering.

The "rules" for making inputs vary with the kind of performance. If testimony is to be offered at a legislative hearing, it is considered courteous to notify the author of the bill being spoken to in advance of the hearing. Again, it is presumed that in such a situation the individual wishing to testify will have notified his or her professional organization in advance. Not to do so will weaken the apparent strength of the organization. A legislative hearing sometimes assumes the character of a morality play, with villains and good guys and innocent maidens to be protected by our heroes, the legislators, Legislators do not take kindly to being made to appear foolish. Although they may speak to each other in public in a critical fashion, these criticisms fall within the rules. Embarrass one legislator and you may well raise the defenses of the others.

The Glory

Few feelings compare with those that come with the successful completion of a political campaign—whether it be the enactment or defeat of a bill or the election or defeat of a candidate. Few feelings can compare with the despair when the victory goes to the opponent. I have had the privilege during the past four years of watching California nurses grow into a more organized and politically effective group. The qualitative changes in their participatory efforts, the growing awareness of their own political muscle, the realization that politics is not only essential, but also fun, have been a wonder to see. The spinoff from these efforts to concern with the quality of patient care being delivered has been heartwarming. We are living in a time of great change. It may be a curse, but it is surely also a blessing.

REFERENCES

1. R. Nuttall, E. Scheuch & C. Gordon, *On the Structure of Influence,* in COMMUNITY STRUCTURE AND DECISION-MAKING: COMPARATIVE ANALYSES (T. Clark, ed., 1968).
2. H. ECKSTEIN, PRESSURE GROUP POLITICS; THE CASE OF THE BRITISH MEDICAL ASSOCIATION (1960).
3. C.F. EPSTEIN, WOMAN'S PLACE, (1971).
4. R.A. DAHL, WHO GOVERNS (1961).
5. H.J. GANS, THE LEVITTOWNERS (1967).
6. E. GOFFMAN, THE PRESENTATION OF SELF IN EVERYDAY LIFE (1959).
7. E. REDMAN, THE DANCE OF LEGISLATION (1973).
8. R. MERTON, SOCIAL THEORY AND SOCIAL STRUCTURE (Rev. & Enlarged ed., 1957).
9. J.G. MARCH & H.A. SIMON, ORGANIZATIONS (1958).

JOAN P. WHINIHAN

14
The Washington
State Success Story

Amendments modernizing Washington state's nurse practice act were signed into law on March 19, 1973. However, the first chapters of this success story were written some two or three years prior to that date. In early 1970 the Washington State Nurses' Association, through its Commission on Nursing Practice, appointed an ad hoc committee to study the state's law regulating the practice of registered nursing. After several months of study and review, the committee recommended that a bill be drafted that would bring the state law into conformity with current nursing practice. As so often happens, practice had preceded the law; every day nurses were being asked and, in fact, expected to perform acts that were clearly outside the scope of nursing practice as was then defined in the state statute.

At the same time that the ad hoc committee was making its recommendation to the WSNA Board of Directors that changes were needed in the law, the Association prepared and submitted a proposal to HEW for a grant to conduct an intensive and collaborative study of the state's nurse practice act. The overall objective of the study was to be the updating and modernizing of the act in order (1) to better define nursing; (2) to reflect the expanded role of the nurse, (3) to clarify the relationship of the professional nurse with others in the health care field; (4) to explore questions of continuing education for licensure; and (5) to explore the question of the composition of the board of licensure. The grant proposal was approved for a one year period—June 23, 1971 through June 22, 1972.

During that year, meetings were held with representatives of the Licensed Practical Nurses Association, the state medical, hospital, and health facilities associations, and various government agencies to obtain advice, support, and cooperation in planning for the proposed changes. Information also was gathered from neighboring states regarding the status of their nurse practice acts and their plans for the future of nursing. Copies of recently revised practice acts were requested from the few states that had already successfully pursued the updating of their state laws.

In addition, in this twelve month period, a series of workshops was held throughout the state to gather input from nurses and to get their reaction to the broad concepts of change. Armed with this information, the ad hoc committee then set about the task of coming up with the actual language of the proposed amendments in consultation with the association's legal advisor.

As the grant period neared its conclusion, it became apparent that it would not be possible in the time allotted to complete either the stated objective of the study or the final report, which was to consist of the proposed legislative package with a draft of a revised nurse practice act. Therefore, the association requested an extension of the contract from HEW and this was granted for an additional six months. Under the extension, the study was then scheduled to be completed at the end of 1972, just prior to the opening of the regular session of the Washington State Legislature in January 1973.

During the last six months of 1972 a draft of an amended nurse practice act was presented to nurses, consumers, other health workers, the public, and state legislators at twelve regional seminars conducted throughout the state. The proposal included a provision for mandatory continuing education as a condition for relicensure.

The meetings were well attended, with several hundred turning out for each of the twelve sessions. As the state legislative campaigns would be underway while the seminars were being held, it was decided to send individual invitations to current legislators and legislative candidates to attend the seminars. Also, a selected legislator was invited to participate in each of the sessions by speaking on the legislative process.

A good percentage of legislators and candidates responded positively to the invitations, and they not only attended but also took an active part in the open discussions. This was extremely advantageous from many standpoints. The large audiences at the seminars demonstrated to the lawmakers that there were vast numbers of nurses in the state; many legislators were introduced to the thrust of the association's legislative proposal before the legislature was in session, thus substantially reducing the time that would be needed by the association's director of government relations to explain the background and rationale for the bill; the seminars offered an excellent opportunity to gain exposure in the media for the need for changes in the nurse practice act.

One very tangible result of the regional meetings was the deletion of the mandatory continuing education provision from the draft of the bill. This decision was based on the nurses' strong opposition to the making continuing education (CE) mandatory, expressed vocally as well as in writing on the seminar evaluation forms. Some legislators at the meetings stated that their support for the bill was contingent on whether or not the CE provision was retained because they had heard objections to this from their nurse constituents.

Although the nurses' stand in opposition to mandatory CE in the proposed bill was loud and clear, it also was clear that nurses overwhelmingly endorsed the concept of mandatory CE. They were unwilling, as some put it, "to buy a pig in a poke." Before they would support the inclusion of this provision in the law nurses demanded to know that there would be ample CE opportunities available where they worked and where they lived.

The culmination of the seminars was an all-day meeting in mid-November of 1972, which focused on nurses' views of the changing role of the nurse and consumer's views of the new roles for nurses. In addition to nurses and consumers, physicians, hospital representatives, and government officials attended this meeting.

Thus, well before the nurse practice act proposal was introduced into both houses of the state legislature a great deal of communication about the need for changes in the law had been accomplished with four important publics—the registered nurses, the state legislators, others in the health care field, and the health consumers.

Because the chairman of the Senate Committee on Social and Health Services was a strong supporter for amending the nurse practice act, the bill was moved first through the Senate. At the Senate committee hearing, the Hospital Association stated its overall objection to the changes being proposed and then requested some minor amendments, which the nurses were willing to accept. The Medical Association, University of Washington School of Medicine, and State Board of

Medical Examiners all presented impassioned statements in opposition to the bill, stressing their particular aversion to that part of the new definition of nursing that gives final authority to the Board of Nursing to determine through its rules and regulations the additional acts that are jointly recognized by the medical and nursing professions as proper to be performed by nurses. As a part of its testimony, the Medical Association insisted on an amendment that would give the Board of Medical Examiners veto power over the Board of Nursing's decisions.

The Senate committee rejected the amendment, voicing grave exception to the idea of one statutory board presuming to take authority over another. The physicians also expressed concern that nurses would venture into areas far beyond their abilities. To allay these anxieties the Senate committee itself wrote and adopted a clarifying amendment:

This chapter shall not be construed as . . . (15) permitting the performance of major surgery, except such minor surgery as the board may have specifically authorized by rule or regulation duly adopted in accordance with the provisions of chapter 34.04 RCW; (16) permitting the prescribing of controlled substances as defined in schedules I through IV of the Uniform Controlled Substances Act, chapter 69.50 RCW.

The testimony presented by the president of the Washington State Nurses' Association and the Chairman of the State Board of Nursing at the hearing before the House of Representatives Committee on Social and Health Services, which follows, summarizes succinctly the rationale for the changes in the law and the amendment accepted by the Senate Committee.

Mr. Chairman, Members of the Committee, I am president of the Washington State Nurses' Association, the professional association for registered nurses. I wish to speak in support of S.B. 2213–amendments to the law regulating the practice of professional nursing in Washington.

In June 1971, WSNA was awarded a grant from the Department of Health, Education and Welfare to conduct a study of the state's Nurse Practice Act. The results of that exhaustive 18 month investigation are the amendments which you have before you in Senate Bill 2213.

Out study indicated that the current Nurse Practice Act had some serious flaws. It not only includes limitations for the expanded role of the nurse, but also contains language explicitly forbidding nurses from doing many of the acts which they now are expected and, in fact, are *required* to do in the regular course of their practice. Because of the serious legal implications, the language in the current law that prohibits nurses from doing "acts of diagnosis or prescription of therapeutic or corrective measures" is deleted and a new definition of nursing has been inserted.

The new definition reads:

The practice of nursing means the performance of acts requiring substantial specialized knowledge, judgment and skill based upon the principles of the biological, physiological, behavioral and sociological sciences in either: (1) the observation, assessment, diagnosis, care or counsel, and health teaching of the ill, injured or infirm, or in the maintanance of health or prevention of illness of others. (2) The performance of such additional acts requiring education and training and which are recognized jointly by the medical and nursing professions as proper to be performed by nurses licensed under this chapter and which shall be authorized by the board of nursing through its rules and regulations. (3) The administration, supervision, delegation and evaluation of nursing practice: PROVIDED, HOWEVER, That nothing herein shall affect the authority of any hospital, hospital district, medical clinic or office, concerning its administration and supervision. (4) The teaching of nursing. (5) The executing of medical regimen as prescribed by a licensed physician, osteopathic physician, dentist, or chiropodist.

In her testimony, the WSNA president continued:

This new definition of nursing more accurately describes the broad scientific knowledge base necessary to give safe nursing care to the public and also reflects the current education and preparation of registered nurses. You will note the definition of nursing includes the words "assessment" and "diagnosis." All professional health workers diagnose—physicians, dentists, nurses, psychologists, social workers, and others. The word "diagnosis" is not limited to medical practice.

The practice of any profession requires assessment of the patient's problem, arriving at conclusions based on this assessment, and action to remedy or alleviate the patient's problem. Such a process can properly be termed "diagnosis" and "prescription or therapeutic or corrective measures."

The expanding responsibilities of the nurse, therefore, represent an evolution in such traditional nursing practice in that they involve primarily more elements of diagnosis and treatment and more sophisticated intervention within the framework of continuing close collaboration with members of the medical profession.

Item 2 of the new definition of nursing provides a mechanism for collaboration between the professions of medicine and nursing and establishes an orderly procedure for identifying the requirements of education and training for nurses to qualify to perform specialized and advanced levels of nursing practice.

Item 3 of the new definition broadens the responsibility of supervision and delegation to include administration and evaluation of nursing practice. In recognition of the concern expressed by the Hospital Association that item 3 would cloud the issue of who was responsible for the administration of the hospital, the Senate Committee on Social and Health Services added the following amendment to clarify item 3: "Provided, however, that nothing herein shall affect the authority of any hospital, hospital district, medical clinic or office, concerning its administration and supervision."

Item 4 of the new definition provides for the inclusion of the teaching of nursing and item 5 deals with the dependent role of nursing in which nurses carry out the medical regimen as prescribed by a licensed physician, osteopathic physician, dentist, or chiropodist.

Sections 4 through 20 of the bill deal with changes in the State Board of Nursing and a redefinition of the Board's responsibilities. The amendments provide for strengthening practitioner input on the Board as well as the addition of a public member. The State Board of Nursing has prepared a statement for presentation at this hearing and its testimony will speak to the specifics of the changes in this area.

In Section 27 the language is deleted from the act that prohibits the conferring of any authority to practice medicine or to undertake the treatment or care of disease, pain, injury, deformity, or physical condition in violation of chapter 18.71; or the conferring of authority to practice osteopathy or osteopathy and surgery in violation of chapter 18.57.

As medicine and nursing have evolved and continue to evolve, nurses have moved and will continue to move into areas of practice previously considered medical practice. The nurse who has been adequately prepared and who knows the cause and effect of her actions is able to contribute effectively to the ongoing development of nursing roles within the ethical and legal framework for practice. Removal of this legal barrier to expanding responsibilities can enhance the opportunity for nursing to make health care more available and accessible to all citizens.

Many tasks that physicians are asking and expecting nurses to do today are considered medical acts. Removal of this restrictive language is needed to protect the nurse from being in violation of the law. I also would call your attention to the fact that the Senate Committee amended Section 27 to set specific prohibitions and limitations as to those additional acts which may be authorized by the Board of Nursing through its rules and regulations to be performed by nurses who have been determined to have the required education and training. In addition, this Senate Committee amendment specifically prohibits nurses from prescribing controlled substances as defined in schedules I through IV of the Uniform Controlled Substances Act.

In the preamble to the act...the statement has been added that "The registered nurse is directly accountable and responsible to the consumer for the quality of nursing care rendered." This statement was amended on the floor of the Senate. For clarification the word "individual" was inserted before "consumer." In fact and in law we know the nurse is responsible and accountable for his or her own acts, as is any professional. This is spelled out in the preamble to reaffirm to the nurse and the public she serves the intent of the Nurse Practice Act which is to assure safe nursing care to the people of our state.

Throughout the law, the word "professional" has been deleted before "registered nurse." This is a housekeeping item to change the title "professional registered nurse" which is redundant to "registered nurse."

The remaining two Senate Committee amendments to SB 2213 will be found in Sections 3 and 27. Language was added to Section 3 to answer the Hospital Association's concern that the practice act for professional nurses not limit the practice of other health workers such as physicians' assistants who are not licensed but who are authorized by state law. A further amendment adds the category nursing home" to the section stating ". . .(4) nor shall it be construed as prohibiting auxiliary services provided by persons carrying out duties necessary for the support of nursing service including those duties which involve minor nursing services for persons performed in hospitals, nursing homes or elsewhere under the direction of licensed physicians or the supervision of licensed, registered nurse...."

It is essential that the Nurse Practice Act be brought into alignment with the practice of nursing and the delivery of health care as it is taking place today. The successful passage of these amendments is important not only to the nurse, but also to the consumer of health care, if in fact, nurses are going to be expected to function to their highest abilities in the health care system.

Following this statement by the WSNA president, the chairman of the State Board of Nursing gave this testimony:

The Washington State Board of Nursing has worked closely with the Washington State Nurses' Association in its study of the practice act and wishes to testify in support of the amendments proposed in Senate Bill 2213.

Sections 4 and 5 of the bill provide for changes in the size and composition of the Board of Nursing. To insure practitioner input on the Board, two members are required to be nurses at the level of direct patient care. Also, because nursing believes it is time the consumer had a voice at an effective, decision-making level, a public member is added to the Board. In making these changes, the Board is enlarged from five to seven members.

In Section 7, the responsibilities of the Board are redefined. In this section, the Board is authorized to be responsible for standard-setting in nursing practice and education and for helping the public to identify those practitioners who are adequately prepared to assume expanded practice responsibilities.

In this same section, the Board is charged with the responsibility of establishing criteria as to the need, type, size, and geographical location of nursing programs. This is done to insure quality of educational programs and capability of practitioners as well as the most efficient use of tax dollars.

In Section 20, the requirement is added that those nurses changing from inactive to active license status after three years on the nonpracticing list must provide proof of reasonable currency of knowledge and skills as a basis of safe practice.

Section 21 deals with the grounds for revocation and suspension of license. The grounds have been clarified and strengthened. This will safeguard the public by providing adequate mechanisms for the Board of Nursing to hold practitioners accountable for performance and quality of nursing practice.

The Nurse Planning Council, Section 18.88.040, is deleted. This is in keeping with the modern philosophy that advisory committees are appointed to accomplish a specific task rather than being perpetuated through statutory provisions. Also, the National Commission on Nursing Education has recommended the appointment of a Statewide Master Planning Committee to assist with planning in nursing education. The nursing profession in this state is moving in this direction.

By busload and carload, nurses converged on the state capital for the Senate and House Committee hearings. In addition to the WSNA president and Board of Nursing Chairman speaking in support of the changes in the nurse practice act, testimony also was given by a staff nurse in a nursing home, a director of nursing service, a coronary care unit nurse, a nurse midwife, a nurse anesthetist, a nurse educator, a public health nurse, and a clinic nurse in a rural setting. Consumers and physicians were also numbered among those giving full support to the nurses' position.

The coronary care nurse said, in part:

With the increasing number of trauma and coronary care units being installed in hospitals, nurses are expected to judge, evaluate, and determine what is needed to be done. Five minutes could mean the patient's life. I and other staff nurses who function in these specialized units find ourselves practicing in gray areas which are not authorized under the current nurse practice act. This is the real world of nursing and patient care and our practice act must reflect this real world. There are those who would like us to believe that what we are doing is covered under those actions permitted in emergency situations. Since we are given specialized training to prepare us to function at this level and we are regularly employed to staff these units, we would have difficulty proving we are dealing with emergencies which were not anticipated.

The staff nurse who practiced in a large nursing home testified:

> Nursing homes are essentially nursing care facilities. There is no full time house staff. Because of this, daily medical leadership by a physician is unavailable.... In the absence of medical direction, professional responsibility for patient care is carried by skilled nursing service.... The nurse is expected to identify that a nursing home patient who has suddenly become confused...probably has a urinary tract infection. The nurse is expected to order a urinalysis for culture and sensitivity and notify the physician. The nurse also is expected to make continual assessment of toxic and therapeutic effects of drugs. Discontinuation or withholding of drugs are the responsibility of the nurse in the nursing home.

The real world of nursing in a small isolated rural town was described by a clinic nurse:

> In the clinic, I do much of the initial screening, referring those needing more complex care to the physicians. Then, on assigned weekends and when the physicians are out of town, I am expected to handle patients problems and emergency situations that arise. What I am allowed and capable of doing on Monday to Friday becomes expanded on the weekend and during physician's vacations.

The historical evolution of the functions of physicians and nurses was cited by one nurse speaking in support of change. She said:

> Nurses and physicians, working together over the years, have faced an onslaught of new knowledge and technology, combined with ever-increasing demands for health care. By mutual agreement, over 50 procedures have been delegated to the nurse that were once carried out only by the physician. These range from taking temperatures to defibrillating patients. If we are to be successful in establishing an effective system for delivering health care services, we must continue working together to define functions as needs change and knowledge emerges. Further, we must describe these functions in such a way as to reflect professional practice for consumer protection.

The president of a visiting nurse service and the chairman of the nurse clinic board in a remote, rural community gave well-documented, yet emotionally charged appeals for passage of the amendments to the nurse practice act. A public health officer and a child psychiatrist in private practice helped complete the nurses' case. The psychiatrist made a telling point when he observed that it was perfectly legal for him to resuscitate heart patients, though he was not at all skilled in this area—but the specially trained and highly skilled CCU nurse who did this was performing an illegal act.

At the House committee hearing the medical association once again attempted to have the bill amended to give veto power to the Board of Medical Examiners. And, once again, it failed in its attempt.

The excitement and ingredients of an old fashioned cliff-hanger existed when the nurse practice act bill came to the floor of the House for final passage on the last day of the regular session. If action was delayed, the bill would be sent back to the house of origin and it would have to go through the entire process again during the special session following adjournment of the regular session. Failure to gain passage of the bill during the regular session would have signalled defeat for that year's session, because the legislature had decided that only bills having budgetary impact would be considered during the special session.

All appeared to be going smoothly until it was noted that several of the representatives had left their desks and were conferring with the Speaker of the House. One of the representatives began scanning the visitors' galleries, caught the eye of the WSNA director of government relations, and motioned her to come to the doors leading to the House floor. This took place as bills were being voted and the nurse practice act was coming up fast on the day's calendar.

A representative who was also a pharmacist had decided to attempt to place a floor amendment on the bill because of his concern over the language dealing with the prescribing of controlled substances. If the bill was amended on the floor of the House this would force it into a conference committee and passage would then require a concurring vote of the Senate—this when the bill was perhaps five minutes away from the House vote. By speaking to the controls in the Board of Nursing, which would have to promulgate rules and regulations for the implementation of this section of the law, and with considerable assistance from nurses' strong supporters in the House, the WSNA director of government relations was successful in persuading the pharmacist-legislator to withdraw his floor amendment.

The representatives who had been huddled with the WSNA director in the hall then returned to their seats in the House. The bill was called, and the votes flashed on the electronic call board—all green, a "go" for the nurse practice act. The bill drew a 100 percent "yes" vote in both the Senate and the House, and was one of the very few bills to successfully pass the legislature during the regular session.

The Governor signed the bill on March 19, 1973, after item-vetoing the subsections that spelled out the criteria for the nurse members of the State Board of Nursing. It was explained that requirements for members of state boards were being deleted whenever possible because this type of detailing could be unduly restrictive.

In his covering letter to the Senate, the Governor wrote, "This act comprehensively reformulates the law relating to the regulation of nursing practice. This legislation has the effect of bringing the law up-to-date with many currently accepted nursing practices and building into the administrative processes sufficient flexibility to meet future needs of the profession."

Nursing in Washington waged a winning campaign for change. However, the true measure of the success of the Washington story will not be known for some years to come, for the challenge lies in implementation, and that challenge is a continuing one.

Implications and Conclusions

The changes in nursing licensure that have been described and analyzed in this book will undoubtedly have a significant, perhaps even revolutionary, impact on nurses and other health professionals both in this country and in others where parallel trends are taking place. For the first time in the modern era nurses are openly accepting independent and collaborative functions in the diagnosis and treatment of patients. Hopefully these developments will result in significant health care improvements. Most of the role expansion that has occurred to date has been either in the acute areas of the hospitals or in the primary care of special groups of ambulatory patients. Other nursing specialties are developing because there are many groups of people who also need better primary care, including most notably the long-term institutionalized patient populations.

Although the new nurse practice acts open new horizons, they have not solved all of the problems of the profession, or even all of the legal problems; the time for relaxation has not yet arrived. Some of the recent revisions may need to be altered to make them more workable, and legislatures that have not yet passed a modern nurse practice act may need some encouragement from their nurse constituents. Moreover, the new laws may create new problems. For example, the growing autonomy of nurses increases the professionalization of nursing, but increasing autonomy will force nurses to be held responsible for their own decisions, increase their burden of worries, and raise the number of malpractice suits brought against them. Already more nurses are feeling that it is necessary to buy malpractice insurance—but insurance often acts as an additional factor encouraging law suits. In the past, the traditional reputation of nurses for near-poverty incomes and lack of insurance were strong deterrents to suits. Thus, a whole new set of problems are evolving. The full impact of the revolution of the seventies with its new problems awaits a new generation of nurses, because most of the nurses who are currently in practice were socialized to accept the protection of a more dependent role and are not moving into expanded practice in great numbers.

There are also some problems which the new laws do not address. None of the new acts certify nurses in specialty roles. Although some board rules may move in this direction, the legislatures felt that certification of the individual practitioner was not a matter for the law to deal with. Some nurses and other health planners had thought that the states might carry out the function of certifying coronary care nurses or nurse practitioners, but the current laws seem to be aimed primarily at removing unnecessary restrictions against nurses, rather than setting up rules for specialty training or practice. This seems like a wise decision on the part of the legislators and the nurses who worked with them as advisors and lobbyists. In the early history of nursing licensure some states wrote the details of education and practice into statutes, but later found that excessive detail can stifle innovation, particularly in the early stages of new programs.

This means that if new nursing specialties are to be certified, other approaches are needed; a variety of options are open. One possibility is to ask that the board rules which are being drawn up include recognition of the individual practitioner who has completed a specified educational program and demonstrated competence through practice or an examination. However, specialty certification has not been a traditional governmental responsibility, even at the less restrictive level of board rules rather than laws. Certification has been the responsibility of the members of the specialized professional group. All of the specialty training in medicine is supervised and controlled by the profession. The individual practitioner is recognized by the members of the appropriate specialty board, and the control of the quality of the residencies and other programs for specialization have been a function of the boards, with support and coordination by committees of the American Medical Association. While the medical system of certification and accreditation of educational programs has been criticized because of its lack of a consumer orientation or representation, there certainly is no serious consideration being given to turning the whole process over to any public body.[1,2]

There are some groups within nursing that have already worked out the mechanisms for certification of members, including the nurse midwives and anesthetists, but the process is not yet as well understood nor as well developed as in medicine. The American Nurses' Association has now set up seven specialty councils, and certification examinations are being offered by some of the groups,[3] but the ANA is hampered by the fact that only about 21 percent of the employed nurses are members of the association.[4]

Inevitably, the members of the new nursing specialties are fragmented and unsure of themselves, and thus self-regulation is difficult to achieve at this time. Such weakness leaves an attractive vacuum, and other groups feel justified, even virtuous, about moving in to establish control. As discussed by Kelly in Section III (Chap.11), the hospital and agency supporters of the concept of institutional licensure feel that their overview of the situation puts them in the best position to handle licensure and certification in the public interest. With equal justification, many physicians feel that they should have some permanent control over the new nursing specialties, since the new roles were carved out of what was medical territory.

Probably the most striking demonstration of this feeling was seen in the recent hiatus in the negotiations between the American Academy of Pediatrics and the American Nurses' Association. Representatives met over a period of years to define the pediatric nurse practitioner (or nurse associate, in the language of the Academy) and issued at least one joint position paper. However, in January 1974 the Academy withdrew and negotiations were not resumed until a year later.[5] In a letter to the ANA, Robert G. Frazier, Executive Director of the Academy, explained one rationale for this action:

It is now apparent that the academy's proposal of a pediatric nurse associate to work under physician direction in performance of both nursing services and delegated medical tasks is not supported by the ANA.[6]

In another letter, which was sent to individual nurse associates on the Academy's mailing list, Frazier did not mention any desire for physician control over nursing functions, but stressed the group's concern about the fact that the ANA had moved ahead unilaterally to establish a certification program for pediatric nurse practitioners, and argued that nurse associates should be jointly taught and jointly certified.[7]

The withdrawal and the tone of the letters suggest feelings of concern, surprise, and perhaps even outrage (on the part of Academy spokesmen) that nurses in a specialty so closely related to pediatrics would move towards self-regulation. The Academy is well within the medical tradition in this regard. The American Medical Association's Council on Medical Education has functioned since 1933 as an accreditation body for a growing number of allied health professions, including at least fifteen different groups of medical technicians and therapists. These occupational groups seem pleased to have the AMA endorsement, and many of their professional associations are open only to graduates of an AMA-approved educational program. From their point of view, members of the medical association feel satisfied that they are performing a significant public service.[1]

Thus, if individual nurses are to be certified and educational programs for the new nursing specialties are to be accredited, a variety of possibilities are open, including: (1) state board regulations, (2) certification by members of a nursing specialty group either under the umbrella of the American Nurses' Association or independently, (3) certification by the American Medical Association or the appropriate medical specialty board, or (5) control by the hospitals or other institutions that employ nurses. It would seem that this might be an auspicious time for serious consideration of the alternatives with some conscious decision making on the part of nurses. Although it is tempting to delay such decision making until the specialties are stronger, the delay might well rule out self-regulation as a viable alternative, because by then the other groups will have preempted the field.

Whichever route is chosen for certification of the new practitioners, all of the new roles imply more education, including the basic specialty education as well as continuing education. The issue of control over the education of nurse practitioners and other expanded role specialists is related to the power struggle over certification, but it is complicated by the original reluctance of the nursing schools to move in these directions. Most of the pioneering educational programs were developed outside of the mainstream of nursing education, under the auspices of health departments, hospitals, medical schools, departments of continuing education, or other institutions. These agencies are now justifiably reluctant to simply bow out and turn their pilot programs over to nursing schools, although many of these experimental programs are terminating because of lack of funds. The nursing schools are finally accepting more responsibility for extended role education, but the transition from pilot to permanent programs is not always smooth. There are disagreements as to who should direct the programs, who should be allowed to teach in them, and what the content should be. There will also undoubtedly be some loss of the innovative spirit as the programs are absorbed into the conservative mainstream of nursing education.

The issue of continuing education is equally controversial. If nurses as a group are to take on more overt decision-making responsibilities, they obviously need to keep their skills and knowledge current. One criticism that has been leveled against professional licensure is that there have been no requirements for continued competence or for the updating of knowledge to keep practitioners abreast of the scientific and technologic advancements in their fields. To remedy this situation the National Advisory Commission on Health Manpower recommended that steps be taken by the professions and the regulatory agencies to provide assistance to practitioners in maintaining competence, and suggested the possibility of using periodic relicensure as a mechanism.[8] The American Pharmaceutical Association has moved to support mandatory continuing education, but most of the other health professions have supported either a voluntary approach, or, like nursing, are ambivalent about the recommendations.[9] California, Colorado, New Hampshire, New Mexico, and South Dakota have enacted laws that mandate continuing education for renewal of nursing licensure. These laws are controversial, and they are said to be difficult to implement. They open up opportunities for the expolitation of practitioners by expensive educational programs, and bring the state into an area that many people feel is the responsibility of the individual professional person.[10,11] As an alternative approach some state nurses associations have experimented with voluntary programs. The Utah effort, which was one of the first, established a comprehensive point system for formal classes, workshops, publications, volunteer work, and a variety of other activities.[12] Similar programs have since been set up in several other states. As the programs evolve they are developing less cumbersome recognition systems, including the use of a standard continuing education unit that is awarded for ten contact hours in any organized educational program.[12] Critics point out that the people who participate in the voluntary programs are the same ones who attended classes and workshops before the programs were established, and that there are still nurses who are not participating and whose skills have become outdated. The debate continues. The American Nurses' Association has announced its support for the voluntary route and the National League for Nursing has stated that it supports the mandatory approach.[9] However, as nursing expands its scope it is clear that the problem of continuing education needs to be faced.

In conclusion, it can be seen that the expanding nursing role and the new laws which facilitate that expansion have far-reaching implications for many of the other issues facing nursing. The changing laws are both a cause and a consequence of revolutionary changes now taking place in the profession, as nurses finally accept a more visible role in the health care delivery system. Yet the full impact of the current changes may not be felt for several years. These years undoubtedly will be both interesting and frustrating, and the way that nurses deal with the problems will be decisive for the future of the profession.

REFERENCES

1. U.S. DEPT. OF HEALTH, EDUCATION AND WELFARE, REPORT ON LICENSURE AND RELATED HEALTH PERSONNEL CREDENTIALING, PUBL NO. (HSM) 72-11 1-26 (1971).
2. H.J. LERNER, MANPOWER ISSUES AND VOLUNTARY REGULATION IN THE MEDICAL SPECIALTY SYSTEM (1974).
3. *Join an ANA Council Today*, 18 AM. NURSE (January 1975).
4. FACTS ABOUT NURSING 72-73, 6 AM. NURSE ASSOC., 64 (1974).
5. ANA and Pediatricians Resume Dialogue, 75 AM. J. NURS. 7-9 (January 1975).
6. *Pediatricians Withdraw Unilaterally from ANA Certification Program*, 74 AM. J. NURS. 387-89 (March 1974).
7. Letter from Robert G. Frazier, M.D. Executive Director, American Academy of Pediatrics, to Pediatric Nurse Associates (January 16, 1974).
8. REPORT OF THE NATIONAL ADVISORY COMMISSION ON HEALTH MANPOWER VOL. 1, 41-44 (1967).
9. J.G. Whitaker, *The Issue of Mandatory Continuing Education*, 9, NURS. CLIN. N. AM. 475-83 (September 1974).
10. G.E. Gibbs, *Will Continuing Education Be Required for License Renewal?* 71 AM. J. NURS. 2175-2179.
11. *Utah Nurses See Their New Certification Plan as Purely Professional Responsibility* 71 AM. J. NURS. 1297 (July 1971).
12. *Continuing Education Guidelines Issued by ANA*, 73 AM. J. NURS. (January 1973).

Index

Administration of nursing practice, 190-191
Age distribution, changing, 59
AHA. See American Hospital Association
AMA. See American Medical Association
American Hospital Association (AHA), 135, 137
American Journal of Nursing, 9, 11
American Medical Association (AMA)
   and certification, 199
   conservatism of, 30
   founding of, 27
   and licensure, 28, 135, 139
American medical schools, 8, 20-22
American Nurses' Association (ANA), 14
   and boards of nursing, 136
   and certification, 200
   and continuing education, 203
   and the definition of nursing, 7, 15-16, 157
   and institutional licensure, 141
   and licensure, 135-136
   origin of, 9
ANA. See American Nurses' Association
Anesthesia, 159
Anesthetists, nurse, 167-168
Apprentice system, 145
Assessment. See Diagnosis
Assistant, physician's, 47-48, 56-57, 165
Associate of arts graduates, 54-55
Australia
   health care in, 40-44
   nursing in, 41-42
   nursing aides in, 41

Barbee, Grace, 38
Barber v. *Reiking,* 18, 34
Belgium, nursing in, 39-40
Berwind, Anita, 2, 82-93
Black, W.L., 67
Board of Medical Examiners
   appointment of, 28
   conservatism of, 29-30
Boards of Nursing, composition of, 154-156
Bullough, Bonnie, 1-3, 53-59, 153-168, 198-203
Bullough, Vern L., 2, 22-32

California Nurse Practice Act, 33-34, 89
Calnen, Terrence, 120
Canada
   health care in, 41, 38-41
   nurse practitioners in, 44-47
   nursing education in, 44
Carner, Jean, 128
Certification. *See also* Licensure, Registration
   by the American Nurses' Association, 199-200

Certification *(cont.)*
  national system of, 138, 147
  programs, 121
  speciality, 138, 199
Change and family nurse practitioners, 116-117
Classification, job, 137
Clinic nurses, 195
Clinical nurses, 118-119, 122
Common law, 36, 91-92
Community college nursing programs, 54-55
Community Nurse Practitioners, 127-128
Competence, medical, 28
Complaints, distribution of *(table)*, 64
Consultation and nurses, 162
Contingent orders, 87-88
Controlled substances, prescribing, 159
Coronary care nurses. *See* Nurses
Coronary care unit
  development of the, 83-85
  law and the, 87
  legality of nurses in the, 93
Creative Health Services, Inc., 128
Credibility gap, 172

Dahl, R. A., 181-182
Dean, Winston, 165
Diagnosis
  definition of
    in California, 163
    general, 90
    in New York, 161
    in Washington state, 191
  delegation of, 164-165
  failure to perform a, 19
  legality of, by state, 158

Diagnosis *(cont.)*
  by nurses, 56, 198
  by protocol, study of, 72-77
Diagnostic functions of physicians, 90-91
Discrimination, sexual. *See* Sexism
Dock, Lavinia, 9, 11
Doctor, origin of the term, 26

Eckstein, H., 173, 181-182
Education, nursing, 53-56
  in America, 8, 26-28
  basic specialty, 201
  in Canada, 44
  continuing, 201-203
  mandatory continuing, 188-189
  requirements, 139-140
  and sexism, 96
Edwards, Charles, 149
Epstein, C. F., 179, 182
Evaluation of nursing practice, 191-192
Expertise, professional, 175-176

Family nurse practitioners (FNP), 95-117. *See also* Nurse Practitioners
  and change, 116-117
  conflicts with physicians, 102-107
  duties of, 100-101
  legal duties of, 109-114
  and protocols, 115-116
  time scheduling of, 107-108
Fenwick, Ethel Gordon Bedford, 11
Field testing of a protocol, 69
Flexner, Abraham, 28
Flexner report, 55
FNP. *See* Family nurse practitioners
Frazier, Robert G., 200

Index 207

Gans, H. J., 181, 182
Geographic aspects of power, 178
Goffman, E., 181
Gordon, C., 173
Greenfield, Sheldon, 2, 62-80
Greenidge, Jocelyn, 127
Group nursing practice, 130

Hatton, Corine L., 2, 118-123
Health care
  in Australia, 40-44
  in Canada, 41, 44-47
  as a human right, concept of, 39
Health maintenance organizations (HMOs)
  development of, 49
  and nurse specialists, 122
Health Services Network, 100
Hersey, Nathan, 136-137
Hiede, Wilma Scott, 58
HMOs. *See* Health maintenance organizations
Hospital
  growing importance of the, 31
  licensure. *See* Institutional licensure
  schools. *See* Education.
  training programs, growth of, 8
Humanitarianism, 97

Influence. *See* Power
Institutional licensure, 135-151
  and the American Medical Association, 139
  and the American Nurses' Association, 141
  in California, 150-151
  certification and, 138, 147
  and dangers for nursing, 144-146
  definition of, 136-137

Institutional licensure *(cont.)*
  in Illinois, 143, 149, 150
  in Massachusetts, 142-143
  in Pennsylvania, 143-144, 149, 150
Insurance, malpractice, 122

Job classifications, 137
Joint statements, purposes of, 31-32

Karmel Committee report, 43
Kelly, Lucie Young, 3, 135-151, 200
Kinlein; M. Lucille, 125, 127, 130
Kohnke, Mary, 127
Koltz, Charles, Jr., 127

Law. *See also* Legal; Legality; Legislation
  common, 36, 91-92
  and the coronary care unit, 87
  implementation of a, 181-186
  and institutional licensure, 151
  and nurse practice acts, 99
  protocol relation to the, 79-80
  purpose of a, 172
  regulating nursing. *See* Nurse practice acts
  respondeat superior, 129-130
  statutory, 92
Legal authorization of nurse practitioners, 48-49
Legal position. *See* Joint statements
Legality of the role of nurses in the coronary care unit, 93
Legislation. *See also* Law
  summary of recent, 168
Lewis, Charles
Licensure. *See also* Certification; Registration

Licensure *(cont.)*
  in America, 26-28
  criticisms of individual, 139-141
  by endorsement, 140
  first phase of, 9-13
  institutional. *See* Institutional licensure
  mandatory, 14
    achievement of, 156-157
    problems with, 135-136
  medical, 22-24
  model, 147
  moratorium on, 148, 149
  reasons for, 23
  second phase of, 14-19
  third phase of, 19-20, 153-168
Lisbin, Arthur D., 23-24
Lloyd, J. J., 138
Lobbyists, 175
London, physicians in, 25

McAdams, D., 137-138
McClure, Patricia J., 2, 125-130
Malpractice.
  coverage, 108
  insurance, 122
  suits, 60, 199
March, J. G., 183
Martin, Leonide L., 2, 3, 95-117
MDs. *See* Physicians
Medex program, 57
Medical
  monopoly, 97-98
  practice acts. *See* Nurse practice acts.
  schools in America, 8, 26-28
  technology, 56
Medicare, 39
Medicine, public power over, 29
Medicine versus nursing. *See* Nursing versus medicine.
Merton, R., 183

Midwives, nurse, 47, 167-168
Miike, Lawrence, 136, 147-148
Model license code, 147
Monopoly, medical, 97-98

National League for Nursing
  on continuing education, 203
  on licensure, 135-136, 139
  origins of the, 9
National League for Nursing Education, 14
National Organization of Public Health Nurses, 14
National Organization of Women, 58
Nations, Wanda C., 2, 33-37
Negligence, 18-19
Nightingale, Florence, 8, 10-11
Nurse anesthetists, 167-168
Nurse associates, 200
Nurse associates, pediatric, 200
Nurse clinicians. *See* Nurse specialists, clinical
Nurse midwives, 47, 167-168
Nurse practice acts, 153-154, 157-168
  in California, 33-34, 99, 163-164
  in Idaho, 158-159
  in New York, 160-162
  state, 11, 160
  in Tennessee, 162-163
  in Washington state, 187-197
Nurse practitioners, 57
  in America, 47-49
  background of, 58-59
  in Canada, 46-47
  family. *See* Family nurse practitioners
  growth in number of, 35
  in health maintenance organizations, 49
  legal authorization of, 48-49
  pediatric, 200
  and physicians, 128-129

Nurse psychotherapists, 122-123
Nurse specialists, clinical, 118-119, 122
  background of, 120-122
  and health maintenance organizations, 122
Nurses. *See also* Nursing
  clinic, 195
  and consultation, 162
  coronary care
    development of, 82-83
    expanded role of, 89-90, 91, 194
    legality of, 93
    role of, 85-87
  diagnosis by,
    expanded role of, 56-59, 126-127, 168, 198
  and institutional licensure, 144-145
  legal restrictions on, 34-35
  outpost, 47
  and physicians. *See* Nursing versus medicine
  practical, education of, 55
  in private practice, 125-130
  public health, 58
  registered, 156
    movement of, 154
    role of, 1
    role expansion of, by state, 160
  role of, 3
  staff, 195
Nurses' Associated Alumnae, 9, 11
Nurses' strike, 177
Nursing. *See also* Nursing
  aides in Australia, 41
  in Belgium, 39-40
  Boards of, composition of, 154-156
  character emphasis in, 10
  definition of
    by American Nurses' Association, 15-16
    in New York in 1938, 15
    professional, 38

Nursing *(cont.)*
  registered, 163
    in Washington state, 191-193
  education, 53-56
    in America, 26-28
    in Australia, 41-43
    in Canada, 44
  functions
    in Australia, 40-44
    in Canada, 41, 44-47
    expanded, 38-39
  homes, 195
  inferiority and sexism, 117
  licensure, history of, 7-9
  practice
    administration and evaluation of, 191-192
    expansion of, 92
    group, 130
  professionalization of, 9
  programs, community college, 54-55
  role expansion of, 56-59, 126-127 168, 198
  roles and sexism, 30
  salaries, 58-59, 107
  schools, *See* Education
Nursing Consultants, Inc., 128
Nursing versus medicine
  on Board veto powers, 190
  in diagnosis, 160-161
  family nurse practitioners versus physicians, 102-107
  in hospitals, 31-32
  nurses practicing medicine, 192, 195
Nuttall, R., 173

Osler, William, 24
Outpost nurses, 47

Palmer, Sophia, 9, 11

Paramedics, 57. *See also* Nurse practitioners, Physician's assistants
Pediatric nurse associates, 200
Pediatric nurse practitioners, 200
Performance, illustration of politics as a, 181–186
Physician's assistants, 47–48, 56–57, 165
Physicians. *See also* Medical; Medicine
 diagnostic functions of, 90–91
 and nurse practitioners, 128–129
 and nurses. *See* Nursing versus medicine
 shortage of, 1
Political process, the, 181–186
Power
 analysis of, 172–173
 geographic aspects of, 178
 importance of, 174–175
 information aspect of, 174–175
 personal attribute aspects of, 178–180
 physical resources aspect of, 176–178
 in the political process, 181–186
 professional expertise aspect of, 175–176
 size aspect of, 174
 struggle, 95–96
 time availability aspect of, 178
Practical nurses, education of, 55
Practitioners, family nurse. *See* Family nurse practitioners
Prescription of therapeutic or corrective measures. *See* Treatment
Prestige, 177
Professions, reasons for, 171–172
Protocol
 acceptance of a, 78
 changing a, 79
 concept, origins of the, 62–63
 construction of a, 69

Protocol *(cont.)*
 definition of a, 62, 65
 development of a, 64–72
 illustration, 65–67
 diagnosis by, study of, 72–77
 family nurse practitioners and, 115–116
 field testing of a, 69
 as a policy, 115
 relation to the law, 79–80
 safety of a, 77
 treatment by, study of, 72–77
 urinary tract infection-vaginitis illustration of a, 65–72
 validation study, 72
Psychiatric nurses, 118–119, 123
Psychiatry, 119
Psychotherapists, nurse, 122–123
Public health nurses, 58
Public power over medicine, 29

Rafferty, Rita, 128
Redman, E., 181–182
Registered nurses. *See* Nurses
Registration, 154. *See also* Certification; Licensure
Resources, physical, 176–177
Respondeat superior law, 129–130
Robb, Isabel Hampton, 9, 11
Roemer, Ruth, 2, 38–50, 138–139
Role of nursing, expansion of, 56–59 126–127, 168, 198

Safety, 139
 of protocols, 77
Salaries, nursing, 57–58, 107
Sarner, Harvey, 18
Scheuch, E., 173
Schmahl, J. A., 120

Schools. *See* Education
Self-discrimination, anticipatory, 17
Sexism
   in meetings, 106
   and nursing inferiority, 117
   and nursing roles, 30
   and the power struggle, 95-96, 98
   and role expansion, 58
Sigerist, Henry, 24
Silver, Henry, 57
Simon, H.A., 183
Smith, Adam, 23
Specialists, clinical nurse. *See* Nurse specialists, clinical
Specialization, 56
   trend toward, 1
Stachyra, Marcia, 120
Staff nurses, 195
Standardized procedure. *See* Protocol
Standing orders, 87-88
Statutory law, 92
Strike, nurses', 177
Supreme Court decision of 1889, 11, 27

Time availability aspect of power, 178
Treatment, 198
   delegation of, 164-165
   exclusion of, 16
   inclusion of, 191
   legality of, by state, 158
   by protocol, study of, 72-77

Ujhely, Gertrud, 123
Urinary tract infection-vaginitis protocol illustration, 65-72

Validation study, protocol, 72
Ver Steeg, Donna F., 3, 171-186

Whinihan, Joan P., 3, 187-197
Women, role of, 30-31
Women's liberation movement, 58

Zimmern, Ann, 127

DATE DUE